UMBERTO ECO

UMBERTO ECO

Philosophy, Semiotics and the Work of Fiction

Michael Caesar

Polity Press

First published in 1999 by Polity Press in association with Blackwell Publishers Ltd.

Editorial office:
Polity Press
65 Bridge Street
Cambridge CB2 1UR, UK

Marketing and production:
Blackwell Publishers Ltd
108 Cowley Road
Oxford OX4 1JF, UK

Published in the USA by
Blackwell Publishers Inc.
Commerce Place
350 Main Street
Malden, MA 02148, USA

ISBN 0-7456-0849-3
ISBN 0-7456-0850-7 (pbk)

A catalogue record for this book is available from the British Library and has been applied for from the Library of Congress.

Typeset in $10\frac{1}{2}$ on 12 pt Palatino
by Best-set Typesetter Ltd, Hong Kong
Printed in Great Britain by MPG Books, Bodmin, Cornwall

This book is printed on acid-free paper.

Key Contemporary Thinkers

Published

Jeremy Ahearne, *Michel de Certeau: Interpretation and its Other*
Peter Burke, *The French Historical Revolution: The Annales School 1929–1989*
Michael Caesar, *Umberto Eco: Philosophy, Semiotics and the Work of Fiction*
Colin Davis, *Levinas: An Introduction*
Simon Evnine, *Donald Davidson*
Edward Fullbrook and Kate Fullbrook, *Simone de Beauvoir: A Critical Introduction*
Andrew Gamble, *Hayek: The Iron Cage of Liberty*
Phillip Hansen, *Hannah Arendt: Politics, History and Citizenship*
Sean Homer, *Fredric Jameson: Marxism, Hermeneutics, Postmodernism*
Christopher Hookway, *Quine: Language, Experience and Reality*
Christina Howells, *Derrida: Deconstruction from Phenomenology to Ethics*
Simon Jarvis, *Adorno: A Critical Introduction*
Douglas Kellner, *Jean Baudrillard: From Marxism to Post-Modernism and Beyond*
Chandran Kukathas and Phillip Pettit, *Rawls: A Theory of Justice and its Critics*
Lois McNay, *Foucault: A Critical Introduction*
Philip Manning, *Erving Goffman and Modern Sociology*
Michael Moriarty, *Roland Barthes*
William Outhwaite, *Habermas: A Critical Introduction*
John Preston, *Feyerabend: Philosophy, Science and Society*
Susan Sellers, *Hélène Cixous: Authorship, Autobiography and Love*
David Silverman, *Harvey Sacks: Social Science and Conversation Analysis*
Geoffrey Stokes, *Popper: Philosophy, Politics and Scientific Method*
Georgia Warnke, *Gadamer: Hermeneutics, Tradition and Reason*
James Williams, *Lyotard: Towards a Postmodern Philosophy*
Jonathan Wolff, *Robert Nozick: Property, Justice and the Minimal State*

Forthcoming

Maria Baghramian, *Hilary Putnam*
Sara Beardsworth, *Kristeva*

James Carey, *Innis and McLuhan*
Thomas D'Andrea, *Alasdair MacIntyre*
Eric Dunning, *Norbert Elias*
Jocelyn Dunphy, *Paul Ricoeur*
Nigel Gibson, *Frantz Fanon*
Graeme Gilloch, *Walter Benjamin*
Espen Hammer, *Stanley Cavell*
Sarah Kay, *Žižek: A Critical Introduction*
Paul Kelly, *Ronald Dworkin*
Valerie Kennedy, *Edward Said*
Carl Levy, *Antonio Gramsci*
James McGilvray, *Chomsky: Language, Mind, and Politics*
Harold Noonan, *Frege*
Wes Sharrock and Rupert Read, *Kuhn*
Nick Smith, *Charles Taylor*
Nicholas Walker, *Heidegger*

Contents

Acknowledgements   ix

Note on References   x

Introduction   1

1   Form, Interpretation and the Open Work   6
    On form and interpretation: from Croce to Pareyson   6
    Art and rationality   10
    The appearance of Opera aperta   15
    The poetics of the open work   18
    Beyond 'openness'   23

2   A Critical View of Culture: Mass Communications,
    Politics and the Avant-garde   28
    The role of the avant-garde   29
    Mass communications and theories of mass culture   37
    Television and semiotic guerrilla war   43
    Openness and structure   47

3   Introducing the Study of Signs   54
    Signals and sense   55
    Ambiguity, self-reflexivity and the aesthetic message   64
    The critique of iconism   67
    Some provisional conclusions on the aesthetic message   69

4 A Theory of Semiotics   76
   From La struttura assente *to* A Theory of Semiotics   76
   Communication, code and signification   81
   Sign and sign-function   83
   Sign production, iconism and the aesthetic message (again)   90

5 Semiotics Bounded and Unbound   100
   The boundaries of semiotics   102
   The dynamics of semiosis   111

6 Theory and Fiction   120
   Readers and worlds   120
   Texts   134

7 Secrets, Paranoia and Critical Reading   145

8 Kant, the Platypus and the Horizon   162

Notes   171

Select Bibliography   184

Index   193

Acknowledgements

I am grateful to Harvard University Press for permission to quote from the English translation of *The Open Work* (1989), to Harcourt Brace and Company for permission to quote from the English translations of *The Name of the Rose* (1983) and *The Island of the Day Before* (1995), and to Indiana University Press for permission to quote from *A Theory of Semiotics* (1976) and *The Role of the Reader* (1979), and to use the diagram from *The Role of the Reader* reproduced here on p. 129.

Every effort has been made to trace the copyright holders, but if any have been inadvertently overlooked, the publishers will be pleased to make the necessary arrangements at the first opportunity.

Note on References

The following forms of referencing are used:

A. Writings by Eco published in volume form (which include many essays first published elsewhere) are referred to by the initial letters of the title and page number. Full details are given in section A of the Select Bibliography, pp. 184–6. In the case of Eco's theoretical works, reference is normally given to editions in both Italian and English, where the latter exists; exceptions to this norm are explained in the text.

B. Shorter writings by Eco not available in volume form: these are indicated by the author's name, date of publication and short title. Full details are given in section B of the Select Bibliography.

C. Writings by authors other than Eco are referred to by the author's name and short title. Full details are given in section C of the Select Bibliography.

Introduction

Umberto Eco was born in Alessandria (Piedmont) in 1932. He graduated in philosophy from Turin University in 1954 with a thesis on the aesthetics of Thomas Aquinas. After that his *curriculum vitae* starts to get complicated. His religious faith began to wane after a militant youth in Catholic Action; the middle and late 1950s were for him a period of religious and political crisis, which finally resolved into that sort of humanist secularism that has characterized his writing ever since (but nobody who has had such an education, he says, ever entirely loses a sense of the religious). It was also a period of professional and intellectual ferment. He was working for a time for the state television company and becoming involved in the artistic and cultural life of Milan at a particularly creative moment of its recent history. The outcome was two books that made Eco's reputation in Italy and, within a short time, more widely in Europe too. *Opera aperta* (*The Open Work*), published in 1962, sought to establish an aesthetics of indeterminacy in modern art, particularly music and the visual arts. *Apocalittici e integrati* ('Apocalyptic and Integrated Intellectuals', 1964) was the first sustained attempt in Italy to understand how the messages transmitted by the media of popular culture actually work. Since the first edition of *Opera aperta* also included a book-length study of James Joyce, and Eco's Joyce shared with his author a not inconsiderable interest in Aquinas, these publications of the early 1960s brought together three strong interests which on the face of it seemed well-nigh incompatible: medieval scholasticism, avant-garde art and contemporary popular culture.

Eco's search for a philosophical discourse which would bring the objects of his research within a unified field took him beyond the post-Crocean aesthetics of his younger years through linguistics and information theory to structuralism and semiotics. The period from the mid-1960s to the mid-1970s was devoted to the construction of a theory of semiotics, of which the most visible outcome was the book of that title, first published in Italy in 1975. The works of the 1960s and 1970s involve a considerable effort of theoretical intensity, but it was never in Eco's case detached from engagement with social praxis. What Eco was undertaking was the construction of a theory of semiotics which would be a theory of the constitution and understanding of human cultural phenomena, an enterprise which in his more tongue-in-cheek moments he cheerily accepted as 'imperialistic' in its scope and ambition. It was during the 1960s too that Eco began to obtain regular employment as an academic, first as a lecturer in aesthetics at Turin (1961–4), then teaching the semiology of visual communication in the Architecture Faculty at Florence (1966–9) and semiotics, again in Architecture, at the Milan Polytechnic (1969–71), before moving in 1971 to the University of Bologna, which has been his academic base ever since.

The itinerary sketched out above is described in greater detail in the first four chapters of this book, which follow Eco's trajectory in broadly chronological sequence. Chapter 1 presents and analyses a series of pre-semiotic aesthetic positions which, though later incorporated into a wider vision, remain formative. Chapter 2 introduces the reader to Eco's reflections on mass culture, reflections which gave the essential impetus to the construction of his semiotics. The principal aim throughout is to present Eco's thought in as clear and accurate a manner as possible, and this aim is particularly evident in the two chapters (chapters 3 and 4) on the evolution of his systematic semiotics between 1967 and 1975: here more than anywhere else the discussion keeps closely to the order and argument of Eco's own text, while essential contextual information is provided in a relatively condensed form.

Chapter 5 represents a transition in the book, as we move from an account of the arguments put forward in *A Theory of Semiotics* to a discussion of some of the more important objections to it and of Eco's clarifications of semiotic issues (some of them in partial, and not always direct, response to his critics). After *A Theory of Semiotics*, three major lines are discernible in Eco's work. Firstly, there is a continuing preoccupation with questions of logic and epistemology, often focused around Eco's continuing reflection on the theories of C. S. Peirce, and with an increasing interest in the work of the cognitive sciences in recent years: *Semiotics and the Philosophy of Language* is an important staging-post in this journey and is discussed here in chapter 5. In the second place, Eco pays particular attention from the late 1970s on to text pragmatics and theories of narrativity (*Lector in fabula* and its English-language cousin *The Role of the Reader* both appeared in 1979); his semiotic concerns loop back here to issues first raised in *Opera aperta* and other essays from his early years, issues that have to do with the nature, scope and limits of interpretation (*The Limits of Interpretation*, 1990). And finally, it is during this same period that Eco conquers planetary fame as a novelist: *The Name of the Rose* was published in Italy in 1980, succeeded by *Foucault's Pendulum* in 1988 and *The Island of the Day Before* in 1994, translations closely following in their wake.

Chapters 6 and 7 examine the relation between the theory and practice of fiction from different points of view. The first discusses Eco's views concerning the construction of model readers and fictional worlds and analyses the three novels together from a meta-textual stance; it resolutely refuses, however, to regard the novels as 'applications' of the theory. Chapter 7 raises two critical questions about the body of work produced between 1979 and 1994, asking how far Eco's denunciation of 'hermetic' interpretation (in the name of limits) might be turned against his own theory, and whether his important distinction between the use and the interpretation of literary texts is adequate to a description of the reading process. The distant origins of this chapter in a public lecture may still be perceptible in the marginally more relaxed tone of its argument. The final chapter (chapter 8) introduces the substantial collection of philosophical essays which Eco published in late 1997 with the intriguing title *Kant e l'ornitorinco* (*Kant and the Platypus*); he particularly recommended it to readers of *A Theory of Semiotics* on the grounds that it contained a rethinking of some of his old positions. As well as giving a brief account of the major issues touched on in *Kant*, chapter 8 ends with a metaphor, perhaps appropriately for a thinker for whom the aesthetic text has always had particular resonance; the metaphor in question is one that is uniquely powerful in the more recent Eco. The reader of this book will, I hope, understand why any greater sense of closure than that would be entirely alien to a practice of thought that over some forty years has not ceased to evolve and deepen.

Eco is a prolific, and highly professional, writer. A study like this, which draws on the most public and monumental of Eco's productions, particularly those in book form, cannot do justice even to all the books. Eco the medievalist, who has written extensively on medieval philosophy and aesthetics (*Art and Beauty in the Middle Ages* was translated into English in 1986), but also edited a lavishly illustrated *Beato di Liébana* for Franco Maria Ricci in 1973, is poorly represented here. So too is the player of experimental literary games (*Vocali*, 1991), the writer of children's books with the painter Eugenio Carmi, the translator of Queneau (*Esercizi di stile*, 1983), the author of a student guide on how to write a degree thesis (*Come si scrive una tesi di laurea*, 1977 – still one of Eco's best-selling books), the organizer and compiler of a CD-ROM on the seventeenth century, above all perhaps the journalist, cultural and social commentator and critic who has hardly ever missed his weekly (now fortnightly) column for *L'Espresso* and has recently started trying his hand at new arts, such as that of interview*ing*.

Still less can it do justice to the mobility, variety, yet interconnectedness of Eco's writing. An anatomy of the body of his work would show the complexity of the system as a whole, at every level. What is striking is not just the big leap between 'theoretical' and 'narrative' writing, but also the way in which ideas are tried out and returned to and revised (and their temperature raised or lowered) in different kinds and at different levels of discourse (which often reappear in written form): seminar, lecture course, conference paper, scientific journal paper, newspaper article, dictionary or encyclopedia entry, foreword, preface, introduction, commentary, postface or afterword to other people's books, interview, collection of essays, treatise, novel, word games, *exercises de style*. Mobility, variety and interconnectedness are features of Eco's thought as well, which in this book we see in its most (relatively) settled form. Although he builds his semiotic model on firmly rationalist and humanistic grounds, he knows that it remains provisional, always to be verified. Having to decide whether semiotics is an ontology or a methodology, he plumps firmly for the latter, which leaves him, and the reader, with the maximum of flexibility – and responsibility.

Many friends and colleagues have helped me in the writing of this book, but I should first thank Umberto Eco who, whenever I have discussed it with him, or indeed talked about other things entirely, has always proved an informative and witty, but also tactful, interlocutor. Vita Fortunati and Giovanna Franci at Bologna provided the vital introduction. Members of the Italian Section at the

University of Kent at Canterbury and of the Department of Italian Studies at the University of Birmingham have been supportive in every way, including enabling me to take sabbatical leave. I am grateful to Jean Petitot for inviting me to the ten-day conference devoted to Eco, with the participation of the author, at Cerisy-la-Salle in June–July 1996, and the British Academy and the Faculty of Arts at Birmingham for providing funds to allow me to go. The British Academy also generously supported a research visit to Rome in June 1994. John Thompson with Gill Motley at Polity Press have shown remarkable forebearance which I have deeply appreciated. The work done on Eco by two of my graduate students, Manuela Barranu and Ruth Glynn, and by another, Stephen Martin, on Peirce has helped me constantly to focus my ideas. I should particularly like to thank Ann Hallamore Caesar whose participation both in the inception of this project and in its completion was decisive.

1

Form, Interpretation and the Open Work

On form and interpretation: from Croce to Pareyson

Eco's aesthetic was formed under the guidance of the Catholic philosopher Luigi Pareyson. Pareyson's theory of 'formativity' was one of several lines of research in the 1940s and 1950s to challenge what for many had become the dogmatic and ultimately sterile idealism of Benedetto Croce. For the post-Crocean generation, there were vast tracts of the artistic and aesthetic landscape which Croce had not simply ignored, but had peremptorily decreed were no concern of the philosopher's. His insistence on imaginative, or lyrical, intuition as the only valid component of the aesthetic experience – 'Let me say straight away, as simply as possible, art is *vision* or *intuition*'[1] – entailed a number of explicit exclusions: art is not a physical fact, it is not a utilitarian act intended to produce pleasure, it is not a moral act. Translated into the perspective of his critics, these exclusions meant that Croce had displayed sovereign indifference to the materiality of the work of art, to the historical conditions of its production, to the processes of conceptualization through which the work of art came into being, to the positive role played by convention and rhetoric (dismissed by Croce as 'precepts', in a rearguard polemic with a long-dead classicism), and to the reception and consumption of the work. All this in spite of the fact that is evident to any reader of Croce that he was a superb historian, an acute reader of literary texts, even, perhaps especially, the most obscure, and a wonderful writer, whom Eco was later to describe, in a 1991 review of a new edition of Croce's *Estetica*, with an adjective that might harbour some ambiguity, as 'overwhelming' (*scrittore travolgente*: *KO*, p. 387).[2]

As Eco's horizons widened beyond his Turinese education in the middle and late 1950s, other alternatives to Croce came into view. From America, where the New Criticism appeared to perform a similar role to Crocean idealism, the pragmatism of John Dewey in *Art as Experience* offered a valuable antidote; already in 1957, on the other hand, Eco could use a review of Wellek and Warren's *Theory of Literature* in Italian translation to regret its lack of interest in the 'consumption' of the work of art on the grounds that: 'to think about the work of art in terms of consumption, extra-aesthetic consumption in and for daily life, is one sign that a given historical period is substantially healthy.'[3] Later, other Italian critics and aestheticians such as Luciano Anceschi, Gillo Dorfles and Dino Formaggio would illuminate further aspects of the 'making' of a work of art – rhetoric, poetics, technique, the fact that it is above all a 'work' – which constitute the key facets of the turn against Croce; a distinctive contribution is made by the Marxist critique of intuitionism elaborated by Galvano Della Volpe in his rigorous polemics for the rationality of art, especially in *Critica del gusto* (1960). But Pareyson was particularly important for the young Eco. He was his teacher in the energetic Department of Philosophy at Turin, and looking back on *Opera aperta* nearly thirty years later Eco would acknowledge its debt to a 'secularized' version of Pareyson's ideas on interpretation (*LII*, p. 20; cf. *LIE*, p. 50, which, however, omits the reference to 'secularization'). It was Pareyson who at the time had proposed the most comprehensive aesthetic after Croce: his *Estetica* had appeared in instalments in the journal *Filosofia* between 1950 and 1954, and was published in book form in the latter year. Pareyson's 'theory of formativity', where the word 'formativity' replaces the 'ambiguous' notion of 'form',[4] emphasized the twofold dynamism of artistic form, as something that is made (or done – the Italian *fare* may cover both senses) and as something organic. This emphasis on the work of art as 'production' rather than 'expression' necessarily affects the mode of its reception: with Pareyson, neither 'intuition' nor 'empathy' plays a part in our response to the work; as readers or viewers or listeners, we 'interpret'. By the same token, at the other end of the line that joins the ordinary reader to the theoretical aesthetician, Pareyson's aesthetics is not 'a metaphysics of art', but 'an analysis of the aesthetic experience'.[5]

Eco's review of *Estetica*, which appeared in *Lettere italiane* in July 1955, was subsequently incorporated into a longer essay on

'L'estetica della formatività e il concetto di interpretazione' (*DA*, pp. 9–31), partially translated into English as 'Form and Interpretation in Luigi Pareyson's Aesthetics' (*OW*, pp. 158–66), and at this point we may join Eco in his account of a theory of interpretation which is at the same time a mapping-out of the territory of aesthetics. The concept of interpretation, which is as central to Pareyson's theory as is that of formativity, occasioned controversy in the 1950s in particular because it did not admit of any substantial difference between the normal appreciation of a work of art and specialized critical discourse. The theory developed as a critique of Croce's views on theatrical and musical performance. Croce regarded the theatrical performance as a new work, as something different from the original text; musical performance, on the other hand, he regarded as a 're-creation' of the original, thus assuming the continuity of the work in its performance, but denying any autonomy to the performer. Pareyson objected, first of all, in the name of the Crocean principle of the unity of all the arts, that the notion of performance (*esecuzione*) should be extended to them all. Notwithstanding the specific and material differences between the arts, Pareyson believed that 'every kind of work requires a performance, even a purely inner one, one that makes it come alive again in the experience of the receiver' (*DA*, p. 19). He also drew attention to the contradiction of Croce's position, whereby the performance was either the faithful rendition of the work or it was the expression of the personality of the performer. Croce could not accommodate both the unity of the work and the multiplicity of its performances because, in his view, 'the spirit neither *interprets* nor *performs*, for either it *creates* new works or *re-evokes* those which it has created' (quoted *DA*, p. 20).

Pareyson, by contrast, puts forward a theory of knowledge which is intimately linked to the process of figuration. Knowledge is a continual exchange between the stimuli offered by reality as 'cues' and the hypotheses that the person puts forward in response to the cues in order to give them a shape and a meaning. The process of figuration leads to a form which is itself the occasion for successive interpretations. The process is actualized in form and this means that it is constantly open to the possibility of being re-interpreted, albeit from the position of the producer ('to interpret means to assume the point of view of the producer'), in following the same tentative path that led to the work. Pareyson points to the gap between 'work' and 'performance'. The two are identical, but at the same time the 'work' (which at this point seems close to an 'idea' of the work) transcends the particular form which the artist has finally achieved:

> Just as the artist could intuit, in the intrinsic disorder of the cues, the outlines of a future order, so will the interpreter refuse to be dominated by the work as a completed physical whole, and will instead try to situate himself at the beginning of the process and to re-apprehend the work as it was meant to be. (*DA*, p. 26/*OW*, p. 163)

We may discern here germs, or more than germs, of future Echian positions. The dialectic between 'order' and 'disorder' will be a constant presence in Eco's thinking from *Opera aperta* on;[6] less immediately, the variable hierarchy suggested in the passage from artist to interpreter and back again may suggest the relation between 'idiolect' and 'lexicon' which will be explored in *La struttura assente* and discussed here in chapter 3. This is not to ignore the strongly personal and interpersonal nature of Pareyson's aesthetics. For the latter the notion of interpretation is closely linked to his idea of style as a 'way of forming', that point at which the process of formation and the personality of the form-giver coincide. The only 'knowledge' which the artist necessarily establishes is that of his or her concrete personality which has become a 'way of forming'. This position enables the sociological critic to approach the historical arena through the personality of the 'form-giver', and it is opposed to the 'impersonality' of the artist argued for by Eliot, Joyce and New Criticism. The permanence of the work in the infinity of its interpretations is made possible for Pareyson precisely by the polarity between the two personalities in play, that of the form-giver and that of the interpreter: 'The work lives only in the interpretations that are given of it' (*DA*, p. 30/*OW*, p. 165). Interpretation takes place in an atmosphere of 'congeniality', based on the fundamental oneness of different forms of human behaviour, but also on an act of trust and loyalty towards the work, and of openness towards the personality of the artist; a trust and openness, however, which are exercised by *another* personality, which would be excluded from interpretation if it were confronted by a work that was closed and defined for ever. The specificity of the personality, experience, likes and dislikes of the receiver is not a barrier to, but an opportunity for interpretation.

There is in Pareyson's aesthetic a very close link between the genesis of the work, its formal properties and possible reactions on the part of the receiver; while the New Criticism formalists tend to keep these three distinct, and to concentrate on the second, they cannot be separated in the theory of formativity. 'A work consists of the interpretive reactions it elicits, and these manifest themselves as a retracing of its inner genetic process – which is none other than the stylistic resolution of a "historical" genetic process' (*DA*, p. 31/*OW*, p. 166).

Art and rationality

Unlike his teacher, Eco does not, at this stage at least, write an aesthetic. The numerous reviews, conference papers, catalogue presentations, articles and more substantial essays that he wrote for both academic publications and cultural periodicals aiming at a wider audience in the 1950s and the early 1960s (many of the ones specifically concerned with aesthetic questions being subsequently collected in *Opera aperta* and *La definizione dell'arte*) approach the problems of the definition of art and the role of aesthetics itself from a particular angle, through the eyes of the critic, the historian or the ordinary reader. Pareyson's commitment to a description of artistic phenomena and processes that is as comprehensive as possible and stresses continuities rather than ruptures is evident also in Eco's multi-directional activity of this period, though it is only later, in the elaboration of a theory of semiotics, that he will come close to the synthesis that Pareyson achieves, and then in substantially different terms. What particularly exercise him in the years leading up to the publication of *Opera aperta* in 1962 and immediately afterwards are the relationships between the work and the reader, stimulus and response, ambiguity and analysis.

As Croce is firmly taken leave of, Eco shores up the defences against a possible return, by himself dismissing the positivism against which Croce's idealism had been (at least in Croce's eyes[7]) such a powerful device. A sociology of art, for example, can only take us so far, as Arnold Hauser himself acknowledges; it has to be 'completed' by 'an organic-structural explanation' (*DA*, pp. 42–3), one, however, that takes full account of the insights already gained by the methods of sociology. A series of essays establishes Eco's distance from the 'positivism' of Raymond Bayer,[8] and he is equally sceptical of Léon Bopp's search for an 'objective' critical methodology at which Bopp hopes to arrive by means of a statistical tabulation of sixty-six 'values' derived from Lanson's (obviously historically limited) *Histoire de la littérature française* (*DA*, pp. 50–5).

In all of these cases, Eco probes the question of what it means to talk about a work of art 'scientifically'. It does not mean, as Eco makes clear in his essay 'Note sui limiti dell'estetica' (a fusion of two reviews, dated 1956 and 1959, now in *DA*, pp. 48–61), simply to list a series of known facts about the work, for a work of art is clearly more than the sum of its parts, and this is acknowledged when people speak of the 'openness' or 'ambiguity' or 'multiple meanings' (*polisegnicità*) of a work of art: the work of art 'constitutes a communicative fact which demands to be *interpreted* [Eco's emphasis], and therefore completed by something that the user [*fruitore*] brings to it' (*DA*, p. 48). To talk scientifically about a work of art may therefore mean a series of different and complementary operations, each of which represents a particular level of use (from pure enjoyment to the most complex critical elaboration). It might mean to see the thing for what it specifically is, an object produced by a person who has given it that distinctive seal which is the manner in which he has produced it (this is Pareyson's formativity). It might mean to try not to resolve the observation into an appreciation that is unexpressed or vague, but rather to clarify one's impression in a way that communicates to others; to see whether there are elements in the work that will persuade others that one's impression is correct, and to make one suppose that the producer actually intended to produce an essentially analogous impression; and to show how he managed to do so. It might mean, finally, analysing the complex and multi-layered structure underlying this impression, which is both formally pleasing and practically efficacious (because it communicates). This approach, Eco concludes, may be considered 'scientific' provided that one accepts that what is in play are human, and often highly subjective, opinions, tastes and desires. The problem of the scientific attitude in relation to works of art is essentially one of balance, of not making ridiculous claims.

This description of 'speaking scientifically about a work of art' is directed precisely at the individual work of art, and what Eco is describing is the relationship between the intentions of the producer, so far as they are discernible, the response of the individual user, and his or her success in communicating this response to others and convincing them of its validity. It is a snapshot of the circulation of the work of art in an interpersonal context, from the group of friends discussing a film to the critic expressing and trying to justify a judgement in a more formal setting. The key figure here, however, is that of the critic ('il fruitore per eccellenza', the user *par excellence*: *DA*, p. 60); the underlying question is the proper definition of the relation between the multiplicity of tastes (which is an indisputable fact) and the status of aesthetic reflection (any claim that aesthetics may have to establish universal rules of taste, or a universal canon of beauty, appears to be undermined by the accepted fact of the multiplicity of taste). In fact, Eco argues, aesthetics, at least since Kant, is not concerned with setting universal standards by following which judgement may be reached, but with establishing the possibility of judgement, that is to say, focalizing the dialectic between the objective properties of the work and the variety of responses to it and identifying within that space the opportunities for judgement. The method by which this is shown is that of the user recounting his or her experience of understanding and interpreting the work and submitting that account to the scrutiny of others. The attitude towards the work should be that of critical understanding, not dogmatic judgement.

I have referred to this little-known essay at some length because it articulates a credo from which Eco will not deviate substantially, as well as being a classic example of his ability to mediate tensions within the culture (in this case between 'science' and 'philosophy', or between Croce and anti-Croce) and to establish a base for his own position within the very act of mediation. The principal features of Eco's aesthetic universe are beginning to appear: the defining complexity, multi-facetedness, 'openness' of the work of art, which, however, must also 'communicate'; the equally open, but analytical, non-judgemental, stance of the 'user'; the constant, and progressive, interaction between user and work.

We shall shortly examine in more detail the crucial idea of 'openness', but first it is necessary to say a few more words on the transaction between user and work, and the choices which it implies. In a 1959 essay on serial music ('Necessità e possibilità delle strutture musicali', now in *DA*, pp. 171–93), in which for the first time Eco suggests an application of information theory to the study of contemporary composers, he addresses the dilemma posed historically to all aesthetics: whether to attempt to define art by its essence, or to do so by its structures. The difficulty in attempting to give an essentialist definition of art is that while art may be named or categorized in a certain way, the definition itself proves to be beyond explanation. The ineffability of art can be described in terms of its effects and the ways in which it might be brought about, but resists attempts to define it in itself. The indefinability of the idea of art becomes the indefinability of an idea of the idea of art in an infinitely regressive begging of the question. Both the desire to give such a definition and the blockage which then ensues are central to aesthetics. But so, Eco argues, reaching elegantly for the authority of a canonical example, is the practical solution adopted by the author of the treatise *On the Sublime*, who switches from definition by essence to a phenomenology of the means of communication and the consequent effects. By examining particular stylemes and devices, pseudo-Longinus establishes how a particular phrase or line can stimulate the reader in specific ways, and, in an early example of stylistic criticism, he analyses the ways in which certain rhetorical devices (the use of asyndeton in the tenth book of the *Odyssey*, the switch from past to present tense in Xenophon, or from third to first person in Hector's speech to the Trojans in Book XV of the *Iliad*) create certain effects and impressions. Longinus's study of the structures of the work provides us both with a key to the aesthetic emotion which it arouses and with the schema of a possible emotion. The ineffable is not in the texture of the analysed work; rather, it is the latter which provides us with the framework of a 'machine for generating the ineffable' (*DA*, p. 173).[9]

Eco believes that Longinus opted for the second horn of the dilemma facing the aesthetician who recognizes the need to address the problem of the definition of art; and faced with the same choice between defining the ineffable 'by essence' and analysing 'the structures which generate the psychological impression of ineffability' (*DA*, p. 173), he too plumps firmly for the latter. In so doing, he allows a certain technologizing rhetoric to seep into his own discourse, but more importantly calls into question the role of philosophy or aesthetics as traditionally understood in speaking about art. If art, that is to say, is only apprehensible through particular features or manifestations, which are themselves relativized historically, then it is difficult to see on what grounds a general statement about art can be made. The same is true for the individual work as for art in general. It is established that the reading of a work of art cannot be a question of the individual sensibility impacting with the art-object and producing a 'poetic' intuition of the work; poetry in this sense will always beg the question. But neither is the apprehension of the work a properly 'scientific' activity, since the conclusions reached can never be wholly verifiable. The activity of analysis and reconstruction which forms the basis of a formative transaction between work and user seems to occupy a third space, between 'poetry' and 'science'. Nevertheless, the definition of art is, as Eco puts it (*DA*, p. 152), a 'gesture' that has to be completed, even at the moment that one recognizes the many ways in which the definition is determined and delimited, historically and culturally.

The reading (viewing, hearing etc.) of a work, then, is a conscious (and self-conscious), analytical process which addresses itself to structures rather than to an irreducible 'thing'. But there may be a price to pay for this relativism, and that is the loss of the function of evaluation. In the important essay 'Due ipotesi sulla morte dell'arte', first published in *Il verri* in June 1963 (that is, after *Opera aperta*) and then in *DA*, pp. 259–77 (and in English as 'Two Hypotheses about the Death of Art' in *OW*, pp. 167–79), Eco explains that, if in his essays he does not evaluate particular works of contemporary art, it is because he is writing as a historian of culture, not as a critic. At the same time, he draws attention to another aspect of the problem. Does the reluctance to make judgements about the value of the work have something to do with the nature of the works in question? Does the replacement of an aesthetic evaluation with a description and justification of a 'poetic' mean simply that the analyst wants to talk about poetics, or does it mean that the works in question can only be understood as examples of a poetic?[10]

Eco's response is twofold. Yes, there does indeed appear to be, in contemporary art, a precedence of 'poetics' over 'poetry', as was already apparent in the Symbolists, especially in Mallarmé. The 'point' of the work appears to be exhausted in the description of it, rather than in the enjoyment of the work itself. Eco refuses to be scandalized by such a development: it simply means that we are again in an age in which art is appreciated rationally, with the intellect, not intuitively. That was the rule in the Middle Ages, and in other periods too, so we should not be frightened of it. But alongside this strong affirmation of the rationality of art, Eco recuperates the concrete experience of reading, seeing and hearing. It is not true that we have fully enjoyed *Finnegans Wake* once we have 'got the idea' of it; the idea has to be realized, or 'formed'. There is in fact

> no contradiction in assuming both (a) that one must appreciate the whole structure of a work as the declaration of a poetics, and (b) that such a work can be considered as fully realized only when its poetic project can be appreciated as the concrete, material, and perceptibly enjoyable result of its underlying project. (*DA*, p. 272/*OW*, p. 176)

But, as Eco goes on to suggest,

to appreciate a work as a perceptible form means to react to the physical stimuli of the object, not just intellectually but also – so to speak – physically. Fraught with a variety of responses, our appreciation of the object will never assume the univocal exactitude characteristic of intellectual understanding and will be at once personal, changeable and open. (*DA*, pp. 272–3/*OW*, pp. 176–7)

Eco thus proposes a combination of a rationalist view of art, with an emphasis on the making of the work and on its structure, complemented by a view of contemporary art as inherently rationalist which allows in practice a synthesis or summary of the work of art (as argued by Della Volpe), with an idea of the reception of the work which maximizes the possibilities of variety, ambiguity and choice. Which, as a definition of the work of art, may be read as a skilful juggling of the pieces or, possibly, as an aporia.

The appearance of *Opera aperta*

In June 1962, Eco published *Opera aperta*, the book that made his name. The essays collected in it grew out of the same terrain that was nurturing the guiding principles of the aesthetics just described. *Opera aperta* has had three editions (1962, 1967 and 1976), each with important variations in content, and each furnished with a different, but always substantive, Introduction by the author. An important intermediate stage between the first and second editions is represented by the 1965 translation into French, published by Seuil, to which we shall return in due course; the English translation of 1989 both omits material from the Italian editions and adds some from elsewhere. The most striking difference between the 1962 edition (and the 1965 translation) and its successors was that, from the second edition on, the substantial essay on the poetics of James Joyce, which made up the whole of the second half of the original book, was omitted, having been published separately in 1966. Since then, in English as well as Italian, the other essays of *Opera aperta* and the essay on Joyce have led independent lives.[11]

Much of what Eco had been feeling his way towards in the essays written in the second half of the 1950s is here distilled into the metaphor of 'openness' around which the essays of *Opera aperta* are clustered.[12] But 'openness' does not just denote a feature of art in general, or an aspect of particular importance in the elaboration of a general aesthetic. It is also a rallying cry. *Opera aperta* imposes itself on the public of 1962 as a statement that is imperiously contemporary. Eco writes about all art, but he also, especially, writes about modern art.

This gives rise to a fruitful tension in the book. At one level, it may be expressed as a tension between different senses of the term 'openness', and to this we shall return. At another, and it is important to pause here for a moment in order to contextualize the work, it is perceptible as a tension between a point of view that is somehow above the fray and one that is deeply embedded in the existing circuit of production and consumption of works of art. The first is far from foreign to aesthetics in general, and to idealist aesthetics in particular, and Eco, for all his commitment to the historicity and the practicality of the work of art, does not always resist it; indeed, he needs to be able to clamber to a position (which at this stage is assured more by key ideas and images than by the kind of systematic theory that will be provided by semiotics) from which it is possible to make authoritative general statements. But the second point of view, that of involvement, is far from alien to Eco either. The essays of *Opera aperta* (and others from the same period not included in the book) are intimately familiar with the milieux of contemporary artistic experimentation, especially in Milan, where Eco trained and worked as a producer of cultural programmes for the newly established state television service (RAI-TV) between 1954 and 1959. He struck up a productive and long-lasting friendship with the composer Luciano Berio, through whom he got to know the work of other contemporary composers as well as the composers themselves (Cage, Boulez, Pousseur) and to be involved with Berio and his then wife, the soprano Cathy Berberian, in experimentation with words and sound in the RAI's electronic music studio (the Studio di fonologia, established in 1955) which would eventually lead to Berio and Berberian's *Thema* (*Omaggio a Joyce*).[13] In 1959 (back from his military service) Eco began to write for *Il verri*, the cultural magazine founded by Luciano Anceschi in 1956, distinguished for its close attention to contemporary art as well as for its nurturing (mainly thanks to Anceschi's discriminating support) of a generation of notable young writers. Among these were Nanni Balestrini, Alfredo Giuliani, Elio Pagliarani, Antonio Porta and Edoardo Sanguineti (with whom Eco had been at university), who in 1961 brought out a group anthology, *I Novissimi*, which made serious claims to mark a new departure in Italian poetry. Both of these experiences not only put Eco in daily contact with highly creative people, an exposure that was only made more frequent by the editorial work that he began, also in 1959, for the publisher Bompiani, but they also provided spaces in which Eco could express his own ideas in print. Although his main contributions to *Il verri* were for the sometimes playful, sometimes satirical 'Diario minimo' series (see chapter 2), the journal also published 'serious' reviews and essays of his, including the study of openness in 'informal' art which appears in *OA* as 'L'opera aperta nelle opere visive'. Two of the *Opera aperta* essays also made their first appearance in Luciano Berio's elusive magazine *Incontri musicali*[14] – and the book itself, of course, was published by Bompiani.

The turn against representational realism in fiction and lyrical intimacy in poetry, renewed attention to the materials, methods and techniques of the arts (as opposed to the 'message' supposedly conveyed by their contents), the analysis of elements (as in Berio's work on phonology or in the colour experiments of the 'informal' painters), the combination and remixing of genres, styles, registers, languages and media (from Balestrini's early experiments with computer-generated poetry to Sanguineti's multilingualism) – all these are part of the excitement of what within a few years will jell, perhaps fatally, into the Italian 'Neo-avant-garde'. The experimentalism which they cultivate and celebrate, however, is very far from being purely formalistic. The problem of political and social responsibility, the relation between avant-garde art and ideology, the question of whether the avant-garde is 'progressive' or 'reactionary' and, more pressingly, of how to get out of the sterile opposition between those two terms was to dominate Italian discussions about the arts and the media throughout the 1960s. We shall return to them later in this study. Within the immediate context of *Opera aperta*, these questions are anxiously addressed in the Introduction to the first edition, and then more extensively in the essay written shortly after its appearance and added to the second, 'Del modo di formare come impegno sulla realtà' ('Form as Social Commitment'). The direction of argument implicit in that title is already adumbrated in Eco's Introduction: the priority of form, with the caveat that form (which is also form*ing*, shaping, making) is not the same thing as formal*ism*: 'if art can choose as many *subjects* of discourse as it likes, the only *content* which matters is a certain way in which man places himself in relation to the world and resolves this attitude at the level of structures in a *way of forming*' (*OA*, pp. 13–14). But with this quotation we have already entered into the question of what it is, in Eco's theory, that constitutes openness.

The poetics of the open work

'La poetica dell'opera aperta', the opening essay in *Opera aperta*, brings three kinds of openness to the attention of the reader. There is, first, a particular kind of modern work which Eco describes as an *opera in movimento*, a 'work in movement'. The examples are drawn from contemporary, post-Webernian, music and illustrate a very specific kind of openness, that in which the performer is required in some way to organize or complete what is left by the composer in a deliberately non-definitive state: in Stockhausen's *Klavierstück XI*, for example, the composer presents the performer with a single large sheet of music paper with a series of note groupings, from amongst which the performer must choose, first the one to start the piece and then the successive units in the order which the performer chooses. Such works are 'characterized by the invitation to *make the work* together with the author' (*OA*, p. 60/*OW*, p. 21). Secondly Eco refers, on a wider level, to works which, 'although organically completed', are nevertheless ' "open" to a continuous generation of internal relations which the addressee must uncover and select in his act of perceiving the totality of incoming stimuli' (ibid.). The examples range from the poetic 'suggestiveness' sought by the Symbolists to Kafka's use of the symbol 'as a communicative channel for the indefinite, open to constantly shifting responses and interpretative stances' (*OA*, p. 41/*OW*, p. 9) to the multiplicity of perspective sought by Joyce in *Ulysses* and the 'Einsteinian' universe of *Finnegans Wake* and to Brecht's use of defamiliarization in his theatre and the responsibility he puts upon the spectators to draw their own conclusions. Finally, Eco acknowledges an even more general sense of 'openness', according to which '*every* work of art, even though it is produced by following an explicit or implicit poetics of necessity, is effectively open to a virtually unlimited range of possible readings' (*OA*, p. 60/*OW*, p. 21): the important example of a 'poetics of necessity' is Dante's, which allowed four levels of reading, but *only* those.

Eco's fundamental point is this: that the activity of interpretation in which every reader (viewer, listener) always engages, necessarily, in any culture, in response to any work of art – this much has already been established on the basis of Eco's reading of Pareyson – is elicited in special and deliberate ways by the modern artist: the need for the addressee actively and consciously to perform (in a Pareysonian sense), to complete, to interpret the work is a priority within the poetics of the artist, within what Eco will later call 'the intention of the work'. The demands made of the addressee vary in degree, as we have seen, but although Eco will continue in his essays to break lances on behalf of the musicians whose work he particularly wants to draw attention to, he will in practice increasingly collapse the 'strong' sense of openness (that of the work to be 'completed', that is, assembled or arranged, by the performer) into the more general one of something that looks suspiciously like a modernist aesthetics.

Here, what will already have become apparent from this brief summary of Eco's argument must be made explicit. The terms in which Eco makes his case in 'The Poetics of the Open Work' are not those of aesthetics, but of cultural history; or, more exactly, readers find themselves deftly guided into the expectation that the settlement of their doubts will have a historical basis.[15] The history, painted in broad strokes, shows two things. The first is the changing relation over time, in Western culture, between the 'definiteness' of the completed work and its 'openness' to interpretation (moving from a relative emphasis on 'definiteness' in the Middle Ages to an increasing emphasis on 'openness' in modernity).[16] The second is a range of resemblances and possible comparisons between the idea of openness in art and aesthetics and what Eco calls 'structural homologies' (*OA*, p. 56/*OW*, p. 18) in other fields of human knowledge. The swift movement through historical periods, perhaps particularly in a cultural environment like Italy's, still at the time steeped in historicism, appears to provide an underpinning of necessity for the broad categorization of modernity that is to follow.

Here the emphasis on openness in the poetics of contemporary art joins with non-Euclidean geometries, multi-value logic, the principle of complementarity in physics (Heisenberg, Bohr), the idea of 'perceptive ambiguities' in modern psychology and phenomenology (Husserl, Sartre, Merleau-Ponty on consciousness as 'the very region of indetermination': *OA*, p. 55/*OW*, p. 17) and the multiple polarity associated with the spatio-temporal conception of the universe which we owe to Einstein to characterize a culture of uncertainty. To an unsympathetic reader of Eco, the broad generalizations and multiple connections may seem less than convincing, a sort of omniumgatherum of anything that might look remotely 'indeterminate'. But the cultural history, and the characterization of the modern, including 'openness', which arises from it is at the heart of the essay, materially and rhetorically. It is the guarantee or promise that a pattern, however provisional, may be discernible, however faintly, and that the addressees of the modern open work are not alone in their unsettledness: it is a constitutive part of their modernity. It is important too that this modernity is not to be construed as ontological: it is not states of the actual world that are being compared, but descriptions of states of the world; we are looking at the relationship between 'a scientific methodology and a poetics' (apropos of Niels Bohr: *OA*, p. 53 n. 13/*OW*, p. 252 n. 9). Eco will return repeatedly to this essentially epistemological basis of the response to the work of art (and to the world), notably in his essay on informal painting. The 'open work' in this context is one before which viewers must choose their own points of view, make their own connections; its forms are epistemological metaphors which confirm, in art, the categories of indeterminacy and statistical distribution that guide the interpretation of natural facts; it is not a narration, but an image – 'it *is* it' – of discontinuity; it represents conjectural freedom, 'the unlimited discovery of contrasts and oppositions that keep multiplying with every new look' (*OA*, pp. 158, 159, 164, 167/*OW*, pp. 86, 87, 90, 93).

Eco makes two points about the poetics of 'openness' and the concomitant freedoms afforded to, or rather demanded of, the addressee (*destinatario*) of the work of art. Firstly, that however 'open' the work of art may be to multiple and even contradictory interpretations, it is still in the end a work, a made object, a thing done. That is the constraint on the interpreter; as Eco will remark thirty years later, 'Joyce's *Ulysses* can stimulate *many* interpretations, but not all possible interpretations . . . In every case, the interpretations had to be of *Ulysses* and not, for example, of the *Odyssey*.'[17] The second, reiterated, point is that the notion of openness does not, in itself, imply a value-judgement. It is not, because our works of art exact more 'openness' from us, that they or we are somehow 'better' than our or their predecessors; it is simply that that is how it is, or rather, it is the common way we think and act in our modernity. Even so, Eco cannot have been entirely surprised that many reviewers read *Opera aperta* in this progressivist or Whiggish light and reacted according to their degree of friendliness or hostility to the perceived thesis.[18] And, to be truthful, it is difficult to avoid an impression of progressive liberation of the reader and a corresponding weakening of the communicative power of classical or traditional art, if only because it is the conditions of *modern* art (its production and reception) that Eco is so keen to explore. Rather than a flaw in Eco's argument, however, this impression suggests the limits of cultural history as a basis for describing aesthetic phenomena.

The strengths and the limitations of the historical approach are most evident in the long essay on Joyce, whose entire work is read as an 'epistemological metaphor'. Eco's interpretation is based on a powerfully argued assessment of Joyce's 'medievalism', in which Eco acknowledged more than a passing personal interest.[19] The creation of the radically decentred universe of *Ulysses* and *Finnegans Wake* is accompanied by a progressive subverting of the conceptual systematicity of Aquinas (and scholasticism in general, and what survives of it in the practices of the Catholic Church), the attraction of which, however, is never entirely dulled in Joyce. Thus, Joyce's poetics, as articulated by him and as realized in the work, are seen by Eco as the site of successive crises of an original medieval order. In *Stephen Hero* Joyce will found his theory of epiphanies, which is largely indebted to Walter Pater, on the teachings of Aquinas, only to kick this pseudo-doctrinal ladder away when he no longer needs it, in the *Portrait*. *Ulysses* is read as an apocalyptic text, one which stresses rupture in the form of a radical and dramatic loss of cultural co-ordinates, whose symbolism Eco puts in sharp contrast with that of the Middle Ages in which meaning is activated on the basis of a shared grammar of bestiaries and lapidaries, grammars and ency-clopedias; yet it is a work which shows its 'medieval nature' (*AC*, p. 48) in its ordering in accordance with 'iron-clad rules' (*AC*, p. 47) that a Geoffroy de Vinsauf or a Matthieu de Vendôme might have sanctioned. In *Finnegans Wake*, finally, the memory of a scholastic order which was present, however 'perversely', in *Ulysses* has now disappeared. But the sense of a crisis has not. Here, it is evoked for Eco by what comes before and after that order: Joyce's indebtedness in the novel to the Irish monastic art of manuscript illustration from which derives a portrait of the artist as 'the last of the medieval monks, protected by his own silence to illuminate illegible, fantastic words, not knowing if for himself or the men of tomorrow' (*AC*, p. 81); and, equally, his fascination with the liberating, and danger-ous, humanistic, potentially hermeticist fantastication and experi-mentation of Giordano Bruno and Nicholas of Cusa.

The sequence of cultural crises mapped around the collapse of medieval 'order', the constant dialectic of order and adventure, is mirrored intriguingly in Eco's own novels, where the theme of the disintegration and reconfiguration of Western thought between the high Middle Ages and the emergence of the 'new' science is a structuring principle.[20] Here indeed is one of the strengths of the essentially cultural-historical basis of Eco's interpretation of Joyce: it provides a narrative, in which each cultural moment comes before or after, providing a link with its neighbours in time. Joyce's own poetics of course proceed in search of a quite different kind of narrative order – a fact of which Eco is well aware and to character-ize which it is precisely the notion of openness that he deploys. But the nostalgia for a narrative sequence is at least as strong in Eco as that for scholastic order – which means that when it is called up, as in the novels, it can never be without irony. At the level of 'Le poetiche di Joyce' in *Opera aperta*, however, the cultural-historical approach also has evident limitations. In the first place, it is liable to a charge of circularity: in so far as we can see in Joyce's work 'a dialectic that belongs not only to his personal intellectual life but to the entire evolution of our culture' (*AC*, p. 85), we have to be satisfied that we are not selecting those features of Western culture which will precisely prove the hypothesis of Joyce's representative-ness. The shadow of the artist or intellectual as 'world-historical individual' may also be discerned in the more prophetic moments of Eco's discourse on Joyce, where historical narrative and analysis give way to a kind of inspired ventriloquism:

> You (Joyce might well say to us) are conscious that the form of the universe has changed, but you can no longer understand it, and neither can I. You are conscious that in this world you will no longer be able to work according to the centuries-old criteria which a whole culture has consecrated, and I am conscious of it too. Very well, I give you an *Ersatz* of this world, which otherwise is divine, eternal and incomprehensible, a 'whorled without aimed' . . . ; but at least it is something of ours, it is established in the human order of language, not in the incomprehensible order of cosmic events, and in this ambit we can confront and understand it. (*PJ*, p. 145[21])

Joyce would not say, I have given you this new world in a single book, which would make him a mystic or a writer of the occult (something that Eco is inclined to reproach Mallarmé with). What he would say is:

> I offer you a possible form of the world realized in language: the form of a new world, built of many relationships, measured by the rhythm of unstoppable mutations which yet always reconfirm the form of every-thing. This is the hypothesis which I put forward on the world, but I put it forward in language. The world as such is not my business. (*PJ*, p. 162)

Which do not just sound like the words the Eco of *Opera aperta* might speak – they actually are.

This is not a solid basis on which to advance a new conception of art and aesthetics. But at the same time Eco is working his way towards other ways of thinking about openness, taking him already in the first edition of *Opera aperta*, and increasingly in the 1965 translation and the second edition of 1967, towards information theory, structural linguistics and theories of communication. Correspondingly, the guidelines provided by an older Anglo-American semantics (C. K. Ogden and I. A. Richards, Charles Morris) begin to diminish in importance. It is to these developments that we must now turn, still, initially, in the company of Joyce.

Beyond 'openness'

The relationship between 'openness' as a characteristic of all art and the programmatic openness of contemporary art is at the centre of the essay placed second in *Opera aperta*, 'Analisi del linguaggio poetico', and is vividly conveyed by what is one of the best passages in the book, where Eco compares a *terzina* from Dante's *Paradiso* with an extract from *Finnegans Wake*. In the *Paradiso* (33, ll. 124–6), at the culmination of the *Divine Comedy*, Dante has to explain the nature of the Trinity, 'the highest and most difficult concept in his entire poem' (*OA*, p. 90/*OW*, p. 40). These are his words:

> O Luce eterna, che sola in te sidi,
> Sola t'intendi, e, da te intelletta
> Ed intendente te, ami e arridi!

(O Light Eternal, who alone abidest in Thyself, / alone knowest Thyself, and known to Thyself / and knowing, lovest and smilest on Thyself![22])

The concept itself is 'univocally' defined by dogma, it is not open to interpretation; Dante's rendering of it in these three lines, however,

> is an absolutely original reformulation in which the ideas are so integrated into the rhythm and phonic material of the lines that they manage to express not just the concept they are supposed to convey, but also the feeling of blissful contemplation that accompanies its comprehension . . . Conversely, at every new reading of the tercet, the idea of the Trinity expands with new emotion and new suggestions, and its meaning, though univocal, gets deeper and richer. (*OA*, pp. 90–1/*OW*, pp. 40–1)

The Joyce passage, on the other hand, from the fifth chapter of *Finnegans Wake*, takes us to the midden-heap where the narrator is trying to describe the mysterious letter found there. Its meaning is undecipherable and obscure because it is multiform. The letter is the linguistic mirror of the universe of the *Wake*, to define which amounts to defining the very nature of the cosmos, as important to Joyce as the Trinity was to Dante. 'But whereas the Trinity of the *Divine Comedy* has only one possible meaning, the cosmos-*Finnegans Wake*-letter is a *chaosmos* that can be defined only in terms of its substantial ambiguity. The author must therefore speak of a nonunivocal object, by using nonunivocal signs and combining them in a nonunivocal fashion' (*OA*, p. 91/*OW*, p. 41). Theoretically, both Dante's tercet and the sentence Eco quotes from Joyce result from an analogous structural procedure: the combination of denotative and connotative meanings with an ensemble of physical linguistic properties to produce an organic form. From an aesthetic point of view, both forms are 'open' 'in that they provoke an ever newer, ever richer enjoyment' (*OA*, p. 92/*OW*, p. 42), though the source of the pleasure is a univocal message in Dante's case, a plurivocal one in Joyce's. At this point in his argument, Eco makes a crucial and difficult move: in the case of Joyce, aesthetic pleasure is 'augmented' by another value that the modern author is trying to attain. The 'value', to judge by the examples given and by the argument elsewhere in the book, is constituted by our being made aware of more and other possibilities (that is, it inheres in the very plurivocality of the form), and Eco acknowledges that, 'theoretically', this value should not be confused with aesthetic value: the latter depends on the project of plurivocal communication being incorporated into the right form, 'since this alone can endow it with the fundamental openness proper to all successful artistic forms' (*OA*, p. 93/*OW*, p. 42). But plurivocality is so much a part of the forms concerned that their aesthetic value can no longer be explained without it. In this sense, the modern open work acquires a 'second order' of openness which, however, seems not to be separable from the 'augmentation' of aesthetic pleasure which its plurivocality entails. It is from arguments such as these that some readers derived their sense of a diminution of the value of the artistic tradition. But, more importantly, from Eco's own point of view, they lead him to force the bounds of aesthetics:

This value, this second degree of openness to which contemporary art aspires, could also be defined as the growth and multiplication of the possible meanings of a given message. But few people are willing to speak of meaning in relation to the kind of communication provided by a nonfigurative pictorial sign or a constellation of sounds. This kind of openness is therefore best defined as an increase in information. (*OA*, p. 93/*OW*, pp. 42–3)

In order to assess what an 'increase in information' might imply, Eco proposes that aesthetics should take a sideways step and see what might be learnt from current researches in information theory.

What Eco learns first and foremost from the lengthy study entitled 'Apertura, informazione, comunicazione' which forms the next chapter of *Opera aperta* is that notions borrowed from information theory, notably that of entropy as a statistical concept, have only limited value when applied to human communication. The question of boundaries is important to Eco's developing methodological search. At the same time as he is inquiring into information theory he is refining his sense of the particularity of the 'aesthetic' or 'poetic' message. Primarily under the influence of Jakobson, and on the strength of a growing familiarity with the Russian Formalists, French structuralism and structural linguistics (he had been introduced to Saussure, he says, by Berio), he begins to introduce a new vocabulary into his essays. The appearance of terms like 'signifier' and 'connotation' and the problematization of others such as 'referent' and 'denotatum' can be traced philologically in the evolution of 'Analisi del linguaggio poetico' from its first published version in 1961, through the first edition of *Opera aperta* and the French translation (where these changes first become noticeable) to the 1967 edition, in which the Jakobsonian criterion of 'ambiguity' also becomes a keyword in the new Introduction. We shall be looking in more detail at the impact of these sources on Eco's aesthetics in chapter 2 – for the moment it is sufficient to register their presence.

The case of information theory is different. Challenged by an important review by Emilio Garroni of the first edition of *Opera aperta*,[23] Eco in the second inserts an interscript into the essay on openness, information and communication. Here he accepts that information theory, which is concerned with calculating the quantity of information contained in a particular message, has little to tell us once it is transposed from an analysis of the transmission of signals to that of communication between human beings. At this point it becomes a theory of communication, in which 'it preserves a basic categorial scheme but . . . loses its algorithmic system' (*OA*, p. 127/*OW*, p. 67). But this does not mean that the exploration of the structures of information has been a blind alley. If the concepts pertaining to information theory had been obviously applicable to language or to art, there would have been no point in trying to find out whether they were applicable or not. That uncertainty has to be tested out by someone like Eco who believes that

> ultimately, the mechanism that underlies a work of art (and this is what needs to be verified) *must* reveal the same behaviour that characterizes the mechanisms of communication, including those types of behavior that involve the mere transmission, along one channel, of signals devoid of all connotative meaning. (*OA*, p. 128/*OW*, p. 68)

The particular problem of 'second-order' openness, with its apparent increase of information, is leading back, through the discriminations made possible by an exploration of information theory coupled with those which come from structural linguistics, to a reconsideration of openness in all aesthetic communication which can only be based on a general theory of meaning. While from information theory Eco has got some sense of what is specific about human communication, from Jakobson and others he has learnt what is specific about 'poetic' communication. But they are all about meaning, and the route to understanding that now lies through semiotics or, as it is still called in the Italian text, semiology. 'The categorial apparatus of information theory appears methodologically fruitful only when inserted in the context of a *general semiotics* . . . Before rejecting informational notions, one must verify them in the light of a semiotic rereading' (*OA*, pp. 129–30/*OW*, p. 69). Information theory is not dismissed out of hand; rather, a wider field is delineated in order, perhaps, to accommodate it. What Eco has done in his 'Postilla'/'Postscript' (dated 1966) is to sketch the working plan for his first semiotic book, *La struttura assente*, which came out in 1968; we shall examine what remains of informational ideas more closely when we come to analyse the relevant part of that book in chapter 3.

Opera aperta is itself an 'open work', subject to change, and above all growth, during its successive editions, particularly in the 1960s; true to itself, it does not offer definitive solutions. Yet it was a book that had enormous impact at the time. Taken, rightly or wrongly, as the manifesto of the group of avant-garde writers who set themselves up in October 1963 as the 'Gruppo 63', 'il best-seller della nostra generazione', the best-seller of our generation, according to the editor and journalist Valerio Riva,[24] *Opera aperta* challenged long-established academic barriers: the fact that it both extended, or exceeded, the bounds of aesthetics in order to open a dialogue with the emerging sciences of communication and was prepared (in

'Chance and Plot') to look at a somehow 'non-artistic' medium like television from the point of view of aesthetics implicitly challenged, and very directly, a view that identified 'culture' with 'great works' and 'great artists'.[25] The fruitfulness of the book both for Eco's developing ideas (what De Lauretis calls its 'valore di ipotesi', its power as hypothesis),[26] and for its early formulation of important themes in subsequent literary theoretical debate,[27] is beyond question. But if it is the case that *Opera aperta* sold 'some tens of thousands of copies',[28] its writ certainly ran beyond the immediate circles of the academy and the avant-garde. It would be surprising, in view of what has just been said, if Eco's book had not aroused the critical reactions which it did. But it is important to get these responses into perspective. Tales of shock and scandal at the appearance of new and challenging modern works (including critical ones) are usually greatly exaggerated, handy though they may be for publicity. If Eco's book was successful, it was also because there was already a public there who needed it, made use of it, was in a sense prepared for it. The artists whom Eco wrote about – Boulez, Berio, Stockhausen, Calder, Wols – were far from unknown. They were *difficult*, and *Opera aperta* provided a way for interested people to talk interestingly about them. The style of the book is for the most part inclusive (as an example one might cite the opening pages of 'The Open Work in the Visual Arts') and, though a serious history of its reception would have to take account of the different constituencies in Eco's readership (for example, the important, and divided, Communist Party readership discussed in *OA*, pp. xv–xvii), it is probably fair to say that the book was important from the beginning, not only because of its specific arguments, but because, beyond those, it helped a wide audience to discern and to adjust to a cultural world in the throes of rapid and perplexing change.

2

A Critical View of Culture: Mass Communications, Politics and the Avant-garde

At one level the essays of *Opera aperta* concentrate on suggesting ways in which difficult modern works work, and providing means for an educated audience to make sense of them. There is at this level a residual moment of pure aesthetic pleasure, or that which corresponds to the studied absorption of the artisan's workshop. Yet the producer, the work and the audience are all implicated in a social process. Throughout the 1960s the interaction between forms of cultural communication and their social environment is articulated in terms of responsibility. Eco is as aware as anybody of the balance that has continually to be re-negotiated within the sphere of cultural production and consumption between freedom and irrelevance, between relevance and subservience, between passivity and critical understanding. He continues to explore these themes in the works of the avant-garde, but they are an important dimension also of his interest in mass culture and mass communications. This interest had been touched on in *Opera aperta* and is the focus of his next, and no less hotly debated, collection of essays, *Apocalittici e integrati* (1964, generally referred to in English as 'Apocalyptic and Integrated Intellectuals', partially translated in *Apocalypse Postponed*, 1994). This important sortie by Eco into the sociology of culture will be our main point of reference in this chapter, which will start by providing some of the background to the questions mentioned above before looking at his propositions in more detail. But a consideration of *Apocalittici e integrati* will lead us back in the end to what is the central theme of the first half of this book, Eco's elaboration of a theoretical model upon which to base the study of cultural phenomena: he has himself indicated that it was the study of mass culture that led him to semiotics (*AI*, p. xiii/*AP*, p. 54); on the way, he had to confront some of the methodological, and ultimately ideological, problems raised by structuralism in general. The chapter will end with a brief mention of the travails of *Quindici*, the journal with which Eco was closely involved and in which the avant-garde came face to face with the street politics of 1967–9.

The role of the avant-garde

It is interesting to turn back for a moment to the essay 'Form as Social Commitment' mentioned in chapter 1, which was written immediately after the publication of *Opera aperta* in 1962 and included in subsequent editions. Although its main focus is on the contemporary artist, and we shall come to that in a moment, it is also concerned with the role of the intellectual in general, and in this respect Eco adopts positions which he will maintain in *Apocalittici e integrati*. It is here, for example, that we find the first formulation of the polemical contrast between 'apocalyptic' intellectuals, the doom-sayers who regard the tendencies of contemporary art (not to mention those of mass communications) as the murder of the human spirit, and the rather more difficult to define 'integrated' intellectuals. The latter are represented in this essay by the idea of a total integration with nature and with one's own activity ascribed to John Dewey, the former with the legacy of the 'beautiful soul' currently residing in the anthropologist and critic Elemire Zolla. Faced with the choice as a critic and a commentator on culture between total surrender to the object à la Dewey and cool detachment from it à la Zolla, Eco is searching for an '"ascetic" stratagem to safeguard my freedom while implicating myself in the object' (*OA*, pp. 253–4/ *OW*, p. 135). This leads him to an identification with the cultural anthropologist perched on a tightrope between regarding the society he is describing as something totally extraneous to himself (and he to it) and being completely taken over by it. What the cultural commentator/anthropologist must do is 'translate' or 'paraphrase', resting his description on 'a sort of metalanguage' (*OA*, p. 271/*OW*, p. 145). To be both inside and outside the object of description is also the task of the artist, evidently with different means: the real content of a work is the vision of the world expressed in its way of forming (*modo di formare*).[1] The avant-garde artist uses the materials of the world from which at the same time he maintains a critical distance: he is 'alienated into' it, as Joyce is alienated into the realities of modern journalism in the Aeolus episode of *Ulysses*, as Antonioni expresses the alienation which he wishes to convey to the public in the very structures of a film like *L'eclisse*. All this should lead to a clearer understanding of the function of the avant-garde and of its descriptive possibilities:

> To understand the world, avant-garde art delves into it and assumes its critical condition from within, adopting, to describe it, the same alienated language in which it expresses itself. But by giving this language a descriptive function and laying it bare as a narrative form, avant-garde art also strips it of its alienating aspects and allows us to demystify it. (*OA*, p. 278/*OW*, p. 150)

Eco's concern is to shift attention away from the supposedly alienating effects of the avant-garde itself to the way in which it exposes the workings of contemporary reality from within so as to enable the human subject to understand or come to terms with them, to master them even, or at least to affect and manipulate them. His approach to mass culture will not be dissimilar: the way to tackle the bogey is to see it for what it is and to understand how it works, without allowing oneself to be taken over by it (this latter being the kind of bureaucratic or managerial enslavement which is what is meant by 'integration' in *Apocalittici e integrati*). The immediate context of his essay is the debate on the relations between literature and industry which took place in the journal *Il menabò* in 1961 and 1962.[2] What was meant by 'industry' was defined by the Marxist critic Gianni Scalia in a fundamental contribution to the debate:

> [Industry] is no longer simply an aspect of economic reality, but the given *totality* of present reality; and it has an impact on all aspects of social and individual life in the 'post-modern' world. Industry is to be understood as scientific and technological decision-making, the planning of production and consumption, the organization of the means of cultural communication, the creation of new kinds of work, new institutions, new models of behaviour.[3]

In short, industry was understood as having to do with the organization of work in general (not just in the factory), the specific forms that it takes in modern capitalism (rational, specialized, proletarian), and its consequences at an individual and social level (analysed particularly in terms of 'alienation').

In fact the exchange of views on literature and industry initiated by Vittorini, and Eco's substantial contribution to it in 'Form as Social Commitment', were only part of a much wider debate going on in the Italian left as a whole which concerned in broad terms the kind of attitude to take, and above all the political responses that needed to be elaborated, in the face of the transformations of the Italian economy (and Italian society) under the aegis of the 'economic miracle' of 1958–63. This is not the place to go into the details of that debate, and in any case one must remember that Eco brings a cultural, not a political, still less social or economic, perspective to bear on the issues – even if it is a cultural perspective which, like that of most of his peers at the time, is politically alert and informed. As usual, Eco offers not a critique, but a description of an artistic process, a 'philosophical investigation concerned with [the possibility conditions of] a certain attitude of contemporary poetics' (*OA*, p. 287/*OW*, p. 155; the English translation omits the words in square brackets). In both *Opera aperta* and *Apocalittici e integrati*, and perhaps especially in 'Form as Social Commitment', which in a way straddles the concerns of both books, Eco is modernizing Crocean idealism by standing it on its head (or 'secularizing Pareyson', as he put it). But he is also responding in particular to the anxieties of a left that is itself run through with Croceo-Gramscian assumptions about the role and direction of contemporary culture, anxieties ranging in intensity from bewilderment through suspicion to downright hostility to one or another or every aspect of the rapid and perplexing cultural (social, economic) transformations of the years of the 'miracle'. There are two aspects of this transformation which particularly exercise the political left, new or old, in so far as it is concerned with culture: the avant-garde on the one hand and the development of mass communications and the mass media (at this moment, television in particular) on the other. From this point of view the avant-garde and the new media really are opposites, or perhaps the 'fatal complement' of each other, as Eco hints in his Preface to the 1977 edition of *Apocalittici e integrati* (*AI*, p. xv/*AP*, p. 56).

The most vocal, and visible, expression of the Italian Neo-avant-garde of the early 1960s was the self-styled Gruppo 63. The group, which calqued its name on and borrowed some of its style of operations from the long-established German Gruppe 47, officially came into being during a series of seminars, readings, lectures and theatrical performances organized by Nanni Balestrini on the fringe of the fourth 'International New Music Week' held in Palermo in

October 1963. The group (which included most of the *Verri* poets as well as novelists like Alberto Arbasino and Germano Lombardi, writers for the theatre, critics and art historians[4]) was more a loose network than a formal organization. The process of inclusion or exclusion, acceptance or rejection, could be a painful one and contributed to a widespread, sometimes frankly envious view of the Gruppo 63 as inward-looking. Eco was present at some of the gatherings of the Gruppo 63, including the founding meeting in Palermo, he was friends with many of the principal people involved, he took part in the debates and his contributions were published along with those of other participants.[5] He was particularly welcomed and appreciated as the author of *Opera aperta* (though his inwardness with the 'culture industry', first with RAI-TV and then with Bompiani, was an added *cachet*). But while *Opera aperta* was almost a theoretical bible for the Neo-avant-garde, Eco consciously limited his involvement to the role of describing what was going on and encouraging from the sidelines. Such reticence was quite understandable, for the Neo-avant-garde, the initiatives of the Gruppo 63 in particular, was of primary concern to the artists themselves, and Eco was not in this category. He thus positions himself in a somewhat oblique relation to the passionate and agonized debates that took place within artistic circles, and particularly amongst writers, during the 1960s on the relation between art and politics, between language and ideology, and on the political role of the artist and of the avant-garde itself. He continues to comment on and to describe what the artists are *doing* and why, but does not, from this perspective, need to take the kind of defined position that those in the midst of the debate like Balestrini, Sanguineti, or Leonetti, from within the Neo-avant-garde, or others like Fortini or Pasolini, from outside it, felt themselves, continuously and repeatedly, constrained to adopt and to defend.

This may help to explain why, subsequently, Eco has been increasingly sceptical about the Neo-avant-garde as a *movement*, and has evolved an increasingly sharp distinction between 'avant-garde' and 'experiment', entirely to the credit of the latter. But the differentiation is a long-standing one, and his position may best be illustrated by a fable invented before the Gruppo 63 even came into existence, in the programmatically entitled essay 'Sperimentalismo e avanguardia' ('Experimentalism and Avant-garde', 1962, subsequently in *La definizione dell'arte*). The fable starts, as good fables should, in the garden, in this case the grounds of a country house, richly, sumptuously, decorated for a wedding. Eco tells us he is there with a friend. This friend is a musician, presumably a rather fashionable, up-and-coming musician, though he is still poor, because he has been invited to create a kind of 'son-et-lumière' for the occasion and he has accepted because he needs the money. He has accepted, but he is irritated by the ostentatious display of wealth. So he takes his revenge. At the height of the party, 'with the guests swarming around the gardens having devoured a buffet of Pantagruelian proportions', from the microphones concealed in the greenery rise the notes of Mozart's K550, the Symphony no. 40 in G minor, to Eco's ears the most subtly tragic, despairing and disquieting of musics. We have a suggestive tableau of a rich, self-indulgent, unthinking, stupid, hypocritical bourgeoisie, with their resident musician employed as entertainer, and the resident musician conforming and at the same time rebelling in his role, trying to turn the tables; plus the young Eco, keeping him company, uncomfortable in his turn, almost angered by the gesture of his friend.

> I remember that my first reaction was one of irritation at the moral alibi which the musician was acquiring on the cheap – because if the music was being consumed cheerfully and distractedly while people were waffling canapés and drinking champagne, it really was being neutralized, emptied of any efficacy, being turned into court music because that was how it was being consumed by a distracted public. It really was an avant-garde on the point of turning into something merely academic. (*DA*, pp. 251–2)

The theme of 'neutralization' is paramount in this essay. Experimentalism in art is here closely connected to the discovery of the experimental method in science. It depends on a radical doubt, a willingness to question everything, a readiness on the part of the artist to begin again, to start afresh, to kick away the support of the existing order. But experimentalism itself becomes the norm, and is readily accepted by a society which is geared to the constant and rapid consumption of the new. 'Experimentalism' finds its place as a term within a negative dialectic, whereby society neutralizes art's threat or challenge to society: if artists can be shown to be just working away in their laboratories, no one need worry. Society has a way of dealing with research products, of putting them to practical use, by blocking their inventiveness, that within them which points towards the future (rather than to present consumption). Using the example of the visual arts and their commercial-industrial application, Eco reveals the paradoxical nature of the avant-garde: its destiny always to challenge the public acceptance of and satisfaction with the products which it has itself just a moment ago brought into being. The inherent revolutionism of the avant-garde is in place, but operates mechanically, turned against itself.

Eco's initial reaction in the garden is a faithful reflection of this pessimistic self-consciousness of the new avant-gardes of the late 1950s and early 1960s. The impotent vengefulness of the musician (by this stage, Eco and his friend, who might be called 'Berio', the principal actors of this story, are obviously fictional entities), the strong element of self-disgust, the spectacle of consumption which recalls scenes from Antonioni on whom (the real) Eco commented so acutely in 'Form as Social Commitment' at much the same time as this essay was written, the consciousness of a complex of powers (perceived mainly as economic, political and social) which bear down on the new, the very sadness of the music which seems to the reader to be a comment not only on the *danse macabre* of the wedding guests, but on the alienation and discomfort of the young revolutionists too – all these form part of the anxious knowledge of the Neo-avant-garde of the processes of normalization and neutralization. This is not a heroic, 'Vulcanic', generation which can hope to shock its bourgeois antagonist by outrageous gesture, as many of the active participants were the first to acknowledge.[6] The avant-gardists are very conscious of themselves being part, and a rather successful part, of the social and cultural establishment and, most fatal of all for an avant-garde, the revolution has already happened, they are the heirs of what is always called in the early 1960s the 'historic avant-garde' of the first quarter of the century, and the latecomers are condemned to repetition. This anxious knowledge pervades the whole non-innocent, non-Edenic, rather guilty experience of the Italian Neo-avant-garde, which is an avant-garde that is formed in the heart of a rapidly modernizing economy, characterized itself by new and rapidly changing patterns of production, distribution and consumption, by fast-developing media of communication, and by sophisticated theories of management and organization, to which the structures of culture are far from impervious.

The point here is not to deny the innovatory ambitions and even, sometimes, achievements, of the Italian Neo-avant-garde, but rather to stress how, even at the beginning, the worm is in the garden, that the consciousness of death, of its own necessary demise, accompanies the Neo-avant-garde throughout, not least in the mind of a watchful and sympathetic observer (the musician's friend) like Eco. This future death is perceived not in a heroic way as the father of Italian Futurism, F. T. Marinetti, imagined it (or pretended to imagine it) in the originating manifesto of the movement in 1909, but in a more downbeat and at the same time rather irritable fashion. Yet, alongside this consciousness of obsolescence, there is too the search for that which will preserve, or reinstate, the authenticity and the integrity of the role and gesture of the avant-garde. Back in the garden – because, of course, the story has not finished yet – Eco thinks again. His initial irritation gives way to the thought that, by writing off the music played and heard in the 'wrong' context, he is not doing justice to Mozart. Mozart could be a court musician when he wanted to be, but nevertheless trusted in the fact that if the form which he produced meant anything it would still count with a public which consumed it with other ideas in mind and thus negated it.

> I could not and should not exclude the possibility that among the hundreds of people present in the park there might not be one who suddenly, stimulated perhaps by the minor mode, felt himself or herself in sympathy with that passage of music and who, through it, saw everything in a different light, the trees, the dancing, even their own presence there. (*DA*, p. 252)

Against the constant cycle of production, consumption and destruction of the new in which the Neo-avant-garde appears to be imprisoned there is the possibility that the 'meaning' of the work, that is, of its very newness, can be received, a possibility dependent not on the occasional emotional effect but on the fact 'that a work of art manifests in its structures a certain vision of the world' (ibid.). The intention of the work, but also that of its addressee, is in play here, in the loop between producer and consumer of the work which is at the heart of Eco's aesthetic reflections from the early, 'pre-semiotic', essays to the later work on interpretation. If the emphasis here is on the producer and the work, what is interesting is that Eco introduces the theme of multiplicity: the work operates on different levels (and not just on the two levels represented in his first reaction to the events: 'correct' rendition, and parodistic rendition); someone, or some few, among the many may pick up the message in some form or another.

In later essays looking back on the experience of the Neo-avant-garde,[7] Eco will prise open this dialectic between an avant-garde which is in some sense dying as soon as it is born and what we might think of as a kind of pluralism (obviously related to the concept of 'openness') which is at its authentic heart. With the increasing radicalization of the negative view of the Neo-avant-garde as a movement, however, especially in the 1984 essay, comes a progressive softening of the positive idea of 'experiment' or 'experimentation'. The notion of experiment in the early 1960s has, for Eco as for others, a scientific or industrial ring about it, associated with the idea of the laboratory: people actually are producing computer-generated poetry and playing with sophisticated electronic equipment to produce new music, as in RAI's Studio di fonologia, and this is a new and exciting situation. But, while the idea of experiment may be triggered by the metaphor of the laboratory, the new avant-gardes quickly come face to face with real industrial production and consumption. Nevertheless, the playing of the Mozart 'out of context' goes to show that the unexpected is not only obligatory (in the logic of the avant-garde, which is required to shock), but it is even possible (in the logic of the experiment). Given this relation, it is not surprising that in the course of the next ten years the idea of experimentalism should move out from its 'scientific' base, without ever wholly abandoning it, and become increasingly associated with ideas of plurality and play. By the 1980s, for Eco, the idea of experimentalism is individualized and dehistoricized, or rather scattered through history (like the ideas of the postmodern and the avant-garde itself, which, according to the Eco of the *Postscript* to *The Name of the Rose*, recur at different moments in history, *PNR*, p. 38/*RNR*, p. 66). It is not clear at this point how necessary it is to conceive a culture imbued with the scientific method in order to produce experiment if, tautologically, any work that we think is important is experimental in one way or another.[8]

This description of Eco's nuanced position towards the Neo-avant-garde may help to clarify what was earlier described as Eco's 'oblique' position in relation to the core activities of the Gruppo 63. The fact that he is not in the thick of the day-to-day concerns of practising writers does not mean that the positions they take or the outcome of the group's debates are a matter of indifference to the cultural critic that Eco is becoming. It should be added that, even while Eco is concentrating on other things, the mass media, for example, or the possibilities and limits of structuralism, he is also in a sense thinking about the avant-garde. It is to these concerns that we must now turn.

Mass communications and theories of mass culture

In the 1962 essay 'Form as Social Commitment', at the same time as tackling the issue of the day – 'Literature and Industry' – Eco was also occupying new territory (for him): that of the relation between the intellectual and contemporary culture in general. These terms are too broad though they evoke the flavour of the times. What is really at issue is the function of those who are paid or take it upon themselves to comment on the phenomena of daily life which are recognizably 'cultural' in an anthropological sense, but equally clearly do not belong to the realms of 'high culture' as codified in three or four centuries of bourgeois hegemony: dress, sport, mass media, films (a borderline case), pulp fiction, taste in cars and so on. In the early 1960s, as now, the principal site for such commentary was journalism, particularly at that time print-journalism, the newspapers, the weeklies (in some ways more influential on a national scale in Italy than the dailies[9]), sometimes magazines. The difference from the present was that such commentary had no academic base, enjoying neither whatever crumbs of social respectability (more in Italy than in Britain) nor, more importantly, the minimal appearance of 'scientific' method or 'objectivity' such a position might confer on it. Cultural commentary was to all intents and purposes educated opinion or prejudice. The mass media, 'popular culture', were a foreign country for all but a handful of those who commented on the phenomena associated with them. Indeed, to visit them often involved the mounting of a mental expedition not dissimilar to the physical 'collecting' of Sicilian folksongs or Tuscan tales a century earlier – hence the appositeness of Eco's critical description of the work of the cultural anthropologist in 'Form as Social Commitment' and his continuing use of a benign form of this model even in *La struttura assente*.

With the publication of *Apocalittici e integrati* in 1964 Eco claimed a distinct position amongst contemporary commentators on that indistinct galaxy of phenomena and events that went variously by the name of popular culture, mass culture, or the culture industry. Eco himself was quick to castigate these labels as 'fetish concepts', by which he meant broad generalizations used by those who were either unconditionally 'for' mass culture, or unconditionally 'against' it in order to obstruct objective consideration of specific phenomena and to scare those who might be tempted to evaluate them for themselves. In a Europe trying to come to terms with the 'invasion' of commercial culture from the United States, for a generation like Eco's own which had 'not grown up from the cradle with mass culture',[10] the initial response tended to be outright rejection or acceptance, and it is these two opposed but complementary attitudes that Eco polemically and elegantly dismisses as, respectively, 'apocalyptic' and 'integrated'. The apocalyptic view is for Eco essentially an aristocratic one, for which culture is by definition something enjoyed by the few and mass culture is anti-culture; behind it lurks the pseudo-Nietzschean figure of the superman, identified by Gramsci with nineteenth-century fictional heroes like the Count of Montecristo, Athos or Eugène Sue's Rodolphe de Gerolstein, whose presence, Eco argues, is a consolation to the reader, allowing him 'to glimpse, against a background of catastrophe, a community of "supermen" capable, if only by rejection, of rising above banal mediocrity' (*AI*, p. 5/*AP*, p. 18); it goes without saying that the reader too may be enrolled in this select band. Set against this is the 'optimistic' response of the integrated intellectual. His integration is often a life-choice as well as an intellectual position and it is worth quoting at some length Eco's description of the rather slippery notion of 'integration' and the basis on which he contrasts it with the splendid isolation of the apocalyptic (and/or its pale petty-bourgeois imitations):

> The combined efforts of TV, newspapers, radio, cinema, comic-strips, popular novels and the *Reader's Digest* have now brought culture within everybody's reach. They have made the absorption of ideas and the reception of information a pleasurable and easy task, with the result that we live in an age in which the cultural arena is at last expanding to include the widespread circulation of a 'popular' art and culture in which the best compete against each other. Whether this culture emerges from below or is processed and packaged from above to be offered to defenceless consumers is not a problem that concerns the integrated intellectual. Not least because, if apocalyptics survive by packaging theories on decadence, the integrated intellectuals rarely theorize. They are more likely to be busy producing and transmitting their own messages in every sphere, on a daily basis. The apocalypse is a preoccupation of the dissenter, integration is the concrete reality of non-dissenters. The image of the Apocalypse is evoked in texts *on* mass culture, while the image of integration emerges in texts which *belong to* mass culture. (*AI*, p. 4/*AP*, p. 18)

The notion of integration is more difficult to pin down because, as he himself is well aware, Eco is himself closer in practice to the integrated than to the apocalyptic position. His opposition to theories of catastrophe, apocalypse, the death of culture is deep-rooted, and the horror of it is vividly recorded in *The Name of the Rose* in the profoundly antipathetic figure of Jorge of Burgos. But, by the same token, Eco is disinclined to see change, the new, as something that is visited on a culture from the outside: we have already noted his own, and his contemporaries', consciousness of the avant-garde as an event emerging from within the established culture. The Eco of 1964, in that apparent dilemma between 'for' and 'against', is 'for', but he wants his 'for' to be more nuanced, and obviously more theorized, than that of the unreflecting *integrati*.

The polemic against the prophets of doom on the one hand and the conformists on the other provided the explosive fuel which powered *Apocalittici e integrati* into orbit, but, once the satellite was launched, Eco had longer-term objectives in view. The idea was precisely to find a method which would enable an informed discussion of the 'culture industry', its products and its means of distribution (the media) to take place: a method, not a theory which in the constantly changing world of phenomena intimately connected to quotidian experience would amount to no more than 'a "theory of next Thursday"' (*AI*, p. 24/*AP*, p. 33). Eco's Preface to the 1964 edition describes the way he intends to proceed in the essays in the book, a procedure which again takes cultural anthropology, informed by a rudimentary information/communication theory, as its model. Eco envisages a three-stage process. Firstly, we must recognize that a new area of anthropological study – that of 'mass civilization' – has come into being with the progress of the working classes towards at least a formal participation in public life and with the broadening of the social base of information consumption. In this mass civilization, 'all members of the community become, to some degree, consumers of an intensively produced and non-stop stream of *messages* which are *generated* industrially and *transmitted* through the appropriate commercial *channels* governed by the laws of supply and demand' (*AI*, p. 22/*AP*, p. 32; emphases added). Once these products are defined as *messages* (and 'mass culture' redefined as 'mass *communication*' or 'mass *media*'), one can proceed to an analysis of their *structure*. This structural analysis not only concentrates on the form of the message, but must also 'define the extent to which the form is determined by the objective conditions of the transmission' (ibid.), which also determine the meaning of the message and its 'informative power', that is, whether it is saying something new or merely repeating what has already been said. The next step concerns the *reception* of the message: having established that it is addressed to a totality of consumers which it is difficult to reduce to a unitary model, the study of reception must be carried forward on an empirical basis, taking account of historical, sociological and individual variations. The third and final step is an essentially political one: 'having established the extent to which the saturation of the various messages may truly contribute to the creation of a model of mass-man, an examination must be carried out to identify what kinds of operation are possible in the current context, and what kinds require different conditions of existence' (ibid.). This last step in particular makes clear that the motivation for all this lies at least in part in the pedagogic traditions of the Italian left. The aim (or at least the justification) is not only understanding, but also 'improvement' at some level (of the messages themselves, or of us as decoders of the messages, for example).

Eco was not a stranger to cultural commentary when *Apocalittici e integrati* appeared in 1964. The previous year had seen the publication of the occasional pieces he had been contributing to *Il verri* over the previous four years; the book took its title, *Diario minimo*, from the feature with which Eco had been particularly associated.[11] It is worth pausing for a moment on the relation between *Il verri* and Eco's interests in popular culture. From its foundation in 1956, *Il verri* had marked out its territory quite clearly as that of 'high' culture. Its principal concerns were literature (primarily poetry and prose fiction, Italian, European and North American), philosophy in general and aesthetics in particular, literary history and criticism, the visual arts (painting above all) and music. There was an occasional film review or article on cinema, but these were not frequent, and 'mass culture' did not feature as such, though increasingly, in the early 1960s, the review focused on the topical problem of the 'culture industry'. This concern arose from the fact that *Il verri* was a periodical which its founder Luciano Anceschi intended from its inception to inform its readers and to take part in and contribute to a contemporary and continuing debate on the arts. The 'Diario minimo' section, which began in February 1959 and was entrusted to Eco from the following issue (thereafter, Eco wrote something for most of the issues in which the 'Diario' appeared and contributed most or all of the pieces, though other people also wrote occasionally for the section), reflected both of these 'souls' of *Il verri*. Some of the pieces are a kind of witty literary play or pastiche that will be appreciated by a literate and cultivated readership. This audience will amuse itself with the up-to-the-minute allusions to *Lolita* or the *nouveau roman*,[12] and will relish the rereadings of classics of nineteenth-century Italian prose like Alessandro Manzoni's *I promessi sposi* (*The Betrothed*), interpreted here as a sequel to *Finnegans Wake*, and Edmondo De Amicis's *Cuore* (*Heart: A Schoolboy's Journal*), whose arch political correctness (1886 vintage) is turned inside out by Eco's entirely convincing eulogy of its smirking schoolboy villain.[13] But there are others which employ a more critical or satirical style in order to make a point about contemporary culture which edges the review beyond its own limits, either by addressing cultural phenomena absent in the main, 'serious' part (striptease in Paris, for example, or the 'phenomenology' of the TV quiz-show presenter Mike Bongiorno),[14] or by chipping away at the bases of even an unconscious resistance to 'mass culture', often through the Enlightenment device of a report by a visitor from distant times or places.[15] The freedom with which Eco uses techniques of estrangement to critical effect owes much, no doubt, to the model of Barthes's *Mythologies*, which had appeared in 1957; at the same time, it should be stressed that the occasional pieces of *Diario minimo* are still largely 'pre-semiological' in character.

At the same time as burrowing away below the surface of the high-cultural garden (whose head gardener happily encouraged the aereating industry of his resident mole), Eco had by now long experience from within of the 'culture industry' fetishized by others from without, and this is important, because the way that cultural products are put together is experienced and recounted by Eco as a living process. One example of this insight, undoubtedly based on personal experience,[16] will suffice. The artisanal world of writing and publishing is becoming industrialized, Eco tells us. Writers do not submit work, they have it commissioned and produce it to time-scales set by the publisher. In return, they may (sometimes) be paid a salary. Eco continues:

> Against that, the writer finds that the publishing firm provides him with new opportunities to work, the possibility of a second job. What is meant by this is not so much the traditional operations of editing and rewriting as the immense activity involved in coeditions of large illustrated works where books are actually manufactured within the publishing firm. The book is thought up and written by an editorial team which chooses the illustrations, writes the captions, conceives, extends, cuts and condenses the texts. . . . But this may often be a killing and mortifying activity, and the writer has to learn how to write a universal history in such a way that the book will be acceptable in Spain and Great Britain, in Germany and in France. This is where he really does learn to write texts capable of being read by the greatest possible variety of readers and always understood without too many misapprehensions; all that is needed is to reduce the meaning to a minimum and put in a lot of repetitions.[17]

Eco's interests and researches in the field of mass communications and mass culture transcend the essays collected in *Apocalittici e integrati*, and it is not my intention to analyse the latter in detail or for their own sake. During the 1960s and the 1970s he is concerned with both texts and media. The texts include nineteenth-century popular fiction (in a series of essays collected in *Il superuomo di massa*, 'Mass Superman', 1976, a title which harks back to the insight into the apocalyptic mentality cited above[18]) and narratives in strip-cartoon format (both the Superman and Steve Canyon strips are analysed in *Apocalittici e integrati*). Certainly the richest is his analysis of narrative structures in Ian Fleming's James Bond novels, which has frequently been reprinted.[19] Tightly and thoroughly argued and extremely perceptive on the ideological substrata of the Bond books, for example on their racism, it remains (except for its last section, on possible nineteenth-century sources or suggestions, of which not even Eco seemed entirely convinced) a wonderful practical application of the structural method to popular fiction. From the mid-1960s onwards, and to this day, Eco has also become a regular contributor to the daily and weekly press on contemporary culture (in the broadest sense) and on issues of the day of every hue (social and behavioural, political, linguistic, ethical, etc.). His articles are often wittily and brilliantly written and, just as the modern writer described above has to learn the skill of writing in a way that will be universally understood, so Eco as a journalist has honed to perfection the rhetorical art of making his point memorably in 700 words. His journalism has been decisive in making of Eco a media figure in Italy (and it has been suggested that this was the cradle where the readership of his novels grew), but it has seldom offered more than occasional insight, and informed opinion, on the media themselves.[20] Yet thinking about the media, the means by which messages are transmitted and received in an era of mass communications, was a decisive aspect of the development of Eco's thinking from what he called the 'pre-semiotic' period of *Opera aperta* and *Apocalittici e integrati* to the systematic exploration of semiology in the second half of the 1960s.[21] We shall now begin to move towards this later period, and firstly look briefly at some of Eco's discussions of actual information media, television in particular, in the 1960s and 1970s. We shall see that there is a progressive 'semiotization' of his description of the media. In the following section, this will be set within the framework of the emergence of a general structural approach in Italy, and in Eco's own work, during the 1960s.

Television and semiotic guerrilla war

In his 1964 preface to *Apocalittici e integrati* Eco drew on a medieval parallel to illustrate the conflict between the apocalyptics and the integrated, telling the story of the battle between Abbot Suger of St Denis and St Bernard of Clairvaux over the appropriateness of frescoing the walls of churches with religious paintings, the *biblia pauperum*, the principle of which Bernard rejected in the name of mystic concentration (the story is repeated in *The Name of the Rose*). He again has recourse to history as a way into problems facing contemporary culture when in the same year he reviews an exhibition devoted to early modern popular prints held at the Castello Sforzesco in Milan. He sees the overall picture as contradictory. On the one hand, these late fifteenth- and sixteenth-century prints did not pursue the primary aim of culture, which is to break established schemas, to teach us to criticize the world around us, but rather a secondary, aberrant, aim, that of helping people to use the mechanisms of fantasy and escape, as a kind of compensation, in order, optimistically, to accept life as it is. And this is exactly the function of much of today's mass communication culture, where the outpouring of news, stories, sensation and entertainment has the sole function of making us forget reality. And yet those prints also played a positive role. They brought the pleasure of the printed text to places where people would otherwise have been satisfied with a straightforward oral communication, with the stories told by their grandparents or by wandering story-tellers. 'Culture transmitted orally is always necessarily static, it does not renew itself'.[22] Culture had to pay the price of producing cheaper, and less worthwhile, books in order for a larger public to be involved.

Eco's earliest comments on television, 'Problemi estetici del fatto televisivo'[23] and 'Appunti sulla televisione',[24] share two features with this excursion into history: its attentiveness to the new and its fundamental optimism. The 1956 paper, given to a conference on aesthetics, is particularly striking, because it passes over the most obviously 'artistic', but in a sense culturally retrospective, products of the infant television service (opera, drama or adaptations of classic novels) in order to focus on 'that very particular kind of communciation which is exclusive to television: live broadcasting' (*OA*, p. 187/*OW*, p. 107 [translation adapted]). In the 1963 paper, it is the evolution of a 'wise cultural policy' that Eco is particularly concerned with, primarily from the point of view of the producer: television should offer a quality product, and trust in the intelligence of its audience (that mass audience which is not the fetishized 'mass' feared by the apocalyptics, but is made up of individuals or groups who in principle are cleverer than the cultural elite would like to believe).

So far we have seen Eco defending and describing the mass media (past and present) in an optimistic and democratic, but also fundamentally 'voluntaristic' spirit, from the point of view of a cultural director or producer who knows how he *wants* the audience to react, and whose wish is to some extent father to the thought. But as Eco gets deeper into the structural study of communication, so his thought on the messages of the media becomes more articulated, and – to anticipate a moment – it is increasingly on the reception, rather than the production, of the message that it will come to focus (a move that is entirely consistent with, or more probably derives from, the disintegration of the fetish-concept of 'the mass'). An important step in this development is a research report published in 1965 and translated into English in 1972 as 'Towards a Semiotic Inquiry into the Television Message'. The report focuses on the communicative aspects of TV, in particular the phenomenon of 'aberrant decoding', the fact that the viewer does not necessarily interpret the message in the way its sender (the TV company) intends it to be decoded, or assumes it will be. The proposed research envisages three phases (the first two of which coincide with the general programme of *Apocalittici e integrati* described above, the third of which differs significantly). The aim of the first is to define terms such as 'code', and to distinguish between the codes of the transmitting organization and those of specific technical operators within it. The second phase comprises field research on actual reception, while the third leads into a comparison of data from phase 2 with the expectations arising from phase 1. The rest of the paper is concerned with establishing the terminology for the first phase (to which we shall return within the context of a more general semiology in chapter 3).

The thrust of this paper is essentially descriptive and methodological, but the exploration of the semiology of mass communications is given a sharp political twist two years later with the proposition of a 'semiotic guerrilla warfare'.[25] Power, Eco states, using a conceit which he will repeat on numerous occasions in the late 1960s, does not lie any longer with those who control the tanks, but with those who control communications. But that control is not absolute. Ambiguity is excluded in ordinary univocal communication, it is sought after in aesthetic communication, and in mass communications it is always present, even if it is unwanted. The problem with mass communications is that up to now the variability of reception has been random; no one regulates the way in which the addressee uses the message. The question for a democratic counter-power is not one of controlling the source or the channel, but is rather one of intervening at the point of reception. Hence the idea of 'guerrilla warfare'. The battle for the survival of man as a responsible being in the Age of Communication will not be won at the point from which the communication departs, but where it arrives. A paradoxical and difficult destiny awaits those who are concerned professionally with communications. Precisely at the moment that communications systems envisage a single industrialized Source and a single message which will reach an audience scattered throughout the world, we have to be able to imagine complementary communications systems which will allow us to reach every single human group, every single member of the universal audience, in order to discuss the message as it arrives in the light of the codes operating at the point of arrival, comparing these with the codes in force at the point of departure. This is not a proposal for a new and more terrible form of control of public opinion, but one for 'action to urge the audience to control the message and its multiple possibilities of interpretation' (*CC*, p. 297/ *TH*, p. 143). In Warsaw a year later, the revolutionary implications of Eco's call to empower the receiver of the mass communications message are spelt out even more clearly. Semiotic observations may help the broadcaster to transmit as univocal a message as possible, eradicating ambiguities, but there is another possibility: that of contesting a form of communication which tends to the flattening of consciousness, the control of opinion and the reinforcement of existing values. This guerrilla function of semiotics means that it is not guilty as charged of justifying existing cultural models, social relations and psychological processes, but that it can become 'one of the forms of revolutionary praxis'.[26]

If there was something utopian in the idea of a semiotic guerrilla war, it did not survive the collapse of the Italian student and workers protest movements at the end of 1969. That Eco is also well aware of the power of tanks is underlined by the unexpected recollection of the Soviet invasion of Czechoslovakia in the preamble to *The Name of the Rose* – an event that had taken place a few days before he delivered his paper in Warsaw. But the progressive semiotization of the study of mass communications continued in Eco's work to go hand in hand with an underlying commitment to a democratic society based on free access to and use of information. Both aspects, semiotic and political, come together in a 1971 essay on the language of newspapers,[27] where the semiotic approach shows its worth in the way that it seeks to give an account of the whole communicative situation rather than just one aspect of it (for example, the intentions of the journalist or the editor, or the reactions of specific readers), and how it tries to offer a structural model of this totality rather than relying on empirical, but partial, data. Later in the 1970s the effects of the no-holds-barred deregulation of Italy's radio and television broadcasting, at one end of the spectrum democratic experimentation in 'counter-culture', at the other the emergence of the Berlusconi media empire, led to a series of penetrating essays from Eco. Once again, he refuses to demonize the real or potential enemy. The underlying continuity of his position is stressed by his concluding remark to a conference sponsored by Thames Television on 'Schools Television' in London in June 1978: 'Don't switch off television, switch on your critical freedom'.[28]

In a closely argued essay on theory and practice in Eco's analysis of the media, David Robey has concluded that 'semiotics, for Eco, is really a high-level metalanguage whose relevance for the work of specific media studies is very much an indirect and mediated one. Its nature is to provide a broad framework for such studies rather than to prescribe precise methods of analysis'.[29] Robey acknowledges that for Eco the study of the media was the way into semiotics rather than vice versa, but then tends to emphasize the limited input of semiotics into Eco's studies of the media. It is legitimate to test Eco's claim in his preface to the 1974 edition of *Apocalittici e integrati* that he used semiotic tools in his post-1964 studies of TV messages, narrative structures in Fleming, rhetoric and ideology in Sue and in the analysis of advertising (this latter in the second section of *La struttura assente*; see *AI*, p. xiii/*AP*, p. 54). A study of the information media such as that sketched above might, however, have led Robey to a more positive conclusion about the relation between theory and practice than the rather limiting one based on Eco's approach to narrative texts (Fleming and Sue) and his work on advertising. Nevertheless, Robey is right when he points to the tension in Eco's work in the late 1960s, particularly in *La struttura assente*, between 'two conflicting lines of research', between what Eco calls specific semiotics, dealing with 'closed', rigorously structured systems seen in synchronic section, and the proposed model of communication as an 'open' process, in which the message varies according to the codes, the codes are brought into play according to ideologies and circumstances, and the whole system of signs is constantly restructuring itself; the tension is 'recognized, and allowed to stand'.[30] The next two chapters will deal in more detail with these questions, but I should like to conclude this one by thinking further about the tension described above in the light of what has already been presented and in that of the rapid absorption, first of structuralism, then of semiotics, by Eco and by Italian culture more widely during the 1960s.

Openness and structure

The variability, and implicit but yet-to-be-defined freedom, of the response which the addressee gives to the messages transmitted by the media recalls the similar, unpredictable, freedom with which the unknown wedding guest may turn a banal and empty gesture of the avant-garde into something meaningful for him or her. Both of these in turn belong to the same family of thought that produces an idea of the openness of the work of art in general and the particularly self-conscious openness of modernism and, even more, the new avant-gardes. But none of these should be understood as a form of critical or theoretical liberalism, in which the meaning of the work depends on purely individual reactions. Openness, after all, is first and foremost a theory concerned with the composition and the intention of the work, while freedom of response, whether to Stockhausen or the nine o'clock news, is a dimension of a total communicative situation which is to be analysed as a whole. There is a constant, and fruitful, oscillation in Eco's work between the demands of interpretative freedom on the one hand and the need to secure statements about culture or communication in general within a clearly visible conceptual structure on the other. The 1960s were a decade in which the demands of structure made themselves felt with particular force in Italian culture as a whole; so too did the limitations of structuralism. It will be helpful to set the general context of the debate before returning to Eco's developing position within it.

For Italian intellectuals, structuralism meant first and foremost a means of entering territory which Crocean aesthetics had marked as out of bounds. These included, so Eco explained to readers of the *Times Literary Supplement* in September 1963, problems of artistic technique, the importance to be attached to calculation, intelligence

and technical know-how in artistic production, and the very structure of the work (which Croce regarded as 'non-poetry').[31] Structuralism was welcomed above all as providing a set of sophisticated
and effective instruments for the analysis of texts: the name of one
of the two most influential academic structuralist journals, the
Pavia-based *Strumenti critici*, is a homage to that view.[32] One of
the founders of *Strumenti critici*, Cesare Segre, was keen to stress the
continuities with the Italian tradition: structuralism had shown
itself capable of grafting onto already established traditions such
as the history of the language, the study of variants pioneered by
Gianfranco Contini, and the stylistics of Leo Spitzer.[33] But this
should not obscure the energy with which Italian linguistics and
criticism were renewed during the early 1960s, not least thanks to
the popularizing efforts of Segre himself and his Pavia colleague
Maria Corti, both of them immensely distinguished critics in their
own right.[34]

Eco's own itinerary is in some ways emblematic. He was introduced to structuralism, he tells us (*OA*, pp. vii–viii), by François
Wahl, who had commissioned the translation of *Opera aperta* for
Seuil. The main parts of the Joyce essay appeared in *Tel quel* in 1962,
but the translation of the book took three years, and went through
three versions. Wahl induced him to read Lévi-Strauss, Saussure
(thoroughly) and the contemporary structuralists. Eco reports that
he had three shock encounters around 1963: Lévi-Strauss's *La pensée
sauvage*, Jakobson's writings published by Minuit (the *Essais de
linguistique générale* appeared in 1963), and the Russian Formalists.
The importance of Jakobson for the clarification of Eco's ideas about
the aesthetic message, and for a structuralist recasting of the notion
of 'openness', will become apparent in chapter 3; his first serious
use of Jakobson comes, rather unexpectedly, in the essay on Kitsch
included in *Apocalittici e integrati* (translated as 'The Structure of Bad
Taste', in *OW*, pp. 180–216; see pp. 194–200 in particular).[35] Eco was
already having Victor Erlich's book on the Formalists translated for
Bompiani; he also tried to secure *Eléments de sémiologie*, the essay
with which Barthes had declared his semiological credentials in
Communications, 4, in 1964, for *Marcatré*.[36] There had been what
Segre describes as an 'explosion' of structuralist criticism between
1963 and 1965 in the wake of Jakobson and Lévi-Strauss's structuralist analysis of Baudelaire's 'Les chats'; at the same time the interest
in the Russian Formalists led to various exercises in story-analysis
(*analyse du récit*), of which Eco's 1965 essay on James Bond was one
conspicuous example.

Structuralism held out the promise of a rigorous method of analysis which might provide the basis for a 'scientific' rather than an 'intuitive' reading of literary texts in particular; and, although Segre argued that structuralism was not incompatible with the historicism which was so important a component of the Italian critical tradition, it was clearly not dependent on it either. Nevertheless, the limitations of structuralism were quickly apparent to the powerful neo-Marxist currents of Italian intellectual life. 'Neo-Marxist' is used here as a broad-brush definition of new left intellectuals, including some, but by no means all, of those who associated themselves with the Neo-avant-garde, who were looking in the 1960s for alternatives to the cultural policy of the Italian Communist Party (PCI) which was still at the time largely influenced by the Soviet Union. A number of these intellectuals were indeed attracted by the analytical rigour of structuralism, but there were drawbacks. In the first place, structuralism in its Italian version was particularly concerned with linguistics and with literary analysis – there was a very large area of cultural experience which it appeared not to touch. Secondly, it appeared in the eyes of many on the new left to be fundamentally idealist in its positing of a structure as immanent to the text, tautological in its concern with verifying structures which are already assumed to be present in the object, and ideologically suspect in its view of the text as a system independent of other social and cultural formations.[37] Eco's work in the 1960s is sensitive to these objections and can be read as a concerted attempt to reinforce the benefits of structural analysis while moving it out of its culturally elite frame of reference and confronting the philosophical and ideological challenge generated from within the political left. The broadening of the agenda to include strip cartoons, comic books, popular song, television and radio programmes is at the heart of *Apocalittici e integrati*, while Eco gets to grips with the philosophical problems in his first sustained attempt to work out a systematic semiology, *La struttura assente*. The book takes its title from its fourth section, which is a detailed argument in favour of a 'methodological' rather than an 'ontological' conception of structure, and while we shall be looking in some detail at the more technical arguments of the book in the next chapter, we should pause here in order to grasp at least the basics of the general position that Eco stakes out in his 'Section D'.

The initial assertion to be demonstrated is that the function of a structural model is to allow the resolution of different cultural levels into homologous parallel series (*SA*, p. 253). The concept of structure is omni-present in Western thought, Eco agrees. The idea of structure which interests structuralism, however, is one in which: (a) a structure is a model as a system of differences; (b) the model is characterized by its being transferable from one phenomenon or order of phenomena to another; (c) a structural methodology is possible when the two preceding postulates are respected, opening the way to interdisciplinary study among the human sciences (*SA*, p. 259). The key move in this definition of the field is the precedence given to the model over the object: what is of interest is the transferable model as described above, not the single object, system or text; one has a structural inquiry, at every level, when one succeeds in resolving the concrete object into a model (*SA*, p. 284). But at this point a second problem arises: is structural analysis concerned with structure as an ontological reality or as an operative model? Eco insists, with Hjemslev, on the point that the structural model is taken as a working hypothesis, with no assumptions implied about the 'real' nature of language or any other object of study: 'for a correct use of structural models, it is not necessary to believe that their choice is determined by the object; it is sufficient to know that it is chosen by the method' (*SA*, p. 286). But there is a powerful alternative, represented by Lévi-Strauss, who in his methodology moves from the operative model to the objective structure; that is to say, Lévi-Strauss posits a homology between thought and world which can only be explained by the existence of an original, transcendental structure, to which the researcher is inevitably drawn.

Eco's sustained debate with Lévi-Strauss on this point in the fourth part of his essay is translated as 'Series and Structure' in *OW*, pp. 217–35. The distinction, and opposition, between 'serial' and 'structural' thought had been posited by Lévi-Strauss in *The Raw and the Cooked*; his definition of serial thought was aimed polemically at Boulez's music and at avant-garde art in general, and it is clear to Eco that he regards the two kinds of thought not just as 'two different methodological stances but two different visions of the world' (*SA*, p. 303/*OW*, p. 217). Eco's solution is to attack the opposition as such and to move the two terms into a dialectical relationship:

> The main problem with the structural method . . . is that, in order not to be confused with an antihistorical science, it must constantly avoid any identification between the Structure it seeks and any given series, taken as the privileged manifestation of the universals of communication. Once this ambiguity is removed, the serial method will appear as the other

dialectic side of the structural method, the side of becoming as opposed to that of permanence. Series will no longer be a negation of structure; rather, it will be the expression of a structure that questions itself and sees itself as a historical phenomenon – and this not so much in order to deny itself all possibility of research as in order to turn the utopia of an ultimate reality into a regulatory principle for an investigation in progress (which should always push beyond the structure, toward its very basis, toward an ulterior code of which the structure is just a message). (*SA*, pp. 318–19/*OW*, p. 232)

With this invocation of a historical dynamics, and the focus on change,[38] Eco seeks to avoid both the chimera of an absolute structure, a Code of Codes, which in the process of inquiry will always necessarily present itself as absent, or at any rate elsewhere, and the bottomless gulf to which the absolute denial of any origin, presence or ontological foundation of structure, carried to its extreme conclusions by Nietzsche, Heidegger and Lacan, must lead.[39] For the Eco of 1968, the 'ontology of Absence' (*SA*, p. 9) which he sees lurking in the anti-structuralism of Derrida and Foucault has a broader, moral or political, connotation: it risks 'blocking any possibility of challenging things as they are'. Eco is mistrustful of the advent of a kind of intellectual paralysis; this theme will return with brio in his polemic with a more developed and extensive deconstruction in the 1980s.

The role of structure in the human sciences is now clear: 'Being absent in any event, structure will no longer be seen as the objective goal [*termine*] of a definitive research, but as the hypothetical instrument with which phenomena can be explored prior to being put into wider correlations' (*SA*, p. 361). This is the foundation of a semiology which, in De Lauretis's words, 'works on systems of inter-subjective cultural conventions based on social relations and history', and in which 'the codes hypothesized as models are propositions that are partial, provisional, linked to changeable historical circumstances, and therefore revisable'.[40] We may see it as a characteristically Echian position, already well-established in his pre-semiotic work, one that allows him the greatest possible flexibility and room for manoeuvre; the structural method is equated with the experimental method; the verb translated above as 'explored', *saggiare*, which might also mean to sample, to test, to assay, is a word beloved of Galileo, whose *Saggiatore* is the very prototype of the scientific explorer. But it is important to remember that this freedom of manoeuvre is established at the very moment that Eco is entering upon the most determinedly systematic phase of his thought, the concentrated effort which, starting from the analyses gathered in *La struttura assente*, will culminate eight years later in his general theory of semiotics. The values of flexibility, openness and experimentation, here re-asserted, must be balanced against the urgent need to construct a system that is as complete and has as much explanatory power as possible.

At the same time as this new chapter was opening, however, another was closing. The events that took place on the streets of Italy between 1967 and 1969 – from the early agitation in the universities, through the reverberations of the protest movements of May 1968, to the factory strikes and occupations during the 'hot autumn' of 1969 and their brutal termination in the Milan bombing in December of that year – cruelly exposed the illusions of the Neo-avant-garde. The avant-garde had already been criticized from the left for its naïve belief that the disruptive power of art in itself could mount a telling challenge to a political and economic system which many within the avant-garde tended to fetishize as omnipotent in any case. The emergence of new social subjects in the late 1960s – students, women, immigrants from the South of Italy – both exposed the real structural weaknesses of 'the system' and the marginalization of writers and intellectuals. Nowhere was this more obvious than in the pages of *Quindici*, a journal set up by the Gruppo 63 in 1967 under the editorship first of Alfredo Giuliani and then of Nanni Balestrini. It was in the pages of this severe publication, with the format of a Chinese wall-newspaper and challengingly lengthy articles, that the crisis of the Neo-avant-garde was played out. The issue became whether to retain the original 'intellectual' tenor of the journal or to hand over an increasing amount of space to the student movement. Eco tried to play a mediating role, but in the face of widening splits within the group tabled a proposal to dissolve it and to cease publication; supported by Balestrini, the motion was carried and *Quindici* ended its brief existence in the autumn of 1969.[41]

That marked the end of the experience of the avant-garde, with which Eco had been productively involved for more than a decade; it marked also the beginning of the violent and ambiguous politics which were to dominate Italy in the 1970s. By this point, however, Eco was already embarked on the attempt to produce a semiotic theory that would do justice to all the multifarious concerns which had occupied him since the mid-1950s. The 'conversion' of structuralism into semiotics in Italy (as opposed to the wholesale rejection of structuralism after 1968 in France) was itself, in Teresa De

Lauretis's view, the result of 'a conscious political shift',[42] a choice that entailed a continuing dialogue with the educated public to a greater extent in Italy than anywhere else (except perhaps in some countries of Latin America, where Italian semiotics was quickly taken up[43]). One of the distinguishing features of Eco's semiotics, and one of its most attractive ones, is the way in which it incorporates the principles of non-dogmatism and anti-absolutism that we have seen him arguing both before and in the course of *La struttura assente*. But dialogue and flexibility occur within the continuing, concentrated effort to construct a semiotic theory on sound systematic foundations; it is with this major project that the next two chapters are primarily concerned.

3

Introducing the Study of Signs

In the end, the essay on structures and structuralism which we have just examined provided the title for Eco's first work of theoretical semiology intended for a wide public.[1] *La struttura assente* (*The Absent Structure*), first published in 1968 and reissued in 1980 with a new introduction but the same text, had emerged, however, from a textbook that Eco had written the previous year for the course which he was teaching on the semiology of visual communications at the University of Florence. The 1967 publication, *Appunti per una semiologia delle comunicazioni visive*, had had a limited circulation but had caught the attention of the literary semiologist Maria Corti, who reviewed it in *Strumenti critici*, and of Pier Paolo Pasolini.[2] The specific provenance of *La struttura assente* helps to explain the emphasis of the first three sections, which are concerned with signal and sense (a tilling of the theoretical ground, to which we shall give particular attention in the following pages), visual codes (notably in cinema and advertising, with particular reference to the problem of 'iconicity') and architecture and communication (to which we have already referred). The last two sections, the essay on the 'absent structure' and a reconnoitring of the 'frontiers' of semiology, extend and deepen Eco's reflections on the nature and status of the emerging field of study. *La struttura assente* was translated into seven European languages; it was while battling with a possible English version that Eco gave up and produced *A Theory of Semiotics* instead (*TSE*, p. vii).

   La struttura assente is, therefore, a book that has been rewritten in the process of translation and in some sense superseded. But it has also been republished, and if it does not achieve the theoretical rigour striven for by *A Theory of Semiotics*, it retains a relative clarity which rigour sometimes obscures. We have already discussed some of its arguments; in this chapter I propose to concentrate on its introductory section, which will explore the basic terms of Eco's semiology before focusing once more on the specific and strategic case of what he calls the 'aesthetic message'. This will serve as an indispensable preliminary to the discussion of *A Theory of Semiotics* that follows in the next chapter.

Signals and sense

Semiology, Eco begins by explaining, is the study of all cultural phenomena as though they were systems of signs; it is based upon the hypothesis that all cultural phenomena are indeed systems of signs, in other words, that they are phenomena having to do with communication. The whole book may be read as a testing of this hypothesis, an assessment, that is to say, of whether and how far the methodology elaborated on the basis of the initial assumption is effective in its explication and clarification of cultural phenomena. The question that is begged in this initial formulation – what is 'culture',[3] and how far does it reach? – though acknowledged, is not pursued in depth on this occasion (it will return again and again).

Eco's first important move, following up the research already embarked upon in *Opera aperta*, is to establish the key notions of semiology (sign, meaning, code, message, etc.) on the basis not of linguistics but of information theory. He is attracted by an approach to communication which stretches across disciplines (psychology, neurophysiology and genetics as well as the human sciences), but his argument for entering the topic from this direction, with its origins in statistics and cybernetics, is an essentially methodological one. If every cultural fact is communication, it is necessary to identify the elementary structure of communication where communication takes place, so to speak, at its most basic level: the transmission of information between two machines. This is not because more complex forms of communication can be reduced to the most simple, but because the latter serves to help us construct an exemplary *model*.

At this most basic level we are concerned with *signals*. The communication model chosen (pp. 17–22) is that of a water catchment area (what in *A Theory of Semiotics* will be dubbed the 'Watergate Model') where one wishes to know when the water reaches a certain level, which is the danger level defined as 0. The water catchment area itself is described as the *source* of the information. In the catchment area there is an apparatus which triggers a *transmitter* when level 0 is reached. The transmitter sends a *signal*, which travels along a *channel* and is received by a *receiver*, which then turns the signal back into a given form which constitutes the *message* addressed to the *addressee* (in this example, another machine which, on receiving the message, activates a mechanism that will change the situation at the point of origin).

To warn the addressee that the water has reached danger level, it is necessary to send a message. For the sake of convenience, this can be thought of as a light-bulb: when lit, it means that level 0 has been reached; when extinguished, it means that the water is below level 0. There is correspondence between signifier and signified. But there is a difference between signified and referent. The signified here is the disposition of the apparatus on the receiving end to respond in a certain way to the signifier: the apparatus does not 'know' that the danger level has been reached, but it has been instructed to respond in a certain way to the signal 'light-bulb lit'.

Communication may be interfered with by *noise* affecting the channel (for example, an interruption in the electricity supply). In order to reduce the risks posed by noise, it is necessary to complicate the code. I might install two light-bulbs: when one is lit it means that the water is below level 0, when the other one comes on it means it has reached it. But that may not be enough to obviate the risk of mistaken information (an electrical fault might cut out both lights, and then I would know that it was a fault, but it might also cause A to come on instead of B, and I would not know that this was the case). Thus it becomes necessary to bring in two more light-bulbs, so I now have ABCD. Elements of *redundancy* have now been brought into the code. This not only makes the message more secure, it also makes other kinds of message possible by combining the four elements in different ways: the code establishes a *repertoire of symbols*, from amongst which I can choose some to attribute to given phenomena, leaving the others as a *reserve*.

A code such as this is based on alternatives: yes or no, lit or extinguished, 1 or 0. Eco is not concerned here with whether the binary method is merely the simplest way of describing the conveying of information, or whether all communication actually is based on a binary mechanism. It is, however, a preferred way of explaining things because of its economy. The binary method is fundamental in information theory in order to show how, starting from a situation in which a number of outcomes are equally probable, the process of arriving at a particular outcome is described mathematically. These methodological reflections serve for Eco to introduce a clarification of the notion of *information*.

Information arises through binary separation and this is true also of more complex systems, such as verbal language: phonemes, the minimum unit of vocal emission, have no meaning in themselves, except that the presence of one phoneme excludes that of another which, had it been present instead of the one actually present, would have changed the meaning of the word ('ship' for 'sheep', for example). An information unit or 'bit' (*binary digit*), information itself, is not to be identified with the notion which is communicated. What counts for information theory is the number of alternatives required to define the event unambiguously, along with the alternatives which are presented at source as equally probable. Information 'is not so much what is said as what can be said' (*SA*, p. 25). Information is a statistical measure of the number of equally probable outcomes present in the source. The information *received* is necessarily a reduction of the huge number of outcomes originally possible before one particular one has been chosen. Information measures a situation of equiprobability which information theorists call *entropy*: as in thermodynamics, 'the entropy of a system is the state of equiprobability to which its elements tend' (*SA*, p. 25). Entropy is also identified with a state of *disorder*, inasmuch as *order* is a system of probability, according to which things 'should' or are likely to happen in one way rather than another (entropy supposes *equal* probability).

The QWERTY keyboard can theoretically generate 85^{1500} messages, a number of possible messages that is expressed by a number containing 2,895 figures. At this point, there comes into play the ordering function of the *code*. The effect of the code is to limit the number of possible combinations. The code represents a system of probability superimposed on the equiprobability of the source in order to ensure communication. It is not 'information' as a statistical measure that requires this element of order, but its transmissibility. Thus the equally possible 85^{1500} messages of the keyboard are reduced to the lesser number of messages allowed by the code known as the Italian language. The code is defined as 'the system which establishes 1) a repertoire of symbols which are distinguished by reciprocal opposition; 2) their rules of transmission; 3) sometimes, but not necessarily, the correspondence, term by term, between each symbol and a given signified' (*SA*, p. 28).

Returning to the example of the water catchment area and the initial model, Eco shows how it is possible to establish a code which selects from among all the possible combinations of the symbols A, B, C and D those which are most probable. The receiving apparatus is instructed to respond in the appropriate way to the foreseeable combinations, those which are not foreseen being understood as noise. This is the selection of *pertinent features*. It is by now clear that the idea of information as possibility and freedom of choice has split into two concepts which are formally the same but denotatively different. The *source information* is corrected by the code which turns equal probabilities into a system of probabilities. But there is now also *code information*. The code has brought order into the physical system and reduced the possibilities of information, but is itself a system of equal probabilities (though reduced in number) in respect of the messages which it can generate.

Notions such as information (as against message), disorder (as against order), equal probability (as against system of probabilities) are all *relative* notions, therefore. The code combats the entropy inherent in the source, but possesses an entropy of its own relative to the indefinite number of messages which it can produce.

The situation described thus far changes if: (1) the receiver is a human being (even though the transmitter is a machine); (2) the source is another human being, in which case source and transmitter (and often code as well) are identified with each other; (3) either source or receiver question the code. When a human being appears on the scene as the receiver of the message, his or her actions will not be restricted to the limited range afforded the machine. Unlike the machine, he or she will 'know' that level 0 means danger and, for example, might be frightened. With the human being we enter the world of sense or meaning, rather than signal (*SA*, p. 30).

Eco sees it as his first task to establish the conditions of use of the term 'meaning' (*significato*), and this entails dissociating the sense of 'meaning' from that of 'referent'. He cites the diagram offered by Ogden and Richards which shows the triangular relationship between symbol ('word'), reference ('thought') and referent ('thing'), according to which there is no direct relationship between symbol and referent.[4] In a semiological perspective, Eco asserts, the problem of the referent is irrelevant (but he will come back to the question in *Theory*). A symbol cannot be verified by checking it against its referent: there are symbols which have a reference but not a referent ('unicorn', for example); there are different symbols with different references which refer to the same referent. The presence or absence of the referent does not affect the study of a symbol as it is used in a given society in relation to determined codes. Semiology is concerned only with the left-hand side of Ogden and Richards's triangle, the line linking symbol and reference. But it looks at it in depth, aware both that numerous phenomena pertaining to meaning occur there and that the relation between a symbol and its meaning can change in a continuous, dynamic process which here is called 'sense' (*senso*) (*SA*, pp. 31–4).

Eco now (*SA*, pp. 34–7) turns to some of the basic distinctions introduced by Saussure which seem particularly useful as the basis of a semiology (a semiology, following Saussure's indication, that might be that more general science of signs of which linguistics 'is only a part'[5]), and to the concept of *interpretant* proposed by the American pragmatist C. S. Peirce. Saussure established that a sign does not join a thing and a name, but a concept and a sound image. The signified is not the thing, but the mental image of the thing; the signifier is not the sound form of the name (which is studied by phonetics), but the image of the sound form. The relation between signifier and signified is arbitrary, but in so far as it is imposed by the language (which is a code) the signified becomes necessary for the speaker. The code establishes that a given signifier denotes a given signified. Once this signified is realized in the mind of a speaker as a concept, or in society as a current usage, it becomes the property of psychology or statistics. At the moment when semiology tries to define the signified, it risks ceasing to be itself, to become, paradoxically, another discipline. Eco suggests that, to some extent, Peirce was trying to avoid this when he introduced the idea of 'interpretant'.

In Peirce, the sign – 'something which stands to somebody for something in some respect or capacity'[6] – is thought of as a triadic structure, like the Ogden–Richards triangle, with the base formed by the symbol or *representamen* and the *object* which it represents, and the apex occupied by the *interpretant*, identified by many with the signified or reference. In any case, the interpretant is not the interpreter; it is that which guarantees the validity of the sign even in the absence of the interpreter. The interpretant has been identified with the signified because it is defined as that which the sign produces in the quasi-mind which is the interpreter; it can also be seen as the definition of the representamen. But the most fruitful hypothesis to Eco's mind is that of taking the interpretant as another representation which refers to the same object. In order to establish the interpretant of a sign it becomes necessary to name it by means of another sign which in its turn has another interpretant that may be named by means of another sign and so on indefinitely in the process which Peirce calls 'unlimited semiosis'. For Eco, it is only by this means that a semiological system can stand on its own two feet; language is seen as a system which clarifies itself through a series of systems of conventions which explain each other. Semiology therefore leads to a hierarchy of metalanguages (there are but few objects whose meaning can be wholly indicated by pointing at them). Eco insists, however, that semiology 'does not study the mental procedures of signifying but only communicative conventions as a phenomenon of *culture* (in the anthropological sense of the term)' (*SA*, p. 37).

Back in the control room, the signifier ABC *denotes* level 0; for the human recipient of the message it *connotes* danger. A connotative relationship is established when the couple formed by a signifier and a denoted signified become the signifier of an additional signified. At this point, having referred back to Barthes's few pages on denotation and connotation (chapter 4 of *Eléments de sémiologie*, which in turn draw primarily on Hjemslev), Eco introduces a distinction between 'codes' and 'lexicons' (*lessici*). Everybody speaking a given language knows what a given word denotes, but not everyone will necessarily be aware of its connotations. He proposes therefore to say that, while denotative meanings are established by the code, connotative ones are established by subcodes or specific 'lexicons' shared by certain groups of speakers, but not necessarily all. He goes on to add to the idea of code by analogy with the Saussurean notion of *langue*. Every diachronic change establishes a new synchronic relationship between the elements of the *langue*. Some codes are imposed (the Morse code, for example), others (like language) are used unconsciously by speakers, but semiology is not immediately concerned with whether the structures that it studies are 'deep' (in the Chomskyan sense) or 'surface' ones.

From code, via *langue*, we have arrived at the notion of *structure*. Eco takes two equally important ideas from Lévi-Strauss (*SA*, p. 42) which he proposes to explore further in order better to define the idea of 'structure' (which is identified with that of 'code'). The first of these is the idea that 'structure is a system supported by internal cohesion', for which he draws first on the theory of double articulation elaborated by André Martinet: the first articulation 'is that whereby every fact of experience to be communicated, every need that one wants to make known to another, is analysed into a succession of units, each of which is endowed with a vocal form and a meaning'.[7] These units are combined to produce syntagms; the 'second articulation' is that of the individual sounds of which these units are made. Martinet insists on the extreme economy of both of these articulatory systems (huge numbers of combinations can be made with relatively few elements). The same differential and oppositional criterion which operates at the level of phoneme also operates at that of larger units.

Continuing with the theme of the internal cohesion of the system, Eco turns to Hjemslev's work on semantics to show that there is a rigorously structural approach to semantics which does not have recourse to the signifier–signified relationship (*SA*, pp. 44–5). Hjemslev is interested in studying not the signified but the positional value of the sign in such a way as to allow the content system to be examined structurally in the same way as the expression system. The point is illustrated by a diagram showing the various positional differences between words signifying /tree/ wood/forest in French, German and Danish.[8] In such a diagram, we are concerned not with 'ideas', but with values emanating from the system. The values correspond to presumed concepts, but they take shape as pure differences and are defined not by content but by how they are opposed to other elements in the system.

These differential choices can be described with binary methods. It does not matter what the meaning is; it is sufficient that, on the basis of a code, it is agreed that certain signifieds are assigned to certain signifiers. That these are then understood as concepts or references is one thing, but at the point at which semiology establishes the existence of a code, the signified is no longer a psychological or ontological or sociological entity: 'it is a cultural phenomenon which is described by the system of relations which the code defines as being accepted by a certain group at a certain time' (*SA*, p. 45). The emphasis here is on that sense (or those senses) in which it is possible to speak both of language (all the examples at this stage are drawn from natural language) and of semiology *qua* discipline as autonomous, self-contained and free-standing. This is done by focusing attention on the internal workings of the code or system or structure (terms which appear at this point to be virtually synonymous).

The second of Lévi-Strauss's ideas about structure which Eco wishes to explore further is the notion that 'structure appears only when it is brought out through the comparison of different phenomena and their reduction to the same system of relations', in other words, structure as a theoretical model. Reserving more detailed observations about structure for another discussion (the essay which constitutes Section D of *La struttura assente*, and which we have already considered in some detail), Eco here wants, firstly, to reiterate the point that a structure is a model constructed according to certain simplifying operations which permit one to bring together different phenomena from a single point of view. He makes it clear that he is dealing with a methodological rather than an ontological structuralism, but the question now arises whether, by such a process of simplification, one might arrive at an Ur-Code, a Code of Codes. This operation, however, does not so much find as *posit* a structure, inventing it as a hypothesis and a theoretical model in such a way as to be able to leap ahead of the interminable work of empirical verification. That is how Eco's book proceeds when speaking of codes: 'The code is the model of a series of communicative conventions which are postulated as existing in such a way as to explain the possibility of communication of certain messages' (*SA*, p. 49). Talking about signifieds does not therefore entail going back to mental events, Platonic ideas or concrete uses (necessarily). There is a code when one assumes that the communicator has a repertoire of given symbols amongst which she or he selects (vertical, paradigmatic, axis) and which she or he combines in ever more complex syntagmatic chains, which constitute the actual discourse. A code may therefore be more conclusively described as 'a structure, elaborated in the form of a model, which is postulated as a rule underlying a series of concrete, individual messages which conform to it and are communicative only in relation to it' (*SA*, p. 50). At this point it is necessary to distinguish further between repertoire, code and lexicon: a *repertoire* entails a list of symbols and may fix their equivalence with given signifieds; a *code* builds these symbols into a system of differences and oppositions and fixes its rules of combination; a *lexicon* is constituted as a system of signifying oppositions, but may not be concerned with the rules of combination, for which it relies on the code of which it is a lexicon.

Turning to the situation in which the sender as well as the recipient of the message is human, Eco puts to one side the question of whether the speaker is free to communicate what he or she thinks or is in some way spoken by the code, determined by it, though he inclines to the latter view.

He also establishes that it is not always the case that sender and receiver always communicate on the basis of the same code. The example of the phrase 'I vitelli dei romani sono belli' shows that it will be understood differently according to whether the recipient believes it to be uttered in the Latin language or in the Italian.[9] If the sender sends it in Latin and the receiver decodes it in Italian, the decoding will be called 'aberrant'. Messages can be ambiguous, polysemous, but this polysemy can be limited by various factors such as the internal context of the syntagm, the circumstance in which the communication is made, or an explicit indication of the code to be adopted.

The *circumstance* in which the communication is made often acts as a kind of referent. The presence of the referent in this sense leads one to select the most appropriate connotative lexicon, and it points one towards the appropriate codes. Circumstance changes the meaning of a message, its function, and the quantity of information which it contains. Semiology is concerned with cultural conventions and circumstance is what anchors the 'abstract vitality' of the systems of codes and messages to social and historical reality (*SA*, p. 55). Uncertainties may be reduced, by taking context and circumstance into consideration, as far as the denotative code is concerned, but they are plentiful at the level of the connotative lexicons. The message as a signifying form appears as an empty form to which the most diverse meanings may be attributed.

Both source and message, notwithstanding the differences of scale previously discussed, can be considered as information, inasmuch as both can be defined as a state of disorder in relation to a subsequent order, as ambiguity in relation to a subsequent shaping, as the possibility of various choices prior to a choice being made. What are the different degrees of semiological information? If the machine receives a message that is not foreseen by the code, it does not respond, it regards it as noise. If human recipients receive such a message when transmitted by a machine, they may well think it is noise. But if the sender is another human being, they may conclude that it is ambiguous and try to puzzle it out. The receiver may also conclude from the ambiguity of the message that it was possible to use the code in a different way: the code is brought into question.

Ambiguity, self-reflexivity and the aesthetic message

Ambiguity and self-reflexivity (leading to the questioning of the code) are for Eco, following Jakobson, the characteristic features of aesthetic or poetic language. Placed in a semiotic context, they offer the most convincing challenge to Crocean intuitionism and at the same time open up new vistas in the mapping of the semiotic continent as a whole. As one might expect from the author of *Opera aperta*, a particular attention to the aesthetic function of language is integral to the development of his semiotics at least until *A Theory of Semiotics* (after which it remains, but with different emphases). The remainder of this chapter is concerned directly or indirectly with the evolution of Eco's thinking on the 'aesthetic message' prior to the *Theory*.

Eco begins his observations with a return to a passage from Croce's 1931 essay on totality as a characteristic of aesthetic expression which he had already considered in 'Analisi del linguaggio poetico' (*OA*, p. 66/*OW*, p. 25). According to Croce, an artistic representation is a reflection of the cosmos, 'at the same time itself and the universe, the universe as individual form, and the individual form as universe'.[10] Croce's affirmation is not rejected out of hand, but serves as a stimulus to Eco to ask how semiology might help us to understand the effect of 'the cosmic' in art. Once again, it is to Jakobson's discussion of the six functions of language (conative, referential, emotive, poetic, phatic, metalingual) that he turns, stressing first the ambiguity of the aesthetic message, structured as it is in an ambiguous way relative to the system of expectations known as the code. A wholly ambiguous message is extremely informative (in the sense already given) because it allows very many different interpretations, but it is close to noise, to pure disorder. A 'productive' ambiguity, as Eco calls it, awakens one's attention and induces one to try and interpret it, but at the same time suggests directions in which one might go in order to decode it. Having done this, the aesthetic message also demands to be understood as itself the principal object of the communication. In Jakobson's words: 'The set (*Einstellung*) toward the MESSAGE as such, focus on the message for its own sake, is the POETIC function of language.'[11] It is not referential; its combination of ambiguity and possible lines of interpretation lead one on to enquire 'how it is made (or done)'.

Certain conditions are necessary for this enquiry to be triggered and to take place: the signifiers acquire appropriate signifieds only from contextual interaction (that is to say, the whole context must support these features of ambiguity and self-reflexivity); the matter (material) of which the signifiers are made must not appear arbitrary in relation to their signifieds and to their contextual relationship. Furthermore, the message is capable of activating different levels of reality: the physical technical level of the substance of which the signifiers are made; the level of the differential nature of the signifiers; the level of the denoted signifieds; that of the connoted signifieds; the level of the various systems of expectations (psychological, logical, scientific) to which the signs direct the addressee. At all of these levels a system of homologous structural relationships is established, inasmuch as all the levels are definable on the basis of one general code which structures them all (*SA*, pp. 61–7).

When stylistic criticism says that a work 'offends the norm', that is, that it is ambiguous in respect of the code, then it must be understood that all levels of the message offend the norm following the same rule. This rule may be described, according to Eco, as an idiolect (in the sense of the private and individual code of a single speaker), an idiolect being the structural diagram which governs all parts of the message. The notion of idiolect is not, as might appear, in conflict with that of ambiguity. The ambiguous message allows one to make a number of interpretative choices. Each signifier takes on new signifieds, not on the basis of the original code (which has been violated), but on that of the idiolect, which organizes the context, and on that of the other signifiers, which react on each other as if to find the support which is no longer offered by the violated code. Thus the work is continually transforming its own denotations into connotations, and its signifieds into the signifiers of other signifieds.

Our first reaction upon engaging in the 'open' process of decoding which is invited by the aesthetic message is to believe that everything that we bring to bear on the message is contained within it, that is, that it 'expresses' the world of semantic connotations, emotive associations and physiological reactions which its ambiguous and self-reflexive nature has aroused in us. But this leads to an aporia. On the one hand we have a message whose structure is such as to allow an 'open' reading; on the other, we have a reading so 'open' that it prevents us from recognizing in the message a formalizable structure. We thus face two problems, which are linked but separable. Firstly, there takes place in the course of aesthetic communication an experience which cannot be reduced either to a quantitative measure or to structural systemization. Yet, secondly, this experience is made possible by something which, at all its levels, must possess a structure; otherwise we would have, not communication, but a purely random stimulation of aleatory responses. What is at stake, therefore, is on the one hand, the structural model of the process of reception (*fruizione*), and on the other the structure of the message at all of its levels (*SA*, p. 69).

To illustrate the first problem Eco takes the example of a Renaissance palace with a facade in ashlar-work. It is clear that the material itself, with its particular tactile feel, adds something above and beyond the plan or section or design of the work. The use of the stone in itself is part of the plan of the work and can be included in a series of relations on which the structure of the work is founded. But the particular sensations which I experience on seeing and touching the stone are not verifiable. That I should feel such sensations is foreseen by the context; they are an effect of the ambiguity of the work, and the work is self-reflexive inasmuch as I can contemplate it as a form which makes the various individual responses possible. But semiology can only grasp the work as a message or source, and thus as code or idiolect, as the starting point for a series of free individual interpretative choices. The work as an individual experience is theorizable but not measurable. Semiology and a semiologically informed aesthetics can tell us what a work may become, but not what it has become. The latter is, if anything, the task of criticism as the account of a reading experience.

The second problem has to do not so much with explicitly 'expressive' aesthetics like Croce's as with those semiotically informed aesthetics which come up against the barrier of the expressive, and Eco is thinking particularly of Morris's view, adapting Peirce, that similarity is concerned with properties which are shared by an icon and its object.[12] What is at stake is this: once the aesthetic message is subjected to a semiological analysis, it is necessary to translate so-called 'expressive' devices (*artifici*) into communication devices on the basis of codes, whether these codes are observed or challenged. Otherwise one is left trying to distinguish between 'semantic information' and 'aesthetic information', the latter being understood as being rooted in the very nature of its materiality and communicable to another person only with the greatest difficulty. The notion of aesthetic idiolect insists on the fact that an homologous structure must be realized at all levels. Such a structure should also allow one to define, in terms of oppositions and differences, the material elements of the work: not only registering their presence, but also structuring, as far as possible, this 'raw' presence. By bringing this too into a system of relations, it should be possible to eliminate the equivocal notion of 'aesthetic information'.

Eco distinguishes between two kinds of sensorial information: the kind that can and has been measured statistically in painting, music, poetry etc., and that which is regarded as somehow much more difficult to grasp, all those elements which contribute to the creation of an emotive, 'pre-semantic' effect, to what is called individual style. Even when faced with such a challenge, the validity of a semiological approach must be judged on its being able to reformulate the motivated, the continuous and the expressive in terms of the arbitrary, the discrete and the conventional. At this point, Eco points forward to the second section of *La struttura assente*, whose title 'Lo sguardo discreto' (*SA*, pp. 107–95) entails the discreteness rather than the discretion of looking; here it will be seen that the problem of the iconic sign becomes the testing-ground for semiology precisely because it has traditionally been seen as impossible to codify in structural terms. It is to this important issue that we must now turn.

The critique of iconism

The best short account of this aspect of Eco's work is that given by Teresa De Lauretis in 1981 and the summary of the question which follows is heavily indebted to her.[13] Eco's critique of iconism, and the systemization of visual phenomena in the universe of signs, is in her view one of his most original contributions to the founding of semiotics. The problem centres on the articulation of sign systems, which was particularly troublesome in the early years of semiotics. In Saussurean linguistics, the principal characteristic of the language system (*langue*) consists in the double articulation of its minimum units, linguistic signs. Since semiology had evolved from Saussurean linguistics, the presence of a double articulation had come to be perceived as a *sine qua non* for every system; an organization of signs which did not possess a double articulation could not be regarded as a sign system. In the opinion of many, the organization of iconic signs – images in painting, advertising, cinema etc. – was such an organization, because it did not have double articulation. Based in part on a hasty reading of Peirce's subdivision of signs into symbols, indices and icons, a distinction had become established between linguistic signs, belonging to verbal language and properly thought of as signs (conventional, codified), and iconic signs, belonging to the 'language of images' and apparently natural, spontaneous, not codified.

The question was felt particularly acutely, according to De Lauretis, in the discussion of cinema in the 1960s. In Peirce's definition, taken up by Morris, the iconic sign has a certain 'native similarity' with the object to which it refers; the relationship between sign and object is not therefore arbitrary or conventional (as in that between signifier and signified in verbal language), but natural and 'motivated' by certain properties which sign and object have in common. Thus it may seem that the images of a film are a direct, 'photographic' representation of people, landscapes, objects as they exist in reality. Their sense is conveyed to the spectator immediately, without recourse to a code, without it being necessary or possible to subdivide the image into discrete units equivalent to the words or sounds of verbal language. Metz had recently argued that cinema is an analogical kind of language, while Pasolini thought that there was a double articulation, but that its minimum units (which he called 'cinémi') were the real objects of which each frame is composed; hence his formula 'la lingua scritta della realtà' (the written language of reality).[14]

Eco's commitment to the 'conventionality' of the sign leads him to challenge both these positions on the grounds that they are based on an intuitionist and Romantic aesthetics, predicated upon the ineffability of aesthetic expression or on its supposed ontological foundation in 'nature'. The problem, as he puts it, is how a graphic or photographic sign can appear to be 'the same' as objects when it has no material element in common with them. The solution he proposes is to abandon the improper transferral of terminology belonging to linguistics and to limit at the same time the notion of double articulation to verbal language. In the case of cinema Eco proposes a threefold articulation at the same time as warning that this cinematic code cannot be isolated from the other codes upon which the whole of the cinema phenomenon rests: spoken language, photography and other codes of perception (for example, the principle of perspective). What have to be established are 'operative points of view'. We are dealing, once again, with a methodological rather than an ontological statement.

From this two further methodological observations flow, as De Lauretis points out. Firstly, the idea of 'discourse', with its postulation of a variety of codes and levels of signification, broadens the theoretical prospect from the purely structural concern with the articulations and minimum units of a system axiomatically given as a homogeneous whole to a much more dynamic and articulated view of signification; to evoke the notion of discourse means to shift the perspective of research from the structure of one particular system to the analysis of the structurings brought about by various codes in different expressive materials and semantic fields. Secondly, the idea of a plurality of codes operating simultaneously in the process of sense production, in *any* communicative situation, allows a more fruitful approach to the question of iconism. If it can be shown that the perception of certain qualities in the image of an object which correspond to certain physical properties of the same object also takes place on the basis of codes, iconism becomes a fact of culture rather than nature. Eco concludes that iconic signs do not reproduce the properties of the object, but rather 'some conditions of the perception of the object'; they exhibit, by means of graphic or gestural conventions, some aspects of the object which are recognized as pertinent. The selection of pertinent traits occurs on the basis of recognition codes, and iconic codes are the graphic conventions which represent them.

Some provisional conclusions on the aesthetic message

La struttura assente marks Eco's first major attempt at delineating a semiological approach to the 'aesthetic message'. He confirms his debt to Jakobson and makes some substantive propositions about the field of inquiry. He tackles head-on the problem of how to overcome the illusion that certain kinds of works of art, or all works potentially at certain levels, are inhabited by 'natural', that is, not culturally coded, features. In general, his research is pushing all the time at what might appear to be the natural or physical boundaries of culture in an attempt to demonstrate the culturally coded character of all our experience. He also makes three broader points which touch on both the creation and the reception of aesthetic messages. Each work challenges or offends the code, but strengthens it at the same time. Each work invites the receiver into the code, to take stock of what has been said and of what has not been said, what can be said (*SA*, p. 79). Finally, harking back to the arguments of *Opera aperta*, he suggests that the understanding of the aesthetic message is based on a dialectic between acceptance and rejection of the codes and lexicons of the sender on the one hand, and of the addressee's own on the other, a dialectic between interpretative freedom and fidelity to the message, between form and openness (at the level of the message), between fidelity and initiative (at the level of the addressee). The 'semiologization' of *Opera aperta*, however, has raised the stakes, as it was meant to do, for now we are asked to conceptualize a more complex kind of interpretation. Put at its simplest, we have to ask what the relation is between interpretation as decoding (which we all have to do to make *any* sense of the message) and interpretation as a kind of exploration and assessment which we have to do to make *better* sense of it.

Deferring further questions to do with interpretation for the moment, let us conclude with two essays written shortly after the publication of *La struttura assente* and included in Eco's next book, *Le forme del contenuto* (*The Forms of Content*, 1971, which will be briefly described in the next chapter). The first of these, 'La semantica della metafora' ('The Semantics of Metaphor') grew out of Eco's chapter on Joyce's 'poetics of the pun' in the essay originally in *Opera aperta* and then published separately as *Le poetiche di Joyce* (*The Aesthetics of Chaosmos*); its central argument, and example, has also appeared in a later paper on Joyce.[15] It is not strictly to do with the aesthetic message, or with the poetic function of language, but it does continue the campaign against the illusion of 'natural expressiveness' mounted in the critique of iconism, this time by dismantling the notion of metaphor. Its argument, furthermore, is strongly supported by a passage from that most 'open' of literary texts for Eco, *Finnegans Wake*, and it draws most of its other main examples from aesthetic texts. If nothing else, 'The Semantics of Metaphor' demonstrates that the aesthetic message continues to be a privileged point of reference for Eco throughout his semiotic evolution. The importance of the essay goes wider than the aesthetic message, but it has implications for it. It is concerned with the workings of rule-governed creativity and the creation of (apparently) new meanings within what is capitalized as the Global Semantic System. But let us proceed in step with Eco's argument.

If a code allowed us only to generate semiotic judgements – that is, those foreseen by the code (example: 'all unmarried men are bachelors') – all our utterances would be ultimately tautological.

But codes allow us to enunciate events that the code did not anticipate – so-called 'factual judgements', for example, 'Luigi is a bachelor' – and also to make metasemiotic judgements which call into
question the legitimacy of the code itself. To the question: how can
it be that 'this code, which in principle ought to have generated the
speaking subject's entire cultural system, is able to generate both
factual messages which refer to original experiences and, above all,
messages which place in doubt the very structure of the code itself?'
(*FC*, p. 95/*RR*, p. 67) there is a quick answer. The fact that the code
allows us to assign new semiotic marks to predictable cultural entities is proper to that feature of the code called 'rule-governed creativity'. Furthermore, the explanation for the fact that the code allows
for factual judgements lies in the arbitrary nature of the code, as a
consequence of which it can manipulate signifiers to refer to new
signifieds produced in response to new experiences; by the same
token, once issued, factual judgements can be integrated into the
code in such a way as to create new possibilities for semiotic judgement. The next question is, how does this rule-governed creativity
work?

As already indicated, this is a discussion which is in a sense prior
to aesthetics, or the aesthetic use of language. The first example of
such creativity is provided in common speech by the use of different
types of metaphors and thus of rhetorical figures. The essay focuses
on the interaction between metaphoric mechanisms and metonymic
mechanisms, to which Eco thinks the entire range of tropes, figures
of speech and figures of thought can probably be ascribed. The goal
of the discussion is 'to show that each metaphor can be traced back
to a subjacent chain of metonymic connections which constitute the
framework of the code and upon which is based the constitution of
any semantic field, whether partial or (in theory) global' (*FC*, p. 96/
RR, p. 68).

In *Finnegans Wake* (part 3, ch. 3), Shaun is referred to as 'Minucius
Mandrake'. Minucius Felix is a Father of the Church and Mandrake,
Eco demonstrates with philological evidence to hand, is probably
the comic-strip character Mandrake the Magician (whose strip only
started appearing in 1934; the name 'Mandrake' does not appear in
the 1924 version of the passage, but shows up in the revision under-
taken by Joyce between 1936 and 1939). What brings the two names
together, Eco argues, is an unnamed third character, Felix the Cat.
In fact, Minucius is surnamed Felix, and the feline Felix is another
cartoon character like Mandrake (*FC*, pp. 98–101/*RR*, pp. 70–2).
This example shows that what appears to be metaphoric is in fact a

coupling by contiguity, except that the middle term has fallen and the contiguity is not therefore apparent. Readers may not find the missing middle term, but they grasp the analogies thanks to the extremely long series of third terms that exist in the general context of the book (*FC*, p. 101/*RR*, p. 72). Eco thinks that it should therefore be possible to show 'that each metaphor produced in *FW* is, in the last analysis, comprehensible because the entire book, read in different directions, actually furnishes the metonymic chains that justify it' (ibid.). This hypothesis is then tested on the 'atomic element' of Joyce's novel, the pun, and specifically the elements of the metaphoric term 'meandertale'.

Eco's contention is that 'all connections were already codified before the artist could recognize them by pretending to institute or discover them' (*FC*, p. 107/*RR*, p. 77). What makes the pun creative is not the series of connections (which precedes it as already codified); it is 'the decision to make the so-called metaphoric short circuit [*la decisione del corto circuito cosiddetto metaforico*]' (ibid.). A metaphor can be invented because language, in its process of unlimited semiosis, constitutes a multidimensional network of metonymies, each of which is explained by a cultural convention rather than by an original resemblance. The imagination would be incapable of inventing (or recognizing) a metaphor if culture, under the form of a possible structure of the Global Semantic System, did not provide it with the subjacent network of arbitrarily stipulated contiguities. 'The imagination', he goes on, 'is nothing other than a ratiocination that traverses the paths of the semantic labyrinth in a hurry and, in its haste, loses the sense of their rigid structure' (*FC*, p. 108/*RR*, p. 78).

In an interesting discussion of this essay Jonathan Culler has argued that Eco's inclination to identify metonymy with the code is a reversal of Jakobson's priorities, mainly, he thinks, because Eco apparently thinks of codes and systems as spatial.[16] The more compelling reason for the privileging of contiguity over similarity, as Culler rightly sees and as we might expect from the argument about the iconic sign, is to combat any privileging of the idea of language, under the shield of metaphor, as 'expressing' things outside language. Eco is primarily concerned to show that no recourse to the referent is necessary in order to explain metaphor or, indeed, to explain metonymy, which may start from the empirical, but becomes metonymy as and when it is codified as such.

> The contiguity on which the metonymic transposition is founded is thus transformed from factual (empirical) contiguity to *contiguity of code*. The

referent no longer carries any weight, and neither does the possibility
of recognizing the metonymized term by a natural kinship with the
metonymizing term. The kinship is not natural, it is *cultural*. The two
terms refer to each other because they are conventionally situated each
in the place of the other. The metonymizing term is already part of
the semantic representation of the metonymized term, as one of its
interpretants. (FC, p. 111/RR, p. 80)

Culler catches effectively the implications of this stance for a theory
of, or an attitude towards, language in general: 'To maintain the
primacy of metaphor is to treat language as a device for the expression of thoughts, perceptions, truth. To posit the dependency of
metaphor on metonymy is to treat what language expresses as the
effect of contingent, conventional relations and a system of mechanical processes' (pp. 201–2).

What has been described is a theoretical construct. In view of
this, or perhaps in spite of it, Eco tries to throw some tentative
light on what makes a 'good' metaphor, on what, amongst good
metaphors, distinguishes the 'rewarding' (Dante's 'selva oscura')
from the merely 'acceptable' (sleep/death), and what makes a
metaphor 'ugly' or 'off-key' (*brutta, stonata* – oddly Englished in *The
Role of the Reader* as 'deceiving' and 'defaulting'). Such exercises
inevitably leave themselves open to criticism,[17] but the final focus
of this rich essay is on the necessary contradictions in the Global
Semantic System. Metaphor is the key to unlocking the subjacent
metonymic chains which show ultimately that contradiction is
possible.

The second essay from *Le forme del contenuto*, likewise included
by Eco in the English-language anthology *The Role of the Reader*, is
Eco's first visit (on paper) to the Garden of Eden (he will make a
brief return trip two decades later in *The Search for the Perfect Language*). In 'Generazione di messaggi estetici in una lingua edenica'
('On the Possibility of Generating Aesthetic Messages in an Edenic
Language'), Eco tries to overcome the problem of always having to
deal with terms like 'ambiguity' and 'self-referentiality', or 'form'
and 'content', in the abstract because, if he wants to give practical
examples, the analyst 'tends to work with aesthetic messages which
have already been elaborated and which therefore present special
complexities' (*OA*, p. 292/*RR*, p. 91). Eco therefore proposes to offer
a small-scale working model of aesthetic language, involving a very
simple language or code and demonstrating the rules by which
aesthetic messages can be generated. Three requirements are made
of the model: (1) These rules will have to arise from inside the code
itself, but then be capable of generating an alteration of the code,

both in its form of expression and in its form of content. The working model must therefore be equipped to demonstrate a language's
own capacity for generating self-contradiction. (2) It must also show
how the aesthetic use of the given language is one of the most
appropriate devices for generating these contradictions. (3) Finally,
the model must prove that any contradictions generated by the
aesthetic use of language at the level of its form of expression
equally involve contradictions in the form of its content; 'ultimately,
they entail a complete reorganizing of our conceptual vision of the
universe' (ibid.).

Adam and Eve start off by devising a restricted series of semantic
units which give preferential status to their emotional responses to
flora and fauna, under six main headings (Yes/No, Edible/Ined-
ible, Good/Bad, Beautiful/Ugly, Red/Blue, Serpent/Apple; this
latter is 'the only antithesis which denotes objects rather than qualities of objects or responses to them' and these objects 'emerge excep-
tionally': they are only incorporated into the code after God's
prohibition: *OA*, p. 293/*RR*, p. 92). One cultural unit leads to another, which produces a series of connotative chains (Red = Edible
= Good = Beautiful; Blue = Inedible = Bad = Ugly), and they have
a repertoire of this language built up out of two sounds, A and B,
which can be arranged in a variety of sequences following the
combinatory rule: X, nY, X (every sequence must start with one of
the two elements, carry on with n repetitions of the other, and end
with one further occurrence of the first element). Whence emerges a
code which fits their needs (though an infinite number of sequences
can potentially be generated). This paradise is thrown into disarray
when God, to his own later detriment, announces to the pair that the
apple is bad.

> In an effort to elaborate a prohibition which would put his creatures to
> the test, God provides the fundamental example of a subversion in the
> presumed natural order of things. Why should an apple which is red be
> inedible as if it were blue? Alas, God wanted to bring into existence the
> cultural tradition, and culture is born, apparently to the sound of an
> institutional taboo. (*OA*, p. 297/*RR*, p. 95)

Things go from bad to worse in Eden: it becomes possible to express
a contradictory fact without obliging the speaker to formulate it in
accordance with the habitual logical rules, which would in fact
exclude it; but this possibility becomes even more fascinating as our
first parents discover that the contradiction resides at the level of the
expression as well as at the level of content, and become acquainted

with the aesthetic use of language. Increasingly excited experimentation with form leads to a reformulation of content (Adam 'discovers that Order, as such, is non-existent; it is just one of the infinite possible states of repose which disorder occasionally arrives at': *OA*, p. 305/*RR*, p. 103).

The pleasure of the piece lies not only in the technical demonstration, but in the discreet parody of poets, poetics, theorists and critics, whose tics and foibles are uncannily foreseen in Adam and Eve's, but essentially Adam's, breakneck career as an experimenter with forms of language and culture: the Romantics, the Baroque, concrete poetry, the Futurists, Mallarmé, Rimbaud, Joyce, Kristeva, Jakobson, Derrida, Hjemslev, Heidegger, they are all there in the garden. Here is Eco enjoying the challenge and delight of building a small-scale, working, model which will sit alongside the huge machine of his *Theory*. (But was God's model, which after all only took him seven days, big or small?) The essay looks forward, but also seems to conclude a phase of Eco's activity. When he reprinted the piece as an appendix to the 1976 edition of *Opera aperta*, a few months after the publication of the Italian edition of the *Theory of Semiotics*, he acknowledged that people might ask him if he would be capable of rewriting *Opera aperta* in the light of his semiotic experience and showing finally how the whole thing works. 'To be blunt,' he replied, 'I already have. In the essay "Generazione di messaggi estetici in una lingua edenica" . . . It's only sixteen pages, but I don't think there is anything to add' (*OA*, p. viii).

4

A Theory of Semiotics

From *La struttura assente* to *A Theory of Semiotics*

Both of the essays discussed at the end of the previous chapter dealt, from different points of view, with ways in which codes are challenged and changed. This was one of the principal concerns of the book in which they appeared in 1971, *Le forme del contenuto*. The other was the modalities of the production of meaning itself, which Eco addressed in the long essay 'I percorsi del senso' ('The routes of sense'). Rather than deal with his argument immediately, however, I propose to look at it from the perspective of his 'treatise' of four years later, published in English in 1976 as *A Theory of Semiotics*. Eco himself tends to look on both *Le forme del contenuto* and his other semiotic book published between *Struttura* and *Theory*, namely *Il segno* (*The Sign*, 1973), as intermediate or transitional works and, in the light of the larger work, not authoritative.

That said, there are differences between them which should be mentioned. The various essays of *Le forme del contenuto* were largely conceived, Eco tells us, as rewrites of parts of *La struttura assente* for possible translations; their being collected together in a book (which has never been republished) served as at least a preliminary focus on the two outstanding problems described above. *Il segno*, on the other hand, was conceived as a whole, but for a particular purpose, as part of a series devoted to classical philosophical terms. This explains its classificatory bent and its close attention to historical uses of the concept 'sign'. Divided into five chapters, it begins by examining the main features of the processes in which the sign is used and making a first attempt at a provisional definition of the sign. The second chapter aims to give as complete a list as possible, one that is 'syncretic' rather than historical, of the different classifications of signs, reflecting the variety of ways in which something is given the attribute of a sign, while the third sets out to summarize the analyses carried out by contemporary linguistics, largely on structuralist lines, of the internal structure of the sign and of the systems in which it occurs. The purpose of the fourth chapter is to review the main positions concerning the nature, purposes and aporias of the sign as they have been considered in the course of Western thought. In his final chapter, Eco outlines a Unified Semiotic Theory of the Sign: in the pages that follow, a number of terms and concepts that recur in his essays of the late 1960s and early 1970s are defined and explained in an almost dictionary-like way, prior to being absorbed into a much more articulated theoretical structure in *A Theory of Semiotics*.

Il segno, then, is a handbook rather than a polemic, a cautious and gradual, but thorough, approach to the topic of the sign, an overview of opinions concerning what a sign is (and is not) and how it works. In the excitement of launching his *Theory*, Eco clearly saw it as too cautious, too slow-moving for his present purposes (see below), and in any case, as was made clear in the book itself, *Il segno* was precisely about that, the sign, and not about semiotics as a whole. Between *Il segno* and *Theory*, but already in the earlier book itself, the notion of the sign as such was becoming increasingly problematic. This may help to explain why *Il segno* seems to have led a semi-clandestine life: it has been republished only once in Italy to the best of my knowledge (by Mondadori in 1980) but is not currently available, and Eco interestingly does not refer to it when he tackles the problem of the sign again in post-*Theory* mode in *Semiotics and the Philosophy of Language*. It has never been translated into English, but it does appear to thrive in French, in which language there have been two editions (1988 and 1992);[1] judging by my own unscientific sampling, it appears to be in constant demand in French public libraries. Its relative unavailability, however, is a shame for, all allowance made for Eco's own understandable reservations, it is both clear, communicating effectively with the untutored reader (very different in tone from the willed 'dryness' (*secchezza*, *TSI*, p. 6) of *Theory*), and very detailed. At the same time, notably in the fourth chapter, it foreshadows Eco's later and growing commitment to the history of semiotics as a necessary and fruitful part of the definition of the discipline.[2]

As Eco approaches the systematization of the field which he will attempt in *Theory*, it is important to remember that the early 1970s were also a hectic time in the process of institutionalization of semiotic studies, both for Eco personally and more generally. In 1971, after a series of appointments in Italy and abroad, Eco received his first permanent academic post at the University of Bologna, where he was engaged to teach semiotics in the Faculty of Letters and Philosophy; this post was to be converted into a full professorship of semiotics in 1975 and the following year Eco became head of a department specializing in the study of communications and performance study. The International Association of Semiotics had been founded in Paris in January 1969, the Italian Association of Semiotics was created in March 1970; and a number of important initiatives quickly followed. In 1971 the International Centre for Semiotics and Linguistics was established at the University of Urbino, with A. J. Greimas nominated as 'scientific director' in charge of a programme of symposia and summer schools. In the same year the journal *VS*, dedicated to semiotic studies under Eco's editorship, published its first issue.[3] The project for a running bibliography of semiotics, initiated in *VS*, was taken up by *Strumenti critici* in 1973, under the direction of D'Arco Silvio Avalle. In June 1974 the first International Congress of Semiotic Studies took place in Milan, with Eco acting as the principal organizer in his capacity as Secretary of the International Association, and in the same year he initiated the 'Il campo semiotico' series with Bompiani (the publisher with whom he has remained throughout in close association as non-fiction senior editor (1959–75) and consultant as well as author).

Eco's 'treatise', as he called it, the *Trattato di semiotica generale*, was published in Italy in 1975; the English version, with its different title, came out as *A Theory of Semiotics* in 1976. Despite the dates of publication, however, the English version is the prior of the two texts, the outcome of failed attempts to translate *La struttura assente* and the decision to rewrite the book directly in English, with the help of David Osmond-Smith; the Italian is 're-translated' from the English (*TSE*, pp. vii–viii). The one place in which the texts differ, as might be expected, is in the prefaces to the respective editions ('Prefazione'/'Foreword') and, as these are important, I shall dwell on them for a moment before entering into the heart of what for all other purposes I shall consider as one book. In view of the priority mentioned above, I shall normally refer in the rest of the chapter only to the English-language edition.

A Theory of Semiotics was Eco's first book in English. About a dozen of his articles on various subjects had been translated into English at this point and three of the specialist essays on semiotics which were to be adapted in this book had been published directly in English in *VS*.[4] Nevertheless, although he had also taught in the United States and lectured there and in Britain, he did not yet possess either the hinterland or the visibility that he enjoyed in Italy. In his home country he had been well known in avant-garde circles since the late 1950s, had become familiar to a wider public with the appearance of and the critical reactions to *Opera aperta* in 1962 and *Apocalittici e integrati* in 1964, had established a formidable academic reputation and at the same time reinforced his presence in the media as both an active journalist and a critic of the media themselves since the mid-1960s on. The American Foreword is therefore briefer and assumes less of the reader than the Italian Prefazione, though it conveys the essential information about the genesis of the book and its structure.

While *Theory* alludes to Eco's earlier semiotic writings and lists a number of ways in which this volume represents a 'partial critique' of them, the author's main concern is to orientate a reader who he knows will be by definition new to his work. The *Trattato*, on the other hand, is preoccupied by the relation between 'revision' and 'novelty'. The direction of the Prefazione is underlined by its epigraph from Pascal ('Qu'on ne dise pas que je n'ai rien dit de nouveau: la disposition des matières est nouvelle'). The dialogue with the reader who, if he or she does not know much about semiotics, has certainly heard of and probably read something of Umberto Eco, goes through four movements:

1 The book is presented as summarizing eight years of work and being born from the remains of four previous books (*Appunti, Struttura, Forme, Segno*): what remains and what is discarded from these previous works is briefly described.

2 The book seeks to reduce, we might say, to distil, all his previous semiotic research into unitary and hopefully more rigorous categories, and to outline the limits and possibilities of a discipline which is taking form as theoretical knowledge only for the purpose of, for the benefit of, a praxis of signs. None of this, neither the idea of 'distillation' nor, more importantly, the politically loaded articulation of theory and practice appears in the English.

3 As to where this book stands, its 'senso', in relation to his other works, Eco describes it as a partial critique of his earlier researches in five respects:

(a)   it makes a clearer distinction between signification sys-
      tems and communication systems (although this item is
      logically omitted from the English text, the distinction
      provides the basic structural organization of the treatise,
      the great bulk of which, 240 pages in the English, is di-
      vided between a 'Theory of Codes' and a 'Theory of Sign
      Production');

(b)   it tries to introduce into the semiotic framework a theory of
      referents that Eco had previously felt he ought to expunge
      on the grounds of theoretical purity;

(c)   it brings together the traditional problems of semantics and
      pragmatics into a single model and seeks to resolve them
      both from a single point of view;

(d)   it criticizes the notion of sign and the typology of signs
      (the 'classical' typology of signs, the English version
      specifies);

(e)   it deals with the notion of iconism by maintaining the cri-
      tique of the naïve assumption that icons are natural, analo-
      gical and non-conventional, but avoiding the equally naïve
      assumption that icons are arbitrary, conventional and fully
      analysable into pertinent features; Eco believes that the re-
      placement of a typology of signs by a typology of modes of
      sign production is one of the strong points of the present
      work, and that this helps to break the umbrella notion of
      iconism down into a number of more complex and variously
      interconnected operations.

4   Finally, in the Italian, Eco presents the new book as 'slightly
more definitive than the others'. Not wholly definitive, he hopes: it
simply 'takes stock' (*fa il punto*: *TSI*, p. 8). Those who are new to
semiotics might prefer to start with *La struttura assente*, but should
not complain if they find it not very rigorous; if they want a rigorous
account, they should read the *Trattato*. But his real addressees are
those who *have* read the previous books, for he stresses that henceforth he will enter into discussion on the limits and possibilities of
semiotics only on the basis of this book. Italian readers, therefore,
are enjoined to swallow all the previous messages they may have
received, and make themselves as pristine as their transatlantic
counterparts.

With the author's guidelines to hand, let us now examine the
ways in which *Theory* seeks to correct and strengthen Eco's evolving
system of thought.

Communication, code and signification

A Theory of Semiotics spells out more explicitly than does *La struttura assente* the relation and difference between communication and signification, and the relevance of the notion of code in this relation. Although there are some important differences between a semiotics of communication and a semiotics of signification, according to Eco, that does not mean that they are mutually exclusive. A *process of communication* is defined as the passage of a signal from a source (via a transmitter, along a channel) to a destination. In the case of communication between two machines, what is happening is the passage of information, but not signification. When the destination is a human being, described here as an 'addressee', regardless of whether the source or transmitter is human, and provided that the signal is not just a stimulus but arouses an interpretative response in the addressee, we have a *process of signification* (the salivation of Pavlov's dog, says Eco, using an example already employed in *Il segno*, would be a sign, rather than a conditioned reflex, if the animal could reverse the process, salivate, and make the conditioned scientist ring the bell). The process is made possible by the existence of a *code*. 'A code is a system of signification, insofar as it couples present entities with absent units. When – on the basis of an underlying rule – something actually presented to the perception of the addressee *stands for* something else, there is *signification*' (*TSE*, p. 8). The abstract nature of this system is underlined by the fact that the addressee does not have to be present or even to exist: 'it is enough that the code should foresee an established correspondence between that which "*stands for*" and its correlate, valid for every possible addressee even if no addressee exists or ever will exist.' A *signification system* is thus an autonomous semiotic construct that has an abstract mode of existence independent of any possible communication act it makes possible; every *act of communication* to or between human beings (excluding stimuli) presupposes a signification system as its necessary condition. It is, in conclusion, possible to have a semiotics of signification independently of a semiotics of communication, but not vice versa. This last assertion clinches the decisively 'humanistic' argument that Eco is advancing in the *Theory*: semiotics is coextensive with signification which occurs only when the communicative act envisages a potential human addressee acting as an interpreter of the message (and not a receiver merely responding to a stimulus). We shall have occasion to return to this humanistic cast of the *Theory*, and of all of Eco's thought, in chapter 5.

As a preliminary to a theory of codes proper, Eco introduces an important refinement to the definition of 'code'. The engineer who designed the communication system which tells the down-stream observer what is happening in the water catchment area probably means by 'code' at least four different phenomena:

(a)   a set of signals ruled by internal combinatory laws, not necessarily conveying any messages or eliciting any responses; such a set could be called a *syntactic* system;

(b)   a set of states of the water which are taken into account as a set of *notions* about the state of the water and which can become a set of possible communicative contents; they can be conveyed by signals, but are independent of them; they could be conveyed by any other type of signal; this set of 'contents' could be called a *semantic* system;

(c)   a set of possible *behavioural responses* on the part of the addressee; they are independent of the (b) system (they could elicit a different behaviour) and can be elicited by another (a) system;

(d)   'A rule coupling some items from the (a) system with some from the (b) or the (c) system. This rule establishes that a given array of syntactic signals refers back to a given state of the water, or to a given "pertinent" segmentation of the semantic system; that both the syntactic and semantic units, once coupled, may correspond to a given response; or that a given array of signals corresponds to a given response even though no semantic unit is supposed to be signalled; and so on' (*TSE*, p. 37).

Only this complex form of *rule* may properly be called a 'code'. Eco therefore proposes to distinguish between what he calls *s-codes* (code as system; a system of elements such as the syntactic, semantic and behavioural ones outlined in (a), (b) and (c)) and *codes* (a rule coupling the items of one s-code with the items of another or several other s-codes, as outlined in (d)).

The importance of this distinction, as will become clear, is that it reserves the notion of code to a communicative situation in which elements of the expression plane are correlated to elements of the content plane (these terms are discussed below, in the section on 'Sign and sign-function'), the code being that which permits this correlation to take place. The idea of 'system', or s-code, allows for the analysis of a structure at one or other of the two levels without any concrete act of communication being implied. By clearing away the clutter which has accumulated around the notion of 'code', Eco is able to begin building a theory of codes which is specifically concerned with the process of signification as previously defined (and, once again, to make a clear separation between semiotics and information theory).

Sign and sign-function

A Theory of Semiotics brings to a head the reconceptualization of the notion of the sign which Eco had begun in *Le forme del contenuto* (in the essay 'I percorsi del segno') and *Il segno*. He makes clear in the Italian Preface that the results achieved at these intermediate stages were not complete: the new book, unlike *Le forme del contenuto*, acknowledges that we use signs to name states of the world, and brings the question of the referent into semiotics; furthermore, and differently from *Il segno*, it deals with semiotic operations which give rise not to isolated signs but to messages and texts. In the spirit of the epigraph to the *Trattato* taken from Pascal, the materials carried forward from 1971–3 are radically reorganized.

If semiotics is the science (or what Locke called the 'doctrine') of signs, Eco is concerned that it should not be hampered in its operations by too restrictive an understanding of the term 'sign'. An important part of the work carried out in *Il segno* consisted in bringing a number of these restricted usages to the surface, principal among them the widespread adoption of the verbal sign as the model for all signs, and the tendency, even when using the Saussurean definition of the sign as the unity of *signifiant* and *signifié*, in practice to identify the sign with the *signifiant* (something that Saussure himself had warned against[5]). In order to have a workable definition of the sign which will match his perception of semiotics as a science dealing with the whole of human culture (at least), Eco needs to be able to give a robust description of the structure of the sign within a theory of codes and at the same time to extend the notion of sign beyond the purely linguistic model.

The basics of his approach are already established in *Il segno*, in particular the insistence on *correlation* which is founded on the model proposed by Louis Hjemslev in his *Prolegomena* of 1943:[6]

	Substance
CONTENT	
	Form

	Form
EXPRESSION	
	Substance

'Every sign', writes Eco,

> correlates the *expression* plane (the signifying plane) with the *content*
> plane (the signified plane), each of these opposing at its own level *sub-*
> *stance* and *form*. No kind of sign escapes this classification. Where signs
> differ is in the articulation of the signifying form: verbal signs have
> articulations which are not necessarily the same as other kinds of sign. In
> this sense the sign never exists as a stable and observable physical entity,
> given that it is the product of a series of relations. What is normally
> observed as a sign is only its signifying form. (*S*, p. 142)

Eco has already therefore established the fundamental *relational*
nature of the sign, as well as its *conventionality* (a signifier is associated with its signified by convention, that is, on the basis of a code;
'conventional', however, is not exactly the same as 'arbitrary', since
this definition includes symptoms and so-called iconic signs).
The main questions that remain to be resolved, or simply better
defined, concern: the interaction of sign and code; the referent; the
description of what is called the 'semantic space'. Let us now see
how these arguments are carried forward in the *Theory*.

Eco proposes to replace the term 'sign' by the notion of
'sign-function' (also borrowed from Hjemslev's *Prolegomena* (see
TSE, p. 49), which serves to underline the relational character of the
phenomenon:

> When a code apportions the elements of a conveying system to the
> elements of a conveyed system, the former becomes the expression of the
> latter and the latter becomes the content of the former. A sign-function
> arises when an expression is correlated to a content, both the correlated
> elements being the functives of such a correlation. (*TSE*, p. 48)[7]

A sign, unlike a signal, is *always* an element of an expression plane
conventionally correlated to one (or several) elements of a content
plane. Only in the sense given by a correlation of this kind,
Eco asserts, is it possible to accept Saussure's definition of the
sign as a 'correspondence' between a signifier and a signified. Two

consequences follow from this position: firstly, that a sign is not a 'fixed physical entity', the physical entity being at most the concrete occurrence of the expressive pertinent element; secondly, it is not a 'fixed semiotic entity' either, coming as it does from two different systems (form, substance) of two different planes (expression, content) meeting on the basis of a coding correlation.

It is at this point that Eco declares that 'Properly speaking there are not signs, but only *sign-functions*' (*TSE*, p. 49). A sign-function is realized when two *functives* (expression and content) enter into a mutual correlation; the same functive can also enter into another correlation, thus becoming a different functive and therefore giving rise to a new sign-function. It is not the case that the code organizes signs: rather, it provides the rules which generate signs. The classical notion of sign now dissolves into a highly complex network of changing relationships: semiotics for Eco suggests a sort of molecular landscape in which what we are accustomed to recognizing as everyday forms turn out to be the result of transitory chemical aggregations and so-called 'things' are only the surface appearance assumed by an underlying network of more elementary units. The metaphor is characteristic: the appearance of 'naturalness' is peeled back to show relationships which are fluid in time and space, but these in turn are populated by 'more elementary' units. Behind familiar naturalness lies complexity, behind complexity lies simplicity: this is the very structure of metaphor itself as described in 'The Semantics of Metaphor'.

On the basis of the pattern of correlation described above, Eco explains the respective roles of codes and sign-functions as follows:

> (a) a code establishes the correlation of an expression plane (in its purely formal and systematic aspect) with a content plane (in its purely formal and systematic aspect); (b) a sign-function establishes the correlation of an abstract element of the expression system with an abstract element of the content system; (c) in this way a code establishes general *types*, therefore producing the rule which generates concrete *tokens*, i.e. signs such as usually appear in communicative processes. (*TSE*, p. 50)

Outside of this activity are zones of non-semiotic matter: in the example of the water catchment area, the light and electrical phenomena underlying the expression plane (the light-bulbs) at the lower threshold, and 'the unshaped continuum of the position of the water along with everything one can think about it' at the upper.

This brings us to the second of the areas on which the *Theory* hopes to shed new light, that of the referent, and by extension the notion, borrowed from Peirce, of the interpretant. The question of the referent, that is to say of the object or thing supposedly corresponding to the sign (as signifier and signified) which 'names' it, haunts Eco's semiotics. Up until *Theory*, he is more or less content to follow what he takes to be the lead of linguistics and exclude the analysis of the relation of the referent to the sign as being outside the proper field of semiotics. His solution does not fundamentally change in *Theory*, but he gives a more fully reasoned account of it.

The problem for a theory of codes is that of the possible states of the world supposedly corresponding to the content of a sign-function, and the first point that Eco makes, launching a formulation that he has since often repeated, is that neither the semiotic function of a message like the ABC (AB in *Theory*) of the water catchment area denoting 'danger level' and connoting 'fear' on the part of its human recipient, nor its semantic import, nor the behavioural response of the recipient will be different even if the sender is not telling the truth. 'Every time there is a possibility of lying, there is a sign-function' (*TSE*, p. 58). It is necessary to distinguish within semiotics between conditions of signification (an *intensional* semantics) and conditions of truth (an *extensional* semantics). The significance of this will become clear later; for the moment it is enough to state that a theory of codes is concerned only with the former. Faced with the classic triangle of the Ogden–Richards type (with all its many variants), a theory of codes focuses on the left-hand side, that is, the relation between symbol and reference or, in Peirce's terms, between representamen and interpretant. The whole triangle, on the other hand, is relevant to a theory of sign production, and in particular to a theory of mentions, which is concerned with statements aiming to indicate something true or false, that is, reference to actual states of the world.

As far as Eco is concerned, from the point of view of the functioning of a code (or many codes), the referent must be excluded as an intrusive and jeopardizing presence which compromises the theory's theoretical purity. Armed with this methodological diktat, he goes on to establish his fundamental, 'culturalist', point:

> Within the framework of a theory of codes it is unnecessary to resort to the notion of extension, nor [*sic*] to that of possible worlds [here in the sense of terms used to deal with the problem of sign-vehicles which refer to non-existent entities such as 'unicorn' or 'mermaid']; the codes, insofar as they are accepted by a society, set up a 'cultural' world which is neither actual nor possible in the ontological sense; its existence is linked to a cultural order, which is the way in which a society thinks, speaks

and, while speaking, explains the 'purport' [Hjemslev] of its thought through other thoughts [Peirce]. (*TSE*, p. 61)

Concerned as it is with such 'cultural' worlds, a theory of codes faces the basic problem of 'how to touch contents'.

From a semiotic point of view (a semiotics that Eco has already stated is mainly concerned with signs as social forces), meaning can only be what he calls a 'cultural unit'. The term is used interchangeably with 'semantic unit': according to *Il segno*, these cultural or semantic units are what interpretants are and 'constitute themselves autonomously in a culture into a system of oppositions whose inter-relation is called the Global Semantic System', this system being the way in which a given culture segments the perceptible and thinkable universe (*S*, p. 148; cf. the 'cultural/semantic units' of Eden in 'On the Possibility of Generating Aesthetic Messages'). A statement such as 'There are two natures in Christ, the human and the divine, and one Person' is one to which a logician or a scientist might object that it has neither extension nor referent, and is therefore a pseudo-statement. But this does not explain why people have fought and died for it. Nor are behavioural responses necessary in order to establish that the expression has a content: the civilization itself elaborated a series of definitions and explanations of the terms involved ('person', 'nature' etc.). The idea of cultural unit, as is clear from the passage cited from *Il segno* above, is intimately linked in Eco's reasoning with the (for him) fruitful notion of *interpretant*, as posited by Peirce, and with it that of *unlimited semiosis*. In fact, 'the series of clarifications which circumscribed the cultural units of a society in continuous progression (always defining them in the form of sign-vehicles) represents the chain of what Peirce called the *interpretants*' (*TSE*, p. 68).

The interpretant in Peirce, as has already been mentioned, is that which guarantees the validity of the sign, even in the absence of the interpreter. In order to establish what the interpretant of a sign is, it is necessary, according to Peirce, to name it by means of another sign which in turn has another interpretant to be named by another sign, and so on. 'At this point there begins a process of *unlimited semiosis* which, paradoxical as it may be, is the only guarantee for the foundation of a semiotic system capable of checking itself entirely by its own means' (*TSE*, p. 68). Eco is persuaded that the idea of the interpretant makes a theory of signification a rigorous science of cultural phenomena, while detaching it from the metaphysics of the referent (*TSE*, p. 70). And his adoption of the notion of unlimited semiosis is almost belligerent:

The very richness of this category [the interpretant] makes it fertile since it shows us how signification (as well as communication), by means of continual shiftings which refer a sign back to another sign or string of signs, circumscribes cultural units in an asymptotic fashion, without ever allowing one to touch them directly, though making them accessible through other units. Thus a cultural unit never obliges me to replace it by means of something which is not a semiotic entity, and never asks to be explained by some Platonic, psychic or objectal entity. *Semiosis explains itself by itself*; this continual circularity is the normal condition of signification and even allows communication to use signs in order to mention things. To call this condition a 'desperate' one is to refuse the human way of signifying, a way that has proved itself fruitful insofar as only through it has cultural history developed. (*TSE*, p. 71)

It should be borne in mind that Peirce develops his theory of the interpretant, and more broadly his semiotics, as 'a general account of meaning and communication within a scientific community which provides the materials for explaining the soundness of inferences and methods',[8] and Christoph Hubig, commenting on the German translation of *La struttura assente*, has argued that the direct application of Peirce's semiotic to the arts is based on a number of misunderstandings stemming from two false assumptions: firstly, 'that Peirce's semiotic represents a scientific method instead of representing a *theory* of a scientific method'; secondly, the overlooking of the fact that in science, 'interpretants carry the sole responsibility for the constitution of meaning, whereas in the arts, divergence from the interpretants upon which a work is based plays the decisive role'.[9]

Eco distinguishes three categories of meaning (what he calls 'three semiotic categories') covered by the function of the interpretant within a theory of codes, all of which are (macro to micro) levels of intensional relations and componential analysis.[10] These are: (i) the *meaning* of a sign-vehicle, understood as a cultural unit displayed through other sign-vehicles and thus showing its semantic independence from the first sign-vehicle; (ii) the *intensional* or componential analysis by which a cultural unit is segmented into its elementary semic components, or semantic markers, and therefore presented as a 'sememe' which can enter, by the amalgamation of its 'readings', into different contextual combinations; (iii) each of the *units* composing the componential tree of a sememe, every unit (or seme or semantic marker) becoming in its turn another cultural unit (represented by another sign-vehicle) which is open to its own componential analysis (*TSE*, p. 72). The following chapters pursue an increasingly sophisticated semantic componential analysis model, dwelling in particular on that proposed indirectly by M. Ross Quillian's model for a semantic memory,[11] henceforth dubbed by Eco 'the Model Q'.

Eco's Model Q is what he describes as an *n*-dimensional model. It is a model of 'linguistic creativity'. The way it works is as follows:

> For the meaning of every lexeme there has to exist, in the memory, a node which has as its 'patriarch' the term to be defined, here called a *type*. The definition of type A foresees the employment, as its interpretants, of a series of other sign-vehicles which are included as *tokens* (and which in the model are other lexemes). The configuration of the meaning of the lexemes is given by the multiplicity of its links with various tokens, each of which, however, becomes in turn a *type* B, that is the patriarch of a new configuration which includes as tokens many other lexemes, some of which were also tokens of type A and which can include as token the same type A. (*TSE*, p. 122)

No graph is in a position to represent the complexity of what is in effect a description of the working of unlimited semiosis, though a diagram is offered to the reader, who should imagine 'a sort of polydimensional network, equipped with topological properties, in which the distances covered are abbreviated or elongated and each term acquires proximity with others by means of short-cuts and immediate contacts' (*TSE*, p. 124).

But what Eco is looking for more specifically is a semiotic model which justifies the *conventional* denotations and connotations attributed to a sign-vehicle, not a box of elements like marbles, jostling randomly, but something more like a box of magnetized marbles. At the same time, it must be possible for the system to be nourished by fresh information (as we have seen in 'The Semantics of Metaphor').

From all of this he reaches the conclusion that what was called the code is better viewed as a complex network of sub-codes, some of which are strong and stable, others weak and transient, as are the systems which they gather together: the durable phonological system, for example, as against many semantic fields and axes, which are transient. If a system is a rule which magnetizes the marbles (as in the analogy above), a code couples different systems and is a *biplanar rule* establishing new attractions and repulsions between items from different planes. 'In other words, every item in the code maintains a double set of relations, a *systematic* one with all the items of its own plane (content or expression) and a *signifying* one with one or more items from the correlated plane' (*TSE*, p. 126). The code is a social convention, the magnetization is a transitory, that is, historical, condition of the marbles box; the magnetization must be understood as a cultural phenomenon, and the box-source must be at best considered as the site of a combinational interplay, of a highly indeterminate *game*. A semiotics of the code is interested in the results of this game. A semiotics of sign production and code-changing, on the other hand, is interested in the process by which a rule is imposed upon the indeterminacy of the source. Thus any graph or representation is *provisional*, 'a working hypothesis that aims to control the immediate semantic environment of given semantic units'. And even if one ever managed to describe a system of this kind, Eco adds, 'it would already have changed, and not merely because of the influence of various historical factors, but also because of the critical erosion to which it would have been submitted by the analysis itself' (*TSE*, p. 128). In conclusion, a semiotics of the code is an *operational device* in the service of a semiotics of sign production.

Sign production, iconism and the aesthetic message (again)

The third of the stated aims of *A Theory of Semiotics* is to 'relate pragmatics to semantics', as is stated in the English Foreword, 'within a single model', as is added in the Italian Preface. The way towards this aim appears to lie through the analysis of sign production. The transition from a theory of codes to one of sign production is effected on p. 142 of *Theory*, where it is stated that 'the very complexity and unpredictability of sign production springs from the format of the semantic universe as it must be outlined by a theory of codes.' Put the other way round, a theory of codes outlines the format of the semantic universe. What is made of the received message, Eco states on the same page, is the proper matter for a theory of sign production, 'which could, from a certain point of view, be regarded as a more highly articulated pragmatics, even if it covers many items of traditional semantics'. In fact, as one works through his reflections on sign production, with their emphasis not only on the physical production, selection and articulation of signs (see below), but also on their interpretation, one can glimpse how the problems, perhaps some of them not wholly resolved or at any rate described to the author's entire satisfaction, may find an outlet in the text pragmatics, including the extensive work on inference and abduction, which increasingly occupies Eco's mental space between 1976 and (at least) the mid-1980s.

The strong, founding, observation that Eco makes about sign production is that the act of uttering presupposes labour, that of producing the signal, then that of choosing from among the signals, then that of articulating the chosen signals in acceptable strings of sign-functions; and that there is a corresponding labour of interpretation. He then proceeds to list the types of labour involved (they are also tabulated in table 31, *TSE*, p. 154 and each is looked at in turn in the course of the remaining 150 pages of this third chapter). They comprise the following:

1   the labour performed on the expression continuum in order physically to produce signals;
2   the labour performed in order to produce expression units;
3   the labour performed in order to correlate for the first time a set of functives with another one, thus making a code;
4   the labour performed when both the sender and the addressee emit or interpret messages observing the rules of a given code;
5   the labour performed in order to change the codes shared by a given society;
6   the labour performed by many rhetorical discourses, above all the so-called 'ideological' ones, in which the entire semantic field is approached in apparent ignorance of the fact that its system of semantic interconnections is more vast and more contradictory than would appear to be the case (code-switching in ideological and aesthetic texts);
7   the labour performed in order to interpret a text by means of a complex inferential process;
8   the labour performed by both sender and addressee to articulate and to interpret sentences whose content must be correctly established and detected;
9   the labour performed in order to check whether or not an expression refers to the actual properties of the things one is speaking of;
10   the labour performed in order to interpret expressions on the basis of certain coded or uncoded circumstances (the labour of inference);
11   the labour which the sender performs in order to focus the attention of the addressee on his attitudes and intentions, and in order to elicit behavioural responses in other people (speech, or rather 'communicational', acts, including illocutionary and perlocutionary as well as locutionary acts).

The replacement of the classical typology of signs by a typology of sign production was also announced in Eco's prefatory remarks. The main conclusion to be anticipated from this exercise is that, while verbal language is the most powerful semiotic device that humanity has invented, nevertheless other devices exist, covering portions of a general semantic space that verbal language does not. It is equally impossible to imagine human communication without words and a world ruled only by words – in which, for example, 'it would be impossible to mention things' (*TSE*, p. 174). Once again, therefore, Eco criticizes the tyranny of the linguistic model in the categorization of signs and goes on to challenge the theoretical consistency of the Peircean (or sub-Peircean) trichotomy of 'symbols', 'icons' and 'indices'. This prepares the way for a further critique of 'index', and in particular 'icon'; the new classification by sign production later in the chapter aims to supersede these categories.

At this point we may pick up the threads of the critique of the iconic sign already well developed in *La struttura assente*, and once again we shall be following closely the account of it given by De Lauretis.[12] The key to a categorization of the so-called iconic sign which avoids either of the naïve assumptions mentioned in the Preface lies, we shall see in a moment, in a rethinking of the relation between 'type' and 'token' (or 'occurrence'). But the question of iconism is in the first place an important test-case for the idea of sign-function itself: given that iconic signs exhibit a natural resemblance or kinship, a relationship that is in some sense motivated, with the referent, the proposed definition of sign-function will only remain valid if it can be shown that in the iconic sign also the correlation of expression and content is conventional and culturally determined. Having analysed the concept of similarity (Morris) and the more precise one, used by Peirce, of 'similitude', Eco goes on to show that they are not based on properties common to the icon and the object but to 'a network of cultural stipulations that determine and direct ingenuous experience' (*TSE*, p. 195). Thus what motivates the organization of the expression is not the object but the corresponding cultural content.

Eco begins by taking into consideration the conditions of replicability of expressions, and says that there are two kinds of relationship linking the concrete occurrence of an expression (or 'token') with its model or type, two kinds of 'ratio'. In *ratio facilis*, the occurrence (token) possesses all or some of the pertinent features or of the properties of the type, as in the case of doubles and replicas (*TSE*, pp. 180–3). We have *ratio facilis* when

> an expression-token is accorded to an expression-type, duly recorded by an expression-system and, as such, foreseen by a given code. There is a case of *ratio difficilis* when an expression-token is directly accorded to its content, whether because the corresponding expression-type does not exist as yet or because the expression-type is identical with the content-type. (*TSE*, p. 183)

This second kind of relation, the *ratio difficilis*, is one that is less immediate: the expression is not modelled on an already existing type but has to be established on the basis of a type (both expression-type and content-type) which does not yet exist in codified form in the culture. As Eco explains on pp. 187–9, what he calls a 'content-nebula' is then formed. The relationship between occurrence ('token') and type, whether *ratio facilis* or *ratio difficilis*, is therefore the aspect of sign production which allows us to explain iconism as a kind of production rather than as an intrinsic quality of certain signs; and, given that the iconic code correlates graphic sign-vehicles to codified cultural and/or perceptual units, Eco concludes, 'iconic signs' are also sign-functions. The importance of the notion of a variable relation between type and token, as De Lauretis stresses (p. 57), lies also in the fact that it makes it possible to cast the question of creativity in semiotic terms – we shall return to this point in a moment when, for the last time, we address the question of 'the aesthetic message'.

The typology of modes of sign production (*TSE*, pp. 217–61) is based on a four-dimensional classification which takes into account the following parameters: (i) the physical labour needed to produce expressions; (ii) the type/token ratio, whether *facilis* or *difficilis*; (iii) the type of continuum to be shaped, whether homomaterial or heteromaterial; (iv) the mode and complexity of articulation. It comprises the following modes (each dealt with in a subsection): recognition (including differentiation between recognition of imprints, that of symptoms and that of clues); ostension; replica and combinational units (computerized reproductions; critique of double articulation model); replica; stylizations and vectors; programmed stimuli and pseudo-combinational units; invention ('a mode of production whereby the producer of the sign-function chooses a new material continuum not yet segmented for that purpose and proposes a new way of organizing (of giving form to) it in order *to map* within it the formal pertinent element of a content-type', (*TSE*, p. 245): this leads to a discussion of Gainsborough's *Mr and Mrs Andrews*). From here Eco goes on to discuss invention as code-making; a continuum of transformations in visual signs; productive features, signs, texts.

The discussion keeps returning to the aesthetic use of language, as Eco acknowledges: 'Any discussion of invention inevitably opens up the problem of the ambiguous, self-focusing and idiolectal use of a code, and compels us to return, once more, to the discussion on aesthetic texts' (*TSE*, p. 258). Eco introduces the section in which this discussion takes place (*TSE*, pp. 261–76) by giving five reasons for the semiotician's interest in the aesthetic text and suggesting how a semiotic approach to aesthetic texts might clarify many problems that traditional philosophical aesthetics has left unsolved. Semiotic interest in the aesthetic text is stimulated by the following facts:

- an aesthetic text involves a particular manipulation of the expression;
- this manipulation of the expression releases (and is released by) a reassessment of the content;
- this double operation, producing an idiosyncratic and highly original instance of sign-function, is to some degree reflected in precisely those codes on which the aesthetic sign-function is based, thus releasing a process of code changing;
- the entire operation, even though focused on codes, frequently produces a new type of awareness about the world;
- insofar as the aesthetic labour aims to be detected and scrutinized repeatedly by the addressee, who thereby engages in a complex labour of interpretation, the aesthetic sender must also focus his or her attention on the addressees' possible reactions, so that the aesthetic text represents a network of diverse communicational acts eliciting highly original responses.

In all these senses the aesthetic text represents a sort of summary and laboratory model of all the aspects of sign-function (*TSE*, p. 261).

Eco begins by addressing the problem of the 'lower levels' of the expression plane – that is, in practice the 'matter' of which the utterances are formed – to which in the aesthetic text both the labour of the sender and the attention of the addressee are directed. The examples given are taken over from *La struttura assente*: the

American political slogan of the 1956 presidential campaign 'I like Ike', commented on by Jakobson in 'Linguistics and Poetics', and the ashlar-work facade of a Renaissance palace (interestingly, here Eco adds another element to his description of the transition in the latter example from the 'design' to the physical encounter with the object, that of time: when the palace is viewed directly, it takes time to comprehend, 'imposing a shifting angle of vision, and thus introducing *time* as one of the indispensable components of the architectural experience' (*TSE*, p. 265)). The upshot is that 'Aesthetics is not only concerned with *hypersystems* such as the various connotations that the work of art conveys above and beyond its immediate communicative appearance; it is also concerned with a whole series of *hypostructures*' (ibid.).

Having registered the aesthetic experiences cited above (one might observe that the 'I like Ike' slogan is at best quasi-aesthetic, but the 'rightness' of the sounds suggests a *je ne sais quoi* effect which attracts Eco's attention and which is what he wants to pin down, to turn precisely into a *j'en sais quelque chose*), Eco now locates this aesthetic attention to hypostructures within the general theory of codes and sign-functions. The examples show that in the aesthetic sign-vehicle matter plays an important part, but it does so because it has been rendered semiotically interesting (as opposed to a mere signal, which is a material fact and can consequently be studied and quantified by information theory). Not only can the sign-vehicle be detected as a pertinent element of the expression system, even the material consistency of the sign-vehicle becomes a field for further segmentation. In aesthetic discourse every free variation introduced in 'uttering' the sign-vehicle has a 'formal' value. An example:

> A red flag on a highway or at a political meeting can be based on various differently manipulated matters in order to be grasped as an expression: but the quality of cloth and the shade of red are in no way relevant. What is important is that the addressee detects /red flag/. Yet a red flag inserted in a pictorial work of art depends, among other things, upon its chromatic quality, in order to be appreciated (and to convey its signification). (*TSE*, p. 266)

Eco, as was already clear in *Opera aperta* and, semiotically, in *La struttura assente*, wants to push as far as possible into the territory of the 'unsayable', the 'not rationally analysable', the *je ne sais quoi*, with both the distribution of sounds, lines, dots etc. and such qualities as 'nuance' and 'tone' becoming susceptible to semiotic analysis.

He turns now to aesthetic overcoding, at the level of expression and then at that of content. At the level of expression, a work of art performs 'a semiotic redemption of its basic matter' (*TSE*, p. 268); in other words, it directs attention, for semiotics as a whole, to what is otherwise regarded as 'hyposemiotic stuff'. This 'pertinentization of matter' forces a reassessment of the expression system as a whole and a rewriting of Hjemslev's diagram, with successive segmentation, and increasing understanding, of the continuum. The first outcome of this further 'culturalization' of matter is a further conventionalization of sign production, of which one immediate consequence for aesthetics and art history is 'that this kind of new knowledge removes many phenomena from the realm of individual "creativity" and "inspiration" and restores them to that of social convention' (*TSE*, p. 269). Eco refers again to Della Volpe's surprising reluctance to apply his rationalist analysis to such features as sound and rhythm, thus running the risk of linking the rational exclusively to the semantic. He also mentions here as one of the main tasks of poetics in the sense given to the term by the Prague School 'the study of all the systems that enrich the expression-continuum of each code (which may already be known, but are never exhaustively *exploited* as far as the flexibility of the expression plane is concerned)' (ibid.).

At the level of content, a reader or viewer questions the text under the pressure of a twofold impression: the sense of a 'surplus of expression' and a corresponding 'surplus of content'. Eco takes the example of Gertrude Stein's rose(s), a text which is glossed as highly informative, therefore ambiguous, therefore open to multiple interpretations (along the lines of the theory of 'openness' expounded in *Opera aperta*). This gives rise to an unexpected statement: 'It is indeed difficult to avoid the conclusion that a work of art *communicates too much* and therefore *does not communicate at all*, simply existing as a magic spell that is radically impermeable to all semiotic approach' (*TSE*, p. 270). But this conclusion is countered when Eco goes on to discuss the aesthetic idiolect.

Deviation from the norm is not random, but springs from a 'general deviational matrix'. Art

> seems to be a way of interconnecting messages in order to produce a text in which: (a) *many* messages, on different levels and planes of the discourse, are *ambiguously* organized; (b) these ambiguities are not realized at random but follow a *precise design*; (c) both the normal and ambiguous devices within a given message exert a *contextual pressure* on both the normal and ambiguous devices within all the others; (d) the way in

which the norms of a given system are offended by one message *is the same* as that in which the norms of other systems are offended by the various messages that they permit. (*TSE*, p. 271)

In a work of art a 'super-system of homologous structural relationships' is established rather as if all levels were definable on the basis of a single structural model which determined all of them, but this does not just make it an admirable complex of interconnecting structures, which would not necessarily have any semiotic status; rather, on the basis of this structural arrangement of mutual homologies, 'the work of art seems to acquire a new status as a *super sign-function*' (ibid.). Thanks to the self-focusing feature of the aesthetic text, its structural arrangement becomes one of the contents that it conveys, and may be the most important one. This represents a new coding possibility. The new code initially seems to have the status of an *idiolect*, that is, a private code or language which Eco describes as (perhaps) expanding (small group round single work, personal style, movement, period, possibly producing new norms accepted by an entire society, in which case the artistic idiolect may act 'as a *meta-semiotic judgement changing common codes*'). The idiolect is more easily identifiable by the critic the more that it is, or becomes, standardized. Even when identified, it cannot be used to produce another work of art; the structural model is a general schema to be embodied in a new substance (like a code and its messages). One reason for the irreproducibility of a work of art is that, however carefully the idiolect is isolated, it will never take full account of the lower levels. This is once again to state that criticism can never fully account for the work of art; when the work is imitated, that is, when the idiolect has been identified, the imitator is keen to emphasize the model that has been isolated. The addressee, in the meantime, '"senses" the surpluses of both expression and content, along with their correlating rule. This rule must exist, but to recognize it requires a complex process of *abduction*: hypotheses, confrontations, rejected and accepted correlations, judgments of appurtenance and extraneity' (*TSE*, p. 273).

Eco turns finally to the changing of aesthetic codes and to the status of the aesthetic text as a communicational act. The effect of 'cosmicity', referred to here in chapter 3, is explained by the process proper to the work of art of constantly changing its denotations into new connotations, by the fact that 'none of its items stop at their first interpretant' (*TSE*, p. 274). The 'headiness' of the aesthetic experience cannot be explained away, or left unexplained, by a notion of 'intuition', not least because experience teaches us that art not only elicits feelings, but also produces new knowledge. It is both a challenge to and a strengthening of the code, as was stated in *La struttura assente*. There is an additional consequence to which Eco draws attention, and it concerns what aesthetics can do for semiotics: 'If aesthetic texts can modify our concrete approach to states of the world then they are of great importance to that branch of a theory of sign production that is concerned with the labour of connecting signs with the states of the world' (*TSE*, p. 275).

From the point of view of communication, all the modes of inference (induction, deduction and abduction) are involved in the process of reading an aesthetic text; the relation between sender and receiver is such that the latter never wants completely to betray the author's intentions: 'in the interpretive reading a dialectic between *fidelity* and inventive *freedom* is established.' The semiotic definition of the work of art explains why a reading takes place that is not entirely predictable, yet does so in something which has a structure at all levels; the semiotic definition 'gives the *structured model* for an *unstructured process of communicative interplay*'. The addressee is required to 'collaborate', and thus the aesthetic text becomes 'a multiple source of *unpredictable "speech acts"* whose real author remains undetermined, sometimes being the sender of the message, at others the addressee who collaborates in its development' (*TSE*, p. 276).

How much 'slightly more definitive', in Eco's charming phrase, is *A Theory of Semiotics* than its predecessors or precursors? The whole text displays a breathtaking control of a subject at the moment that it is taking shape in the author's hands, a creative mastery, surely the most difficult. Eco in the *Theory* undoubtedly increases the amount and complexity of knowledge at the disposal of his readers and still leaves them asking for more. Yet there seems to be something wrong. On the one hand, there is the inevitable circularity of a theory aspiring to be a general theory of culture which excludes anything that cannot be interpreted culturally. On the other hand, the nature of the evidence, perhaps the very layout of the text, suggest a kind of *bricolage*, with extra pieces being constantly accumulated, all of them good, yet not obviously combining into a whole. It seems that the bigger and more complete the model becomes, and the faster it goes, the greater is the risk of pieces falling off or of some minute but consequential piece of the matter holding it together succumbing to fatigue. The next chapter will begin by looking at some of the more important comments on and critiques of the *Theory* – doubts about the scope of Eco's notion of 'codes', or about the boundaries he draws around his 'field' or 'discipline', or about his allegedly 'pre-Freudian' treatment of the human subject. But it will also lead into what might be construed as Eco's own response to the limits reached by his most purely semiotic research, notably his increasing (but far from exclusive) interest in text pragmatics. It would be consistent with the entire pattern of Eco's work to see the next phase of his activity emerging dialectically, neither uncritically nor yet dismissively, out of what had just preceded it.

5

Semiotics Bounded and Unbound

Eco's research in the years immediately following the publication of
A Theory of Semiotics followed two, interweaving, paths which very
crudely may be described as follows. In the first instance, a rereading of Peirce in the light of the increasingly pragmaticist bent of his
own interests enabled Eco to refine in important ways his deploy-
ment of key strategic terms like 'sign' and 'code'. The defining role
now given to inference and interpretation in cognitive activity of all
kinds had to do with semiosis in general as a social, and perhaps
biological, process. Secondly, however, in an apparent shift of
emphasis from the primarily semantic (and syntactic) concerns of
Theory, Eco directed his attention to the semiotics of texts, and to the
pragmatic aspects of text-interpretation in particular. This new
direction of research reflected a felt need to extend the scope of
semiotic inquiry from the single utterance to the larger and much
more complex unit represented by the text; it was also a point
of contact between semiotics and the current concerns in the mid-
1970s of related disciplines such as literary theory and narratology,
and may not have been unconnected with the novelist burgeoning
within Eco himself (*The Name of the Rose* was published in Italy
in 1980); for Eco explicitly it was a question of re-establishing
contact with the problematics of interpretation which had underlain
his work in the early 1960s. The two lines of research overlap
to a very considerable extent: much of the material treated in the
first is textual, while general rules of inference are continually
invoked in the second. Most important, perhaps, is the constant
concern with 'interpretation', whether the interpretation of per-

ceptual data or that of texts, which comes increasingly to the fore in the late 1980s.

These topics, and their many ramifications, have been addressed by Eco in numerous essays and articles, as well as conference papers and lectures. These, together with his unstinting delivery of courses and seminars, and supervision of research doctorates, at Bologna and elsewhere, have constituted the bulk of his scientific output since the late 1970s. Although both *Lector in fabula* (1979) and *Kant e l'ornitorinco* (1997) advance sustained arguments, it is noticeable that Eco has not attempted to reproduce the synthesis aimed at by *A Theory of Semiotics* (or even, to some extent, *La struttura assente* before it).[1] His preferred form of publication, as at the beginning of his career, remains the collection of normally already published essays, articles or papers, reformatted as necessary to ensure the coherence of the ensuing volume. The emphasis is once again, and characteristically, on the scientific work in progress rather than the achieved systematization. But 'the book', conceived and realized as such, having been kicked out of the door, has come back through the window in the shape of the three novels which Eco has published to date (*Il nome della rosa*, 1980, translated in 1983 as *The Name of the Rose*; *Il pendolo di Foucault*, 1988, translated in 1989 as *Foucault's Pendulum*; and *L'isola del giorno prima*, 1994, translated in 1995 as *The Island of the Day Before* – all translations by William Weaver). And we might note that his scholarly study of 'perfect languages', *La ricerca della lingua perfetta* (1993, translated by James Fentress in 1995 as *The Search for the Perfect Language*), though certainly not a fiction, is conceived of as a *storia* (a story and a history) and is a kind of quest-narrative in its own right, while *Kant e l'ornitorinco* makes more extensive use than any of Eco's previous philosophical works of parables and invented dialogues.

This chapter and the next will draw particularly on the three collections of academic essays which Eco published during what we might be permitted to call his 'long 1980s' and two lecture series published in the early 1990s. The first of the collections, chronologically, is *Lector in fabula* (1979), where Eco first explores the terrain of text pragmatics and in particular the notion of 'interpretative cooperation' in narrative texts to which his subtitle draws attention.[2] *Semiotica e filosofia del linguaggio* (1984, translated the same year as *Semiotics and the Philosophy of Language*[3]) is based on five entries written by Eco for the Einaudi *Enciclopedia* between 1976 and 1980 dealing with the concepts of sign, meaning, metaphor, symbol and code: the *Enciclopedia* itself, a major intellectual undertaking of the time, aimed at a remapping of contemporary knowledge through the detailed and expanded high-quality treatment of certain selected 'keywords' in the culture.[4] *I limiti dell'interpretazione* (1990), from which the English translation *The Limits of Interpretation* differs in part, gathers fourteen essays dealing with different aspects of the theme announced in the title; the study of hermetic semiosis, which is not in the English version, was to form the backbone of Eco's Tanner Lectures given at Cambridge (England) in 1990 and published, with the contributions of others, as *Interpretation and Overinterpretation* in 1992. Much of his previous work on the interpretation of narrative texts also found its way into the Harvard lectures of 1993–4, published as *Six Walks in the Fictional Woods* in 1994. Finally, it should be added that amongst Eco's several volumes of occasional and journalistic writing published during the past two decades, the 1985 collection *Sugli specchi* in particular includes several important semiotic essays.[5]

The boundaries of semiotics

The lines of research sketched out above seem by and large to have developed independently of the various objections and reservations advanced by others in respect of *Trattato/Theory* and *Lector in fabula* (or, in Britain and America, the contemporaneous but differently constituted *The Role of the Reader*). These were the two books which in quick succession were widely reviewed and commented on in the late 1970s, especially in the United States, but Eco has not always responded directly or immediately to the points made. An exception to this was his willingness in the early 1980s to engage with issues bearing on the definition or scientific status of semiotics.

Although criticisms were made of Eco's handling of linguistic categories,[6] critics have felt more unease about what Eco left out than about what he put in. The recurrent anxiety concerned the boundaries that Eco chose to draw in *Theory* between 'culture' and 'nature', given that semiotics is described axiomatically as the study of cultural phenomena, and cultural phenomena are seen as semiotic. When Eco defines the 'natural boundaries' of semiotics in terms, *inter alia*, of a 'lower threshold', he senses that he is drawing a line in the sand: 'Probably it would be prudent to say that neurophysiological and genetic phenomena are not a matter for semioticians, but that neurophysiological and genetic informational theories are so' (*TSE*, p. 21); ten years later, on the occasion of an address to a conference on 'The semiotics of cellular communication', the caution is still there, but so is the enduring curiosity as to how far into the natural world the semiotic activity might reach: having advanced a series of arguments at the start of the conference which discouraged the direct application of semiotics to immunology, Eco ends by conceding that 'I still feel unable to say whether semiotics can help immunology, but I have discovered that immunology can help semiotics' (*LII*, p. 215).[7] A number of his semiotic colleagues, as he acknowledges, would be more optimistic. But one does not have to go as far as the level of the immune system to see how jagged is the line that has to be drawn. It is argued by Sollace Mitchell, for example, that any discussion of 'the material world of signs' is prevented by the exclusion of a consideration of the referent,[8] and even though the sensation of materiality, the semiotization of it, is engaged with by Eco, in, for example, his account of the 'hypostructures' which underpin our tactile and temporal experience of a Renaissance building (see above, p. 95), Mitchell is not the only reader to discern in Eco's theory a potential drift away from matter. Robert Scholes, for example, in an interesting comment, observes that Eco runs into difficulty when he tries to make Shklovsky's formulation of the doctrine of 'de-familiarization' support Jakobson's notion that poetic discourse directs the attention of the reader primarily to its own formal structure:

> Shklovsky said that the language was made strange to restore objects to us, to 'make the stone stony'. He emphasized the perceptual, cognitive, and even referential quality of poetic estrangement. To move from this bold and elegant position back to Jakobsonian self-referentiality seems like an unnecessary retreat for semiotics, and indeed, it is not Eco's ultimate position in this book.[9]

Scholes's conclusion may or may not be true.

We have already stressed the importance for Eco's semiotic theory of his critique of iconism, and the reasons for it: these are questioned in a trenchant review of *Theory* by Michael McCanles which depicts Eco's endeavour as being primarily concerned with defining a theory of sign production that is independent of all motivations and naturalizations, 'a process of inventing and communicating meaning wherein "meaning" itself is wholly internal to the process itself'.[10] That is why the critique of iconism assumes such importance: if semiotics is to exist as an intelligible theory of signs, any assumption that there is some sort of *a priori* natural code motivated by analogy with the transhuman, natural world must be destroyed. McCanles questions whether Eco's demonstration that the iconic sign is unmotivated is wholly convincing. In *Theory* he describes a fourfold process of sign production: relevant elements are picked up from an unshaped perceptual field and organized in order to build a percept; by means of abstractive procedures the percept is mapped onto a semantic representation; this semantic representation is either arbitrarily associated with a set of expressive devices or mapped onto a transformation according to conventional rules of similitude (*TSE*, p. 252 and table 43, p. 253). But at each point of the mapping from perception to abstraction, and from abstraction to similitude, McCanles observes, what is left out is governed semiotically, but what is left in still results from motivated analogy or similitude to the object itself. The flaw in Eco's argument, it seems, is that while he at least implies that human beings 'naturally' take their conventions as natural, he does not explain why this should be so, and from this flows a potentially endless recursivity:

> The problem is that the concept of the natural has been trivialized by semiotics at the very moment that it becomes the ultimate norm to be appealed to, since for Eco 'nature' is both something that stands noumenally beyond all codes (or perhaps does not exist), and that which semiotics must continually use to demystify all other naturalizations.[11]

The various observations summarized above amount to a series of reservations about a perceived circularity in Eco's thinking which ensures that semiotics presents itself as the science of phenomena which have been defined *a priori* as semiotic. Eco might answer any of the objections raised by claiming that his theory is by definition only concerned with matter or the natural object precisely at the moment when it *is* semiotized; it is a matter of argument whether such a response would dispose of or confirm the objection. The difficulty comes from knowing whether one is dealing with a purely territorial dispute (an argument about what can and cannot, should and should not, be included within the purview of semiotics as a discipline for the latter to be able to function effectively) or with a fundamental objection pointing to a lacuna in the theory itself. The most searching questions in the immediate aftermath of *Theory* (reinforced subsequently by the appearance of *Lector in fabula*) were posed from the perspective of psychoanalytic criticism. In order to grasp the point at issue, it is necessary to go back briefly to *A Theory of Semiotics*, and particularly its last, very brief, section, 'The Subject of Semiotics', which we have not yet considered.

Eco introduces his last chapter by acknowledging a 'ghostly presence', that of the acting subject of every semiosic act, who now
makes 'an unavoidable appearance'; the author recognizes that a
theory of the relationship between sender and addressee should
also take into account the role of the 'speaking' subject not only as
a communicational figment but as a concrete historical, biological,
psychic subject, as it is approached by psychoanalysis and related
disciplines. But he immediately lays his cards on the table. The
subject of an act of utterance (the *sujet de l'énonciation* as opposed to
the *sujet de l'énoncé*) must be considered as one among the possible
referents of the message, and thus one of the objects of the possible
mentions the message performs; as such, it has to be studied by the
disciplines concerned with the various physical or psychic objects of
which languages speak. In so far as the subject, along with some of
its properties and attitudes, is presupposed by the utterance, then it
has to be 'read' as an element of the conveyed content. 'Any other
attempt to introduce a consideration of the subject into the semiotic
discourse would make semiotics trespass on one of its "natural"
boundaries' (*TSE*, pp. 314–15). Eco is aware of the fact that some
semiotic approaches do 'trespass' on this threshold and make
semiotics the study of this creative activity of a semiosis-making
subject – and here, in a long note, Julia Kristeva is finally identified
as the target of Eco's observations: a Kristeva who describes semiotics as having come to a fork in the road, and who believes that a
critique of the previously dominant 'semiology of systems' and its
phenomenological foundations 'is possible only if it starts from
a theory of meaning which must necessarily be a theory of the
speaking subject' (cited *TSE*, p. 317 n. 2). Eco does not rule out, at
least on paper, the possibility that semiotics might overcome one
of its 'natural boundaries', but asserts that from the point of view of
his book

> the most reliable grasp that semiotics can have on such a subjective
> activity is the one provided by a theory of codes: *the subject of any semiotic
> enquiry being no more than the semiotic subject of semiosis, that is, the historical
> and social result of the segmentation of the world that a survey on Semantic
> Space makes available.* . . . . Semiotics can define the subject of every act of
> semiosis only by semiotic categories; thus the subject of signification is
> nothing more than the continuously unaccomplished system of systems
> of signification that reflects back on itself. (*TSE*, p. 315; emphases in the
> original)

What is odd about 'The Subject of Semiotics' is that, while Eco
clearly took Kristeva's position seriously enough to confront it in

the final pages of his treatise, he did not take it so seriously that he
felt the need to deal with it except in territorial terms – as perhaps
another, future, kind of semiotics, or not semiotics: Kristeva herself
called her approach 'sémanalyse' rather than 'semiotics', he points
out (*TSE*, p. 318). And there is something defensive about the way
in which Eco states, modestly, that semiotics can only deal with
phenomena semiotically (they may have other aspects which are the
province of other forms of human inquiry), but at the same time
establishes, immodestly, for semiotics a 'paramount subject matter',
semiosis, which is no less than 'the process by which empirical
subjects communicate, communication processes being made possible by the organization of signification systems' (*TSE*, p. 316).
When he adds, shortly after, that, for semiotics, subjects of semiosic
acts can either 'be defined in terms of semiotic structures or – from
this point of view – they do not exist at all', one recognizes the
methodological rigour of the definition, and circumscription, of the
scientific discipline, but is at the same time not only left wondering
what has been left out but sorely tempted to see if there is anything
that ought to be put in. It is a sensation similar to that engendered
by the sharp discrimination between 'interpretation' (in) and 'use'
(out) which will feature prominently in Eco's theory of reading.

More important, however, is the critique first mounted by De
Lauretis and then taken up by others which regards Eco's treatment
of the subject as entailing a 'pre-Freudian' vision of the relation
between nature and culture, between mind and body, matter and
intellect. The force of this critique lies not so much in the lances
which De Lauretis breaks on behalf of Lacanian psychoanalysis
(still less in those which she conspicuously refuses to break on
behalf of Kristevan *sémanalyse*) as in the identification of the problematic exclusion in Eco's semiotics of what only for the sake of
convenience can be described as 'the body', since it is precisely
the dichotomy between 'body' and 'non-body' implicit in Eco's
approach that she denounces. She draws attention efficaciously to
the capacity of semiotics as described by Eco to absorb all aspects of
social behaviour (those studied by cultural anthropology or what in
due course would become 'cultural studies' as well as aesthetics or
political science or rhetoric or the study of ideologies), while firmly
drawing the line at 'that area where human physicality becomes
culture, represents itself, becomes semiosis – the area defined by the
work of Freud'.[12] This may simply betoken a cultural limitation on
Eco's part: his treatment of the body, the female body in particular,
and, I would add, the body 'as' female in the first two at least of his

novels has occasioned reactions ranging from embarrassment to irritation.[13] But it also strongly underpins what De Lauretis herself recognizes as a semiotics concerned, as Eco's is, 'to stress the social aspect of signification, its practical, aesthetic or ideological use in interpersonal communication, where meaning is construed as semantic value produced through culturally shared codes' as opposed to an emerging Kristevan semiotics 'focused on the subjective aspects of signification . . . where meaning is construed as a subject-effect'.[14] To this extent, the emphasis that Eco gives to what is in effect already established by Western science as the human cultural world seems *necessary*, and not incidental, to his projected outline of a theory of semiotics which identifies culture with signification and communication, which bases itself on a methodological and not an ontological structuralism, but which is extremely sensitive to, and permanently on guard against, any suggestion of idealism or mentalism in its own procedures or assumptions (cf. *TSE*, p. 315, and *passim*). So much so that Eco will not fundamentally change his position even with the more flexible notion of sign, and therefore, he argues, of the human subject, which he presents in *Semiotics and the Philosophy of Language*; he might even be said to dig in deeper. While the sign (as the constantly interrogated locus for the semiosic process) and the subject ('constantly reshaped by the endless resegmentation of the content') are dynamic, the relation between history, the social, the semiosic process and some unspecified 'deep impulse' remains dominated by the former:

> As subjects, we are what the shape of the world produced by signs makes us become. Perhaps we are, somewhere, the deep impulse which generates semiosis. And yet we recognize ourselves only as semiosis in progress, signifying systems and communicational processes. The map of semiosis, as defined at a given stage of historical development (with the debris carried over from previous semiosis), tells us who we are and what (or how) we think. (*SFL*, pp. 53–4; *SPL*, p. 45; note that in the Italian the last sentence begins 'Only the map . . .')

This is not determinism; the keyword remains 'recognize'; we are what we know, even though what we know is not necessarily, ultimately, what we are. Nevertheless, there is no strong invitation here for semiotics to concern itself with any deep impulse.

The question of how semiotics deals with its 'lower threshold' on the one hand, and its claim to account for the whole range of human communication on the other, raise the issue of its 'scientificity' or otherwise. The provocation seems to lie in the combination of the huge range of topics and issues to which professed semioticians devote their explanatory efforts and the pretended scientific character of their discourse. A benign response might begin by acknowledging the existence of 'a field burgeoning with such a bewildering array of pursuits as to all but belie its claims to the possibility of an over-arching, systematic discipline'; the array in fact has all the appearance of a *dis*array.[15] For John N. Deely, who wants to make people understand that semiotics is not the jargon-ridden ragbag which so many benighted souls seem to think it is, but rather 'the nascent form of a perspective and discipline powerful and encompassing enough to achieve a major revolution in our understanding of the intellectual life and its diverse roles in culture' (ibid., p. 174), Eco's *Theory* is a major contribution and a 'clarifying landmark'. A less well-disposed survey of the burgeoning field might simply point to the confusion and the babble at every level:

> Semiotics, semiology, hermeneutics, structuralist criticism – so many labels, but how many things? . . . 'methods' which regard Mickey Mouse and the *Mona Lisa*, Superman and *King Lear*, advertising jingles and the works of Schoenberg, as equally legitimate objects of inquiry. Is this movement . . . the first step towards some new critical method, a method sufficiently general as to assign an interpretation to everything that could be regarded as a 'sign'?[16]

In this perspective, semiosis [*sic*] is a disease and the kind of theoretical tools deployed in the last chapter of *The Role of the Reader* (the volume under review) no more than the rhetoric of technicality, a smokescreen.

Both the benign and the less benign versions of this critique led Eco to formulate a careful response in an essay for *Semiotica*;[17] the essay was reproduced in abbreviated form (with only a brief reference to Scruton) as the Introduction to *Semiotics and the Philosophy of Language* the same year; the Italian version of this Introduction has a slightly different emphasis, as we shall see. It is necessary, he argues, to make a crude distinction between *specific semiotics* (in the plural) and *general semiotics* (in the singular).[18] A specific semiotics is the 'grammar' of a particular sign system and 'proves to be successful insofar as it describes a given field of communicative phenomena as ruled by a system of signification' (*SPL*, p. 5). There are grammars of sign language for the deaf, of traffic signals, of a playing-card 'matrix' for different games or of a particular game, such as poker. In its study of such systems – from a syntactic, semantic or pragmatic point of view – a specific semiotic may aspire to, and may achieve, the status of a 'science', which means that it can have predictive power and may have effects in terms of social engineering. Eco further distinguishes *specific* from *applied semiotics*, describing the latter as a

> hardly definable 'twilight zone' of semiotically oriented practices, such as the application of semiotic notions to literary criticism, the analysis of political discourses, perhaps a great part of the so-called linguistic philosophy . . . Frequently, these semiotic practices rely on the set of knowledge provided by specific semiotics, sometimes they contribute to enriching them, and, in many other cases, they borrow their fundamental ideas from a general semiotics. (*SPL*, p. 6)

In Eco's view the task and nature of a general semiotics are different; in fact such a general semiotics partakes of the nature of philosophy rather than of science. A general semiotics does not study a particular system but *posits* general categories in the light of which different systems can be compared. It sets about this philosophical task in one of two ways (and here I follow the Italian version, which is interestingly more historicist in orientation than its American cousin; the latter omits some of the historical material contained in *Semiotica e filosofia del linguaggio*, which itself is related, in an ancillary way, to Eco's growing interest, at the same time as his distinction between the 'philosophical' and 'scientific' aspects of semiotics, in the history of the subject as part of the task of 'looking for a disciplinary object'[19]). One way is that taken traditionally by many philosophies of language, which is the attempt to deduce in some way a system of semiosis or to construct a philosophy of man as a symbolic animal. The other way may be construed as an 'archaeology' of semiotic concepts, in the manner of the Aristotle of the *Metaphysics*: having established that the object of the first philosophy is being, you find out what others before you have said about it and, if people have never spoken about it in the same way, why it is that this object, always described differently, is always felt as though it were the same thing. If 'being can be said in many ways', Aristotle wants to know if it is possible to put oneself in the position of the deep unity which governs the surface discrepancies. This unity is not found, but posited. Eco believes that the same task faces the philosopher of a general semiotics, who inherits a tradition of more than two thousand years in which the sign 'has been said in many ways'. The philosopher seeks to posit a concept which allows a series of phenomena to be interpreted globally and allows others to found their own partial interpretations. The philosopher does not discover the substance, he posits its concept' (*SFL*, p. xiv). When semiotics posits such concepts as 'sign' it acts like philosophy does when it posits such abstractions as subject, good and evil, truth or revolution (*SPL*, p. 10). 'Good or bad are theoretical stipulations according to which, by a philosophical decision, many scattered instances of the most different facts or acts become *the same thing*' (*SPL*, pp. 10–11; emphases in the original). Because a philosophy is true only in so far as it satisfies a need to provide a coherent form to the world, it has both great explanatory power and practical power, in that its followers are enabled to deal coherently with the world, but this is neither the 'engineering' power of the sciences, or of a specific semiotics, nor is it a predictive power: the key example of this difference is Marxism, which displayed both explanatory and practical power, but 'failed when, assuming to be a science, it claimed to have a predictive power' (*SPL*, p. 12).

This important clarification of the status of an inquiry partaking, in its different manifestations, of both a scientific and a philosophical calling forms part of Umberto Eco's continuing reflection on the nature, the foundation and the boundaries of semiotics. The philosophical character of general semiotics echoes his choice in *Theory* of the approach to semiotics as a 'field', 'in all its many and varied forms and in all its disorder' (*TSE*, p. 7), rather than a 'discipline': in the first case, semiotics is defined inductively by extrapolating from the field of studies a series of constant tendencies and therefore a unified model; in the second, the expectation would be that the researcher would propose a semiotic model deductively on which the inclusion or exclusion of various studies from the field of semiotics would be decided (ibid.). For the past hundred years, as Ugo Volli has pointed out in an invaluable essay on Eco's definition of the object of this philosophy/science, semiotics has been in a permanent state of 'being born' and at the same time has occupied a borderland status between the human sciences and philosophy, linguistics and the cognitive sciences, literary criticism and theory, anthropology and mathematical logic, computer science and epistemology.[20] Eco's metasemiotic worrying-through of the choice between a view of the world of culture as being modelled on a methodological framework furnished with the notion of sign and the assertion that cultural phenomena actually are systems of signs is an early example of his search for definition in this borderland. Eco takes the ontological problem seriously, as we have seen, and adopts a gradualist approach to its solution in the pre-*Theory* semiotic writings. But his anti-idealism is constantly reaffirmed, and with it his insistence on connecting semiotics with the real world and his preference for 'surface' over 'depth'; Volli will go on to argue that his 1980s positions on hermeticism and interpretation can be attributed to 'this idea that semiotics is a theory of the *phenomena* of communication and signification and not of their improbable 'deep' *noumena*'.[21] At that pass Eco has made his stand.

The dynamics of semiosis

I should like in the second part of this chapter to focus on further important developments, or refinements, in Eco's thinking about signs and codes which are at least logically if not chronologically prior to his propositions in the area of text pragmatics. At the same time they contribute to that linkage between 'semiosis' and 'the real world' which Volli mentions, and which Eco sees as one of the strengths of Peirce's pragmaticist semiotics. Four topics are concerned, and we shall look at them in turn: unlimited semiosis and 'habit'; sign and inference; dictionary and encyclopedia; abduction.

1 Unlimited semiosis and 'habit' The notion of 'unlimited semiosis' is clarified in an important essay first published in *VS* in 1976,[22] and then in *RR* as 'Peirce and the Semiotic Foundations of Openness' (as well as in *LF*); the clarification tends to emphasize its dynamic and above all dialectical nature. The fact that semiosis is unlimited does not mean that it does not in some sense stop, or pause, in real life. This feature is accounted for by the Peircean notion of 'habit', which Eco describes as both a behavioural attitude to act in some regular way and the rule or prescription of that action. Here, summarizing Peirce, is the example he gives:

> A sign can produce an emotional and an energetical interpretant. If we consider a musical piece, the emotional interpretant is our normal reaction to the charming power of music, but this emotional reaction may elicit a sort of muscular or mental effort. This kind of response is the energetic interpretant. But an energetic response does not need to be interpreted; rather, it produces (I guess, by further repetitions) a change of habit. This means that, after having received a series of signs and having variously interpreted them, our way of acting within the world is either transitorily or permanently changed. (*RR*, p. 194)

But, argues Eco, Peirce is also a dialectical thinker. The final interpretant (such as the energetical one just described) is not final in a chronological sense. Semiosis dies at every moment but at every moment is reborn. Peirce asks how otherwise a habit can be described than by a description of the kind of action to which it gives rise, with the specification of the conditions and the motive. Thus, adds Eco, 'the repeated action responding to a given sign becomes in its turn a new sign, the representamen of a law interpreting the former sign and giving rise to new processes of interpretation' (ibid., p. 195).

2 Sign and inference   Eco's further thoughts on the sign and codes should be read against this background idea of semiosis as a process that is dynamic but not idealistic, not free to flow, as it were, without any check. In Eco's most comprehensive statement of his position on the sign, in *Semiotics and the Philosophy of Language*, with slight variations between the English and Italian versions, Eco emphasizes the way that the sign can be seen to fit into an inferential process. In the Introduction to the Italian edition he talks about a crisis of the concept of 'sign' and it is in this connection that he outlines the historical approach described above (and already adumbrated in the 1973 textbook *Il segno*). Is the sign the proper focus of semiotics, as it was from the Geneva School of Saussure and Bally up to the 1960s, or is that focus the process of semiosis itself, as seems increasingly to be the case, with the growing interest in the generation of texts, their interpretation, the drift of interpretations, the drives which produce them, the actual pleasure of semiosis? (*SFL*, p. xiv). In a preliminary stab at the problem, Eco argues that he wants to get beyond this either/or by showing, precisely through a return to the history of the concept of sign, that the alternative was formulated very late: the original idea of sign was not based on equality, on a fixed correlation established by the code, on the equivalence between expression and content, but on inference, interpretation and the dynamics of semiosis; if one looks back in history, one finds that the sign, rather than corresponding to the model '*a* is the same as *b*', corresponds to 'if *a* then *b*' (ibid., p. xv). And for Peirce, in a formulation that Eco particularly likes to repeat, the sign is that which always makes us know something more.[23]

It seems that in this revisiting of the concept of sign (see especially the chapter 'Signs' in *SPL*) Eco focuses even more than in *Theory* on the cognitive aspects of our manipulation of signs. In order to know the meaning of a sign we engage in a process that does not only involve recognizing in certain cases that something stands for something else, but also and necessarily inferring that such is the case and interpreting accordingly. A single formal structure underlies all signifying phenomena, that of 'implication' or entailment, which generates interpretation (*SPL*, p. 51). A sign is a clue from which inferences must be made;[24] if we interpret, rather than recognize, signs, that means we perceive various paths which we might follow in order to make sense of them (or, more pragmatically, to use them in the world); the sign itself includes instructions for its insertion in the possible contexts within which it is interpretable. The position reached is formulated as follows:

> A sign is not only something which stands for something else; it is also something that can and must be interpreted. . . . The criterion of interpretability . . . held for the classical notion of natural signs, based on an inferential model . . . but it should hold also for linguistic signs, even though they were based, by a long historical tradition, on the model of equivalence . . . This latter idea of sign as identity was due to the persuasion that the meaning or the content of a given linguistic expression was either a synonymous expression or its definition. (*SPL*, p. 46).

This mention of definition leads us to consider the opposition developed by Eco between 'dictionary' and 'encyclopedia' thanks to which the notion of code also undergoes some revision.

3 *Dictionary and encyclopedia*   The opposition between 'dictionary' and 'encyclopedia' as forms of semantic representation is adumbrated in *A Theory of Semiotics*, sections 2.10.2. (where there is criticism of the 'simple dictionary' representation afforded by the KF model) and 2.11.3. The idea of 'encyclopedia' is explored further in 'Testo e enciclopedia' (in *LF* but not in *RR*[25]) and in the essay on Peirce and the semiotic foundations of openness quoted from above. In his exploration of text and encyclopedia Eco remarks that, as proposed in *Theory*, a componential analysis in encyclopedia form is fundamentally oriented towards the text because it takes into account both contextual and circumstantial selections (*LF*, p. 16).

One of the things that Eco is doing in this essay is trying to distinguish between context, co-text and circumstance, a refinement which need not detain us at this point. But his main aim is to extend his theory, or, as he would see it, to release the potential within it, to deal semantically with *texts*. To this end, the notion of 'encyclopedia' is enriched by that of 'frame':

> In this way we postulate a semantic description in terms of structure of the code constructed in such a way as to enable the understanding of

texts; at the same time we postulate a theory of the text which includes
(through the notion of encyclopedia or thesaurus and that of frame)
rather than excludes the results of an enlarged componential analysis
[along the lines of the model of a global semantic field, Model Q,
suggested in *Theory*]. (*LF*, p. 23)

The theory of codes and the theory of texts thus become closely
interrelated: the sememe appears as a virtual text, and the text is
simply the expansion of a sememe. This key phrase is taken up
again at the beginning of the Peirce essay (*LF*, p. 27; cf. *RR*, p. 175,
where the Italian adjective *virtuale* is substituted by 'inchoative'):
the idea is argued to be implicit in Peirce's semiotic theory. The
Peirce essay also draws attention to the 'logical limit' to the encyclopedia, which cannot be infinite: its limit 'is just the *universe of
discourse*' (*RR*, p. 189); this leads Eco to make a contact with the
theory of 'possible worlds' which will be discussed in the next
chapter.

Eco's remarks on the notion of 'encyclopedia' in *Lector in fabula*
and *The Role of the Reader* are inevitably tinged by his particular
interest in these essays in extending his semiotics, including its
semantic aspect, in a more comprehensive way beyond single utterances to texts. But a series of essays on the topic written during the
early 1980s locate it in the wider context of Eco's semiotics as a
whole, without losing sight of its particular relevance for a semiotics
of the text in particular. His next important statement on the
notion of 'encyclopedia' comes in the programmatically entitled
'Dall'albero al labirinto' ('From the Tree to the Labyrinth') of 1981.
Eco begins by describing three 'models' of actual or possible ency-
clopedias, at any rate models in some respect corresponding to
historical phenomena – the primitive 'pile' form like the *Physiologus*,
the 'tree' form like Vincent de Beauvais's *Speculum Mundi* or
Aquinas's *Summa theologiae*, and finally the case of the *Encyclopédie*,
which d'Alembert describes both as a tree, for the first time acknowledging its purely hypothetical structure, and as a map. But
the fourth form, the 'semiotic encyclopedia', does not exist as an
object and could never be published. Passing from 'models' of actual encyclopedias Eco has arrived at the 'encyclopedia' as model.
He explains clearly the problem which arises in semantics 'when
you have to construct a code, or a system of equivalences which
make a given portion of content (or meaning) correspond to physical expressions (words, or other signs in non-verbal semiotic systems)' (p. 45). He points to the difficulties with 'dictionary' models
and with the Porphyrian tree. There are linguists who insist that the

analysis of semes can only be conducted in terms of 'dictionary', that is, ascribing to an expression only its strictly linguistic properties; all the rest belongs to the sphere of empirical knowledge and belongs to an 'encyclopedia'. Eco's objection to this is that there is no such thing as a 'pure' dictionary description; even actual dictionaries cannot avoid giving some encyclopedic information in their definitions. He insists that semantic representations depend on context, and that at this point the idea of dictionary collapses. The idea of encyclopedia becomes more useful, but he underlines that an encyclopedia cannot (should not) be given a hierarchical (tree-like) form.

The most helpful structural representation of the semiotic encyclopedia, he suggests, is the metaphor of the *rhizome* proposed by Deleuze and Guattari in their 1978 book of that title. Eco lists the main characteristics of a rhizomatic structure as described by Deleuze and Guattari, and from this he concludes that a semantic representation in the form of an encyclopedia is structured according to a 'network of interpretants', that is, definitions which substitute other definitions, situations which clarify the sense of a term, visual representations which explain verbal expressions and vice versa, chains of synonyms. The chain of interpretants operates in such a way that some of the variously described properties assigned to a linguistic expression, or to an expression belonging to another semiotic system, appear to be mutually contradictory, and only the context establishes which needs to be activated in accord with the dominant theme of the discourse. A semantic representation of this kind does not take the form of a hierarchically structured tree, but that of a network or labyrinth. It allows various pathways and different choices which may be defined on the basis of context or precise textual rules. It is potentially infinite, because it must take account of all the properties which all cultures have attributed to the different expressions. And finally, it is not concerned with recording what 'is true' but rather that which has been said by and in society, not only what is accepted as true but also what is accepted as imaginary.[26] This notion of encyclopedia does not deny the existence of knowledge: it denies that it can be organized in a definite and permanent way. It can be organized locally but not globally; if it thinks that its local organization is global, it is 'ideological' (in the sense of displaying 'false consciousness'). Such an encyclopedia does not physically exist, yet it is the whole of what humanity has said.

This description and the rather wide-ranging conclusions Eco draws from it are included in his account of the structure of the encyclopedia in *SFL*, pp. 109–12 and *SPL*, pp. 80–4 (which is differently organized from the Italian). 'Dictionary vs. Encyclopedia', the second essay in *SPL*, deals specifically with the 'battle' between dictionary and encyclopedia and in particular summarizes the weaknesses of the 'dictionary'. The other occasion in this book on which Eco comes back strongly to the idea of 'encyclopedia' is in the chapter on 'Codes', equivalent to the final chapter in the Italian edition, which presents itself as in part a critique of Eco's original (1976) article on 'Codice' in the Einaudi *Enciclopedia* (*SFL*, pp. 255–8). It should be noted that this self-criticism and the conclusions to the essay from which I will quote are either absent or toned down in the American edition.

The search for codes is justified in the end by the revisionist Eco as part of that life-long struggle against the 'ineffable', against some creative urge that cannot be explained. 'The life of culture is the life of texts sustained by intertextual laws where everything that "has already been said" acts as a possible rule. The *already said* constitutes the thesaurus of the encyclopedia' (*SFL*, p. 300; emphases in the original). In accordance with the bulwarks he is erecting against semiotic drift in the mid-1980s, Eco argues here that the 'anticodism' of post-structuralism is a return to the orgy of ineffability. To speak of codes means accepting that we are not gods and that we are moved by rules – whether these are social and historical, produced by us, or imposed on us from outside remains to be decided. Even if we think of the encyclopedia as a labyrinth, this does not mean that we cannot describe it or describe the pathways through it, or, as the English has it, 'explain its modes of birth and development' (*SPL*, p. 188).

There are a number of other interesting occasions on which the topic of the encyclopedia is raised explicitly in Eco's work in the 1980s, beyond informing his textual pragmatics through and through. There is an exploration of where Greimas fits between dictionary and encyclopedia in the article co-written with Patrizia Magli, 'Sémantique greimassienne et encyclopédie' (originally published in 1985, English translation 1989). 'L'Antiporfirio' in *Sugli specchi*, originally written for Vattimo and Rovatti's *Il pensiero debole* (1983), ably adapts the notion of the encyclopedia to the positive associations of 'weak thought' ('What makes the encyclopedia fruitfully weak is the fact that no closed and definitive representation of it is ever given', etc.: pp. 356–7). Finally, one should mention Eco's article on 'Dictionary vs. Encyclopedia' in Sebeok's *Encyclopedic Dictionary of Semiotics* (1986). This entry is less meta-textual than one might expect in the circumstances. It gives particular attention in its later pages to the 'encyclopedia-like' semantics of Putnam and Petöfi, at the same time as stating what have now become the fundamentals of Eco's position on the encyclopedia: the encyclopedia is a semiotic postulate, a regulative hypothesis which encourages partial and local exploration of the encyclopedic universe; and there is no difference between linguistic knowledge and factual knowledge because the knowledge represented by an encyclopedia is a 'cultural' knowledge, as reflected by interpretants. 'It is not an idiosyncratic competence but a cultural competence, recorded by an intertextual body'.[27]

Eco's developing ideas on the encyclopedia as cultural knowledge, and its rhizome-like structure, mark a shift from the idea of code as rule to that of code as a system of possible inferences, in important ways analogous to that from sign as equivalence to sign as implication or entailment. What they have in common is the replacement of a relatively static moment of interpretation (that of recognition or decoding) with the dynamic process of 'abduction'.[28] 'Abduction' is a term which Eco borrows, and strategically elaborates, from Peirce, and it would be useful to pause over it for a moment before going on to see in the next chapter how all this links with Eco's textual semiotics.

4. Abduction   Peirce introduces the notion of 'abduction' (or hypothetical inference) as a third mode of reasoning, alongside deduction and induction. The three modes of reasoning are seen as processes of argumentation; the distinction between them is based in part on Peirce's analysis of syllogistic figures, where he demonstrates how each figure is based on an independent principle of inference.[29] The example which Eco uses repeatedly (cf. *TSE*, p. 131) is taken from Peirce's *Collected Papers* 2.623.; Peirce here calls 'hypothesis' what he elsewhere and Eco habitually calls 'abduction':

> Suppose I enter a room and there find a number of bags, containing different kinds of beans. On the table there is a handful of white beans; and, after some searching, I find one of the bags contains white beans only. I at once infer as a probability, or as a fair guess, that this handful was taken out of that bag. This sort of inference is called *making an hypothesis*. It is the inference of a *case* from a *rule* and a *result*. We have, then – DEDUCTION. *Rule.* – All the beans from this bag are white. *Case.* – These beans are from this bag. Therefore *Result.* – These beans are white. INDUCTION. *Case.* – These beans are from this bag. *Result.* – These beans are white. Therefore *Rule.* – All the beans from this bag are white. ABDUCTION [HYPOTHESIS]. *Rule.* – All the beans from this bag are white.

Result. – These beans are white. Therefore *Case.* – These beans are from this bag.

After 1891, Peirce modifies his ideas on inferences slightly by considering the three modes of reasoning not only as processes of argumentation, but as methodological steps taken in a scientific investigation.

> Abduction is described as the first step in an investigation, the invention or proposal of a hypothesis. Deduction, the second step, stands for the analysis of the hypothesis by inferring the necessary consequences from it. The third step, induction, refers to the testing of the hypothesis by experiment. Thus only abduction introduces new ideas in our thinking. (Schillemans, pp. 264–5)

Eco uses the term 'abduction' in a broad sense, as synonymous with hypothesis and conjecture (*LII*, p. 132), and as constituting 'a typical procedure thanks to which in semiosis one is able to take difficult decisions when following ambiguous instructions' (*LII*, p. 225). In his contribution to *The Sign of Three*, a volume that he co-edited with Thomas Sebeok in 1983, Eco discusses four kinds of abduction.[30] In hypothesis or 'overcoded abduction' the rule is almost automatically given to us during the interpretation of the sign; in most cases we are not even conscious of the fact that we are making an inference. In 'undercoded abduction' we have to select the rule among a number of equivalent alternatives made available by the actual, shared knowledge; the point is to select the most plausible one. In 'creative abduction' the signifying rule has to be invented; this is the kind of interpretation of signs typical of detectives and scientists. In meta-abduction we ask ourselves if the possible universe suggested by creative abduction is compatible with the universe we experience (cf. Schillemans, p. 266, for this summary). Amongst these four, Eco's overcoded abduction seems to be founded on the same mechanism as Peirce's deduction: reasoning from a general law to a particular case. Meta-abduction is comparable with Peircean induction: the testing of a hypothesis. Peirce's abduction is divided between undercoded abduction, which depends on cultural convention, and creative abduction, which is the only kind that can allow the possibility of escape from the cultural system: 'Creative abduction can break through the ideologically structured world-view. It is an adventurous walk in the rhizomatic labyrinth, with new significations as a result' (Schillemans, p. 266).[31]

Schillemans insists on the point that if Eco holds 'stubbornly' to the term 'abduction' to cover this range of modes of reasoning, it is because, while Peirce is concerned with a semiotics of 'true representation' where, as we have seen, abduction functions as the first step towards truth, Eco is concerned with a semiotics of cultural representation, in which it is the work of abduction to recognize or to introduce order. For Eco abduction lies behind each decoding and interpretation of a sign; but in the Peirce essay in *Lector in fabula* (this passage appears to be omitted in the English) he reminds us that 'for Peirce a sign can be not just a word or an image, but a proposition or even a whole book' (*LF*, p. 35). Texts in Eco are conceived of as signs, and the interpretation of texts becomes an inferential process of selecting between possible alternatives. How this is done is a matter for a theory of reading and interpretation.

6

Theory and Fiction

Readers and worlds

Lector in fabula and *The Role of the Reader*, both published in 1979, appeared at a time when the first post-structuralist wave of theoretical interest in readers and reading was reaching its apogee.[1] Eco was in line with a broad consensus in assigning to the reader the role of actualizing or realizing the text, in some sense, albeit with the particular semiotic inflection deriving from the earlier *Trattato/ Theory*. His approach was far from unproblematical, as we shall see.[2]

Eco starts from the proposition that the surface (or manifest) appearance of a text, the words on the page, represents a chain of expressive devices which the addressee must actualize. A text, defined by Eco as 'a network of different messages depending on different codes and working at different levels of signification' (*RR*, p. 5), has to be actualized, and is therefore incomplete, for two reasons. The first has to do with any (not just a textual) message. An expression is empty (a *flatus vocis*) until it is correlated with its conventional content with reference to a given code. The addressee is postulated as an operator capable of opening the dictionary, so to speak, at every word that he or she encounters and drawing on a series of pre-existing syntactical rules in order to recognize the reciprocal function of the terms within the context of the sentence. Every message postulates grammatical competence on the part of the addressee. Opening the dictionary also means accepting a series of what, following Carnap, Eco calls 'meaning postulates': a term is incomplete in itself even when it is given a minimum dictionary definition.

A (written) text is distinguished from other kinds of expression by reason of its greater complexity. The main reason for its complexity is that it is run through with *what is not said*, in other words with what is not manifest on the surface, at the level of expression. This is what has to be actualized at the moment of the actualization of the content. A text, more than any other message, requires active and conscious co-operation on the part of the reader. Even a simple narrative text is full of blank spaces needing to be filled in, omissions which the reader has to make good. Eco offers two reasons for this feature. Firstly, a text is as a general rule 'a lazy (or economical) mechanism which lives on the surplus value of sense introduced by the addressee' (*LF*, p. 52). Secondly, the more one moves along the line from a purely didactic text to an aesthetic one, the more the text wants to leave the reader free to interpret, even if generally it wants to be interpreted with a reasonable margin of unambiguousness (*univocità*). A text needs someone to help it work. A text, finally, postulates its addressee not only as an indispensable condition of its ability to communicate, but also of its power to signify. A text is emitted in the hope or expectation that someone will actualize it (whether or not that someone actually exists).

Eco's initial focusing on gaps in the text and the process of actualization calls to mind other prominent theories of reading and particularly the phenomenological approach elaborated by Wolfgang Iser in the 1970s on the basis of the work of Roman Ingarden.[3] This almost automatic association bundles together both real overlap and significant difference between Iser's phenomenological and Eco's semiotic perspectives. In a valuable overview of 'semiotics since Eco', Gregory C. Colomb declared that Ingarden 'was a most semiotic phenomenologist, and in this as in so much else Iser has followed his lead', while at the same time 'the increasingly large role of pragmatics in semiotic theory can be seen as an attempt to accommodate within semiotics some of the questions central to phenomenology',[4] before going on to suggest what the two approaches could usefully learn from each other. But a fundamental difference remains in the fact that for Iser actualization is the result of an interaction between text and reader which produces a 'virtual' work, and that '[a]s the reader passes through the various perspectives offered by the text, and relates the different views and patterns to one another, he sets the work in motion, and so sets himself in motion, too.'[5] Eco's view of the reader's operations, on the other hand, has some similarities with the structure proposed for the avant-garde 'open work', based on post-serial musical composition, in which the interpreter enjoys interpretative freedom, but only within a gamut of interpretations 'foreseen' by the composition itself.[6] Eco himself has insisted on this difference while acknowledging the similarity between his 'model reader' and Iser's 'implied reader'. For him the model reader is 'a set of textual instructions, displayed by the text's linear manifestation precisely as a set of sentences or other signals'. While Iser underlines the point (in *The Act of Reading*) that the concept of implied reader is a textual structure anticipating the presence of a recipient 'without necessarily defining him', Eco's concern is to focus on the 'fictitious reader' portrayed in the text, on the assumption that 'the main business of interpretation is to figure out the nature of this reader, in spite of its ghostly existence' (*SWFW*, pp. 15–16).

If it is an obvious condition of the existence of texts that a text is emitted in the expectation that it will be actualized, that its empty spaces will be filled, it seems equally evident, in a pragmatic sense, that the competence of the addressee is not necessarily the same as that of the sender. In chapter 2 of this book it has been shown how, in a political and ideological perspective, this gap can be exploited as a form of resistance to an imposed or hegemonic message. In any case, apart from considerations of use-value, the view that the message, even more the textual message, is not the crystalline object supposed by the classic model of sender–message–addressee is a constant of Eco's semiotic reflections. *A Theory of Semiotics* (2.15) had argued against such a simplistic model of communication and had demonstrated how the codes of the addressee can vary, in whole or in part, from those of the sender, how the code is not a simple entity but more frequently a complex system of systems of rules, and how the linguistic code is not enough to understand a linguistic message. In order to 'decode' a linguistic message the receiver needs circumstantial as well as linguistic competence and has to be able to trigger presuppositions, discard idiosyncrasies, and so on. In spoken communication the possibilities of 'aberrant' interpretation are guarded against by all sorts of other, non-linguistic, signs given; different sign systems complement each other in order to guide interpretation. What happens in a written text, 'which the author generates and entrusts to a range of possible interpretative acts, like a message in a bottle' (*LF*, p. 53)?

At this point Eco reformulates the proposition that the text postulates the co-operation of the reader as a condition of its actualization. It would be more accurate to say that the text is a product whose 'interpretative fate' (*sorte interpretativa*) must be part of its own generative mechanism. To generate a text means putting into action a strategy which foresees the other side's moves, as in war or chess. The only difference is that generally (not always) the author wants his or her 'adversary' to win. The author must also foresee accidents or mistakes or lack of information on the part of the reader and deal with them sooner or later. It seems, therefore, at this point that the author has to refer to a series of competences (a phrase which Eco describes as being 'wider' than 'a knowledge of codes') which confer content on the expressions which he uses. He has to assume that the series of competences to which he refers are the same as those referred to by the reader. So he foresees a Model Reader capable of making interpretative moves which correspond to his, the author's, generative moves. The sort of reader required is signalled by a number of different means: language, the choice of a particular kind of encyclopedia or ensemble of cultural references, particular vocabulary or style, genre.

It will be apparent that the summary of this part of Eco's theory in the preceding paragraph assumes the presence of an author, and that this author is to all intents and purposes the 'empirical' one, the flesh-and-blood being who sets pen to paper. Is this a purely rhetorical device, or even a grammatical necessity, in so far as the business of presupposing or expecting a reading requires a subject? But that subject (in Eco's account) is sometimes the text and sometimes the author, which suggests that authorship itself may on occasion be conceived as a textual strategy (that disposition of the materials, in terms of classical rhetoric, which will elicit the most satisfactory, and satisfying, interpretation) and on others as an authorial intention (the empirical author disposing the materials in order to achieve a desired effect, or effects). While on the one hand the empirical existence of an actual and active author seems, and is, an indispensable condition for the communication of a text, it is also a persistent embarrassment for theories of textual meaning which regard the contribution of the empirical author to interpretation as at best marginal, if not downright misleading. The author foresees a model reader, whose interpretative competence and co-operation are part and parcel of the generative mechanism of the text. The empirical reader constructs a model author and the empirical author is ritually and regularly disposed of. 'I'll tell you at once that I couldn't really care less about the empirical author of a narrative text (or, indeed, of any text),' Eco tells his Harvard audience in 1993,

an audience whom he playfully assumes to spend its time reading biographies of Proust and Jane Austen and therefore likely to
be shocked at such a proposition (*SWFW*, p. 11). In the tripar-
tite division of intentions mapped out in *Interpretation and Overinterpretation*, the *intentio auctoris* receives equally short shrift, and
what matters is the 'dialectical link between *intentio operis* and
intentio lectoris' (*IO*, pp. 63–4). Yet the empirical author is not so easy
to get rid of. Not only may he be asked, if still alive, how far he
was aware 'of the manifold interpretations his text supported' (not
in order to validate this or that reading, 'but to show the discrepancies between the author's intention and the intention of the text')
(*IO*, p. 73), he is, in *Lector in fabula* at least, the founder or origin of
the figure of the model reader foreseen and constructed in the text.
The text enacts a certain idea of the reader which originates with the
empirical author, even as at the same time it can only be enacted in
and through the text. The author remains a shadowy presence (in
IO, borrowing an idea of one of his students, Mauro Ferraresi, Eco
puts forward the idea of a 'liminal author', a figure on the threshold
'between the intention of a given human being and the linguistic
intention displayed by a textual strategy': p. 69), and as long as this
uncertainty, this undecidability between its empirical and its textual
status, attaches to it, the notion of author appears to result in an
imbalance or an asymmetry in the whole process of reading and
interpretation. The possible implications of this asymmetry between author (empirical or model) and reader (empirical or model)
will become more apparent as we proceed in our analysis of Eco's
theory of (co-operative) interpretation.

It must be acknowledged, however, that even while the empirical
author retains a shadowy presence in Eco's text, Eco's own authorial intention is certainly to reconceptualize the author as a textual
strategy and as what he calls an 'interpretative hypothesis'. In a
simplified communicative process we have a sender, a message and
an addressee. Eco distinguishes between a message with a referential function, where the addressee uses grammatical traces such as
'I' as referential indices ('I' = the sender of this message), and occasions when the text is considered as a text, and especially when it is
addressed to a wider audience (a novel, a political speech). In this
case sender and addressee are present in the text not so much as
poles of the act of utterance as 'actantial roles' of the enunciated.[7] In
such cases the author is manifested textually only as (i) a recogniz-
able style (or idiolect, cf. *Theory* 3.7.6.); (ii) a pure actantial role ('I' =
the subject of this utterance); (iii) an illocutive occurrence, or a

perlocutive operator stating an 'instance of utterance', or the statement of a subject which is extraneous to the uttered but is in some way present in the larger fabric of the text. An example taken from Wittgenstein's *Philosophical Investigations* shows that in this text Wittgenstein is none other than a 'philosophical style' and the Model Reader is none other than the intellectual ability to share this style and co-operate in realizing it (*RR*, p. 11). The Model Reader is an ensemble of 'happiness conditions', established by the text, which must be satisfied for a text to be wholly realizable in respect of its potential content.

When the empirical author fashions a model reader he designates himself as the subject of the uttered as a mode of textual operation, in a way that is equally 'strategic', therefore. The figure of the author is not always clear to the empirical reader, who tends to flatten it, to fit it into what she or he already knows about the empirical subject of the utterance. This can make textual co-operation uncertain. Textual co-operation does not mean the actualization of the intentions of the empirical subject of the utterance, but the intentions that are virtually contained by the uttered. The example proffered by Eco (the use of 'Russian' instead of 'Soviet': *LF*, p. 63) seems to suggest a kind of 'unconscious of the text'. If an author uses the term 'Russian' instead of 'Soviet', readers have the right to give that term an ideological connotation. They have the right because the connotation is activated textually, and this is the connotation which readers have to attribute to their own Model Author, independently of the intentions of the empirical author. Textual co-operation takes place between two discursive strategies, not two individual subjects. The Model Author exists as an interpretative hypothesis when we give shape to the subject of a textual strategy, as it appears from the text in question, and not when one hypothesizes an empirical subject behind the textual strategy who perhaps thought or wished or wished to think differently from what the text, measured against the codes to which it refers, says to its own Model Reader.

The author makes assumptions about his or her model reader and about the knowledge and competences which writer and reader share. But at the same time he or she creates those competences. 'Thus it seems that a well-organized text on the one hand presupposes a model of competence coming, so to speak, from outside the text, but on the other hand works to build up, by merely textual means, such a competence' (*RR*, p. 8). What is meant by 'build up' in this case? The question points to two further questions.

The first, more general, one asks whether the text is less 'lazy' and the co-operation sought is less free than might appear or, as Eco puts it in an appropriately constructivist but strangely limiting simile, whether the text is an assembly-kit allowing only one possible outcome or a box of Lego bricks from which it is feasible to make many different combinations. Eco graphically describes the gap between the message-expression as source of information and the message-content as an interpreted text, a gap which corresponds to the difference between the knowledge that the addressee should supposedly share with the sender and the real patrimony of the addressee's knowledge (diagram, *LF*, p. 54/*RR*, p. 6). The second question, however, is more focused and takes us back to the earlier distinction between 'open' and 'closed' texts: one can readily think of a process of construction of the reader of a closed text, but what of open texts? To what extent do they play on, suggest, expect the gaps mentioned above, constituting themselves as texts which can be read in a thousand, infinitely enjoyable, ways? Do such texts forgo the postulating of a Model Reader, or do they postulate one of a different nature?

With the notion of 'closed', Eco is thinking of texts that are produced for a specific market, with the intention of stimulating a precise effect which will be clearly signalled to the readership. Of course, the more a text works to establish a particular readership, the more open it is to aberrant reading. Certainly such texts can be read perversely – if we can imagine the work of the late nineteenth-century popular novelist Carolina Invernizio being plundered for hitherto unimagined decadentist frissons, for example.[8] In other instances the author can 'misread' his readers: the example is Sue's *Les mystères de Paris* (the analysis in *SM* is translated in *RR*, pp. 125–43). Nothing is more open than a closed text – but this openness is something that is done to the text from outside, it is a way of using the text. The notion of 'use', and its opposition to 'interpretation', is an important point to which we shall return in a moment.

The author of an 'open' work is aware of, accepts and works on the gap between the source of information and the interpreted text mentioned above. He decides up to what point he must control the co-operation of the reader, where it has to be stimulated, where it has to be led, where it has to become free interpretative adventure. The one thing that the author will try to achieve is to ensure that, while many interpretations are possible, they will echo each other, in such a way as not to exclude but to reinforce each other. Thus, the Model Reader of *Finnegans Wake*, to return to a favourite example, is the operator capable of realizing, in time, the greatest possible number of criss-crossing readings. At this point the reader (of Eco) may entertain a doubt. Eco may be describing the ideal reader envisaged by Joyce, at least the Joyce whom Eco quotes repeatedly. But is the ideal reader the same as a model reader, and what is the relation of either, or both, with the empirical reader? Does a model reader not also have in some sense to 'grasp' the work at first reading, and in the time of reading? No doubt the model reader is a potentially endless re-reader. But she or he is also a first reader. Eco makes a sharp distinction between the empirical and the theoretical, and he describes a theoretical model, yet, if he seeks to make a general point about interpretative co-operation, he cannot help all the time being pulled back towards the empirical. The one who reads *Finnegans Wake* is neither Joyce's insomniac (nor did Joyce seriously expect that he or she would be, that is why that person is 'ideal') nor only the reader who makes the fullest possible reading of the text (Eco's model reader). She or he is also, first and foremost, the one whose reading is partial, tentative and progressive: if the model envisages that only as part of its prehistory, as stages in the 'becoming' of the model reader, then such a reader and such a reading can only be described as empirical. Since elsewhere, however, Eco describes the process of actualization precisely in these tentative and progressive terms, it is arguable that the notion of model reader has a double sense, designating both the realization of any possible number of readings (even very few, though Eco is hardly likely to be interested in these) and the realization of the greatest number of possible readings.

The reference to Joyce, however, also makes the point that even with the most open work imaginable a model reader is constructed by means of a textual strategy. If the text is picked up by readers whom the text neither postulates nor helps to produce, it will be illegible, or another book. This is as true of an open as of a closed text. 'The reader', as Eco puts it in *The Role of the Reader* (p. 10), 'is strictly defined by the lexical and the syntactical organization of the text: the text is nothing else but the semantic-pragmatic production of its own Model Reader.' The value of such a statement, however, may lie more in its emphasis on limits and necessary choices (the text allows A but not B, or, if it appears to allow B, it is because it is being misappropriated) – an emphasis to which Eco returns again and again in the coming years, and in different contexts – than in its filling-out of the contours of the reader figure. Once again, Eco returns to his distinction between 'use' and 'interpretation'. We must distinguish between the free use of a text that is taken as a stimulus to the imagination and the interpretation of an open text. The chain of interpretations may be infinite, but, as Peirce shows, the universe of discourse intervenes to limit the format of the encyclopedia (cf. chapter 5 above). A text is nothing other than the strategy which constitutes the universe of its legitimizable, if not 'legitimate', interpretations. One can decide to enlarge the universe of discourse, as the process of unlimited semiosis encourages one to do. But it has to be decided whether what one is about is keeping semiosis going or interpreting a text. These, it should be noted, are decisions of the empirical, not the model, reader.

In the course of this and the next chapter we shall return to the as yet unresolved imprecisions surrounding the notions of 'empirical' and 'model', and those of 'use' and 'interpretation'. But before we do so we should focus on what is undoubtedly the primary strength of Eco's analysis in *Lector in fabula* and (in abbreviated form) in *The Role of the Reader*. This is the description and representation of the narrative text as a system of nodes or junctures, from which we discern the points at which the co-operation of the model reader is expected and stimulated. Eco's model (reproduced in figure 1) is based on Petöfi's textual grammar,[9] but is focused on the co-operation of the reader, not on text generation; what particularly interests Eco in Petöfi's model is 'the double consideration of both an intensional and an extensional approach' (*RR*, p. 14). Despite the seemingly vertical structure of the model, Eco is at pains, both in his introductory remarks and in the detail of his description, to undermine its appearance as a sequentially organized series of 'levels'. The 'boxes' in the diagram may be entered from different directions and exited from in others, and Eco stresses this rhizomatic and multi-directional character of the model, which is not hierarchical except as concerns the lower levels: the starting point has to be the linear text manifestation, the 'words on the page'.

Eco's contribution to textual theory here is to show how far the concept of code can be developed.[10] The diagram offers a view, however provisional, of everything that enters into a (any) communication and at the same time into the realization (concretization, actualization) of a text. Starting necessarily from the linear text manifestation (box 3),[11] Eco looks next at the circumstances of utterance (box 2) and then moves up the extensional side of his diagram, crossing the line into 'actualized content', to discuss what he calls '(bracketed) extensions' (box 5). This is the point at which the reader makes some initial hypotheses:

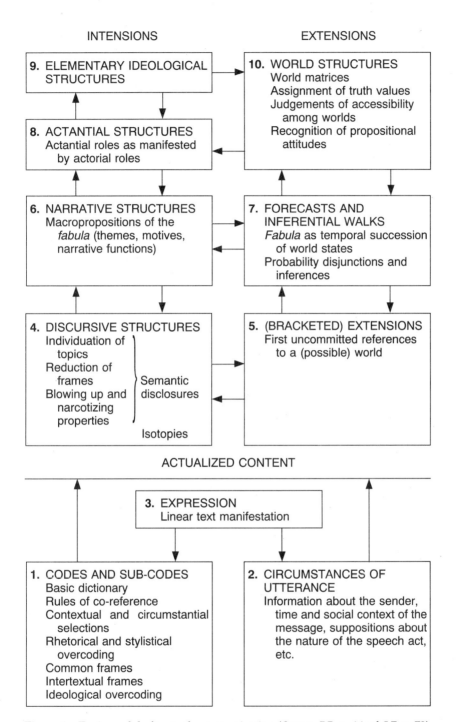

INTENSIONS   EXTENSIONS

9. ELEMENTARY IDEOLOGICAL STRUCTURES

10. WORLD STRUCTURES
World matrices
Assignment of truth values
Judgements of accessibility among worlds
Recognition of propositional attitudes

8. ACTANTIAL STRUCTURES
Actantial roles as manifested by actorial roles

6. NARRATIVE STRUCTURES
Macropropositions of the *fabula* (themes, motives, narrative functions)

7. FORECASTS AND INFERENTIAL WALKS
Fabula as temporal succession of world states
Probability disjunctions and inferences

4. DISCURSIVE STRUCTURES
Individuation of topics
Reduction of frames
Blowing up and narcotizing properties
Semantic disclosures
Isotopies

5. (BRACKETED) EXTENSIONS
First uncommitted references to a (possible) world

ACTUALIZED CONTENT

3. EXPRESSION
Linear text manifestation

1. CODES AND SUB-CODES
Basic dictionary
Rules of co-reference
Contextual and circumstantial selections
Rhetorical and stylistical overcoding
Common frames
Intertextual frames
Ideological overcoding

2. CIRCUMSTANCES OF UTTERANCE
Information about the sender, time and social context of the message, suppositions about the nature of the speech act, etc.

Figure 1   Eco's model of textual communication (*Source*: RR, p. 14; cf. LF, p. 72)

As far as the reader recognizes the existence of certain individuals (be they animate or not) furnished with certain properties (among which the possible properties of performing certain actions), he probably makes some indexical presuppositions, that is, he assigns those subjects to a possible world. In order to apply the information provided by the lexicon, he assumes a transitory identity between this world and the world of his experience (reflected by the lexicon). (*RR*, p. 17)

If in the course of reading readers discover discrepancies between the world of their experience and the world of the text, they either go straight to box 10 or put the extension into brackets, that is, they suspend disbelief and wait for more semantic information that will be actualized in box 4.

Eco's presentation continues by returning to codes and sub-codes properly so called (box 1). In order to actualize the discursive structures of the text the reader compares its linear manifestation with the system of codes and sub-codes furnished by the language in which the text is written and by the encyclopedic competence to which by tradition that language refers: this competence is what in *TSI/TSE* is represented by Model Q. At the level of the basic dictionary we have minimum 'postulates of meaning', the laws of entailment, based on the recognition of the elementary semantic properties of expressions, and the attempt to produce provisional amalgams, at least at the level of syntax. The example that Eco gives is of the elementary meanings entailed by 'princess' (living, human, female). What the reader does not yet know is which 'synthetic' properties attaching to living female humans are to be actualized: he or she will leave this open for the time being. Passing rapidly over rules of co-reference and contextual and circumstantial selections, Eco dwells at greater length on rhetorical and stylistic overcoding (discussed in *TSI/TSE* 2.14.), a sub-level at which the reader is capable of decoding a whole number of ready-made expressions recorded by the rhetorical tradition without inferential effort, and, more extensively, the notion of inferences drawn from common and intertextual 'frames' (a term borrowed from research in Artificial Intelligence). Husband and wife are shown in a domestic scene. The husband raises his hand in fury. Although the linear text manifestation describes neither the intention nor the act, it is clear that the husband intends to strike his wife. We do not infer, as Eco puts it, that he is raising his hand in order to register his vote. Our inference is made possible by a pre-established 'frame' which we call 'violent quarrel'.[12] Eco's view is that textual understanding is dominated to a considerable extent by the application of pertinent frames, just as interpretations destined to failure depend on the application of 'wrong' frames.

No less important to the hypotheses we make about the text we are reading are the inferences we draw based on intertextual frames. No text is read independently of the reader's experience of other texts. Eco, however, is concerned to extend the idea of intertextual frames beyond the favoured structuralist notion of 'motifs' and suggests a possible hierarchy of such frames: (i) ready-made *fabulae* such as standard thrillers or fairy tales with (Proppian) functions recurring in the same order; (ii) 'motif' frames, which are fairly flexible frames such as 'the girl pursued' with certain recurrent elements but no fixed sequence; (iii) situational frames, classic scenes like the Western shoot-out or the custard-pie fight in slapstick comedy; (iv) rhetorical topoi, for example the 'locus amoenus'. Intertextual frames circulate within the encyclopedia, they can be combined in various ways, and the author can choose to frustrate as well as to confirm our expectations (Eco mentions the 'Scenes we'd like to see' series in *Mad* magazine in the 1950s which made a point of upsetting our intertextual expectations: the kidnap victim is tied to the railway track; the rescuers gallop up to save her; the kidnap victim is run over by the train[13]). What Eco refers to as 'common' frames come to readers from their normal encyclopedic competence which they share with most members of the culture to which they belong and which for the most part are 'rules for practical action'.

Intertextual frames, however, are rhetorical or narrative schemas which are part of a restricted and selective band of knowledge which is not shared by all members of a culture. That is why some people are able to recognize when the rules of a genre are being broken, or to predict more easily how a story is going to end, while others, who do not have enough frames at their disposal, are destined to enjoy or endure surprises, *coups de scène* and outcomes which the sophisticated reader regards as banal. This hierarchical distinction between levels of readerly competence seems both an intrusion of empirical considerations (sociological, perhaps psychological) into a structural description of the interaction between text and reader and a weakening of the complex and fluid notion of the reading process which is being advanced. Quite apart from the question whether this 'intrusion' is to be welcomed or not, the point needs to be made that the distinction between the 'naïve' and the 'sophisticated' reader is one that recurs in Eco's writing of this period and it is one that seems to raise more problems than it solves: we shall return to this theme in some detail in the next chapter.

As if to emphasize the non-linear and non-hierarchical nature of his presentation, Eco in the remaining pages dedicated to his model zig-zags from side to side of the diagram reproduced here (the order followed in his exposition is in fact: 4, 6, 7, 8, 10, 9). On the intensional side, he considers in turn what is needed for the reader to make the right choices in order to determine what the story is about and the sense or senses that it makes, to work out the *fabula*, and, by a further abstraction, to reduce the *fabula* and every other narrative structure to pure formal positions (subject, object, sender and addressee) which produce actantial roles. The work of the reader in establishing discursive and narrative structures (see boxes 4 and 6) is extremely energetic, consisting in a constant process of abduction, confirmation, modification, elimination and adjustment in the light of experience (of the text). The *fabula* is not established at the end of the reading, but is built up as the reader goes along through this series of abductions resulting in a number of macropropositions. At each step the reader is led to conduct an intermediate extensional operation:

> he considers the various macropropositions [of the *fabula*] as statements about events taking place in a still-bracketed possible world. Each of these statements concerns the way in which a given individual deter- mines or undergoes a certain change of state, and the reader is induced to wonder what could happen at the next step of the story. (*RR*, p. 31)

In the act of reading, the traffic between boxes 6 and 7 appears to be particularly intense, and Eco acknowledges that at this point his diagram 'becomes very stiff vis-à-vis the flexibility of movements presumably accomplished by the reader' (*RR*, p. 37). The process reaches a (provisional) conclusion with the relation of the *fabula* to states of the 'real' world (box 10), the moment at which the reader unbrackets the suspension of disbelief entered into in box 5. Even if the text is a fictional one, the comparison with the 'real' world is indispensable, Eco argues, in order to acknowledge the 'verisimili- tude' of the *fabula* (cf. *RR*, p. 37). Box 9, which is concerned with 'elementary ideological structures', is the intensional counter- part of box 10: 'every reader is moving within box 9 when making interpretative decisions about the ideology of a given text, and within box 10 when making decisions about the credibility of the reported events and of the beliefs, lies, or wishes of the characters' (*RR*, p. 38).

The reference to 'worlds', both fictional and real, leads us to another important component of Eco's textual theory, namely, the notion of 'possible worlds', which is borrowed, to admittedly different ends, from modal logic. The problems that arise from such transference from one discourse to another (not only, or even principally, in Eco's specific case) have been carefully set out by Ruth Ronen, who, however, also acknowledges the benefits acquired by literary theory's illicit trade in logical concepts. While recognizing that the interest in the broad topic of possible worlds in the past twenty years or so has had to do with a widespread redefining of fictionality in its pragmatic and contextual (rather than purely textual) aspects – and Eco's 1979 books were already a sign of this shift – Ronen points out the fundamental differences of interest between the philosophical and the literary-theoretical uses of the same terms. 'Possible worlds [in philosophy]', she writes, 'are based on a logic of ramification determining the range of possibilities that emerge from an actual state of affairs; fictional worlds are based on a logic of parallelism that guarantees their autonomy in relation to the actual world';[14] in logic, possibility refers to abstract logical probabilities of occurrence which exclude, by necessity, impossibilities; literary theorists interpret possibility and impossibility as alternative world-constructing conventions applied to concrete worlds. Fictional worlds are not possible (in the philosophers' sense): they are not alternative ways the world might have been (but this does not seem to bother literary theorists).[15]

In fact, when first introducing the notion of possible worlds in *Lector in fabula* and *The Role of the Reader*, Eco is careful to distinguish the different uses, primarily through the idea that while modal logic thinks of possible worlds as empty, for textual semiotics they are individual, full, 'furnished' worlds, ' "pregnant" worlds of which one must know all the acting individuals and their properties' (*RR*, p. 218); as Ronen says, the literary interpretation of possibility makes use of possible world notions 'in a way that intensifies the autonomy of fictional worlds at the expense of doing justice to the logical meaning of possibility'.[16] Nevertheless, the idea of possible worlds, which for modal logic is a metaphor and for textual semiotics is an operational category functioning as 'a structural representation of concrete semantic actualizations' (*LF*, p. 125), is a suggestive one. When Eco returns to the question in a paper first given in 1986 and then reprinted in *The Limits of Interpretation* as 'Small Worlds', it is not so much the functionality of the concept in view of a structural analysis that engages his interest as the light which is thrown by the smallness and the 'handicapped' conditions of characters' worlds on the likely dimensions and distortions of our own, 'real', one (*LIE*, p. 74). In the lectures published as *Six Walks in the Fictional Woods* he formulates this idea slightly differently. Fictional worlds are 'parasites' of the actual one, 'but they are in effect "small worlds" which bracket most of our competence of the actual world and allow us to concentrate on a finite, enclosed world, very similar to ours but ontologically poorer. Since we cannot wander outside its boundaries, we are led to explore it in depth' (*SWFW*, p. 85). In the same lecture (p. 87) he floats the idea of fiction as a small world in the same way as a child's toy or game is a scaled-down version of objects or actions in the real world, and of its being similarly used to therapeutic, or learning, ends – a questionable doctrine to which we shall return in the next chapter.

One other aspect of the question which Eco dwells on in *The Limits of Interpretation* concerns the notion of 'impossible possible worlds'. These are the kinds of world with which Eco was particularly concerned at the time of his analysis of Alphonse Allais in *Lector in fabula* and *The Role of the Reader*. Allais was a master at eliciting from the reader the same kind of response that Douglas R. Hofstadter describes us as making to the pictures of M. C. Escher, which 'rely heavily upon the recognition of certain basic forms, which are then put together in nonstandard ways; and by the time the observer sees the paradox on a high level, it is too late – he can't go back and change his mind about how to interpret the lower-level objects'.[17] Eco will tend to distinguish sharply between lower- and higher-level interpretations, a point which will be taken up in chapter 7. The notion of 'self-voiding texts' and 'self-disclosing metafiction'[18] to explain 'worlds that the Model Reader is led to conceive of just to understand that it is impossible to do so' (*LIE*, p. 76) may be relevant to Eco's own fiction, and particularly to his third novel. It is to the novels that we now turn: not with the intention of applying or testing the theoretical principles we have just reviewed – a task which would require far greater space than that available here – but in order to suggest that Eco's narrative, which has always played on the paradoxes of fiction, may risk becoming silenced by them.

Texts

Eco devotes a number of pages, in his *Reflections on 'The Name of the Rose'*,[19] to the construction of a world ('furnished as much as possible, down to the smallest details') and to the construction of the reader. This reader would be formed by the first one hundred, demanding, pages, would play the author's game as his accomplice, and would be a type of reader who, 'once the initiation was past, would become my prey – or, rather, the prey of the text – and would think he wanted nothing but what the text was offering him' (*RNR*, p. 53). Much has been written since 1980 about the 'world' of *The Name of the Rose* – to limit ourselves briefly to that first novel alone – and many critical pages have been devoted to the topic of the semiotic education of the reader which the novel enacts.[20] But it is now possible to look back on that first, extraordinarily successful, venture into narrative from a distance, across a space occupied by two further, no less furnished and exacting, novels,[21] and ask oneself, in a way that was obviously not possible for Eco's first readers, whether, through the three fictions taken together, one may begin to discern a story which links them. If there is such a story, it is almost certainly a meta-textual one.

It would begin in the cloistered world of *The Name of the Rose*, with its snow-bound mountain abbey, the regulated repetition of its liturgical hours, the disciplined murmur of its scholarly routine. This is a closed world which is under threat, from the awful acts of violence triggered within the community itself, from religious and political disputes which challenge the very foundations of the monastic life and at a crucial moment are brought inside the abbey gates, from the rise of new social orders and new ways of thinking which cannot for ever be kept outside the walls. It is a spatially closed world, mentally and spiritually circumscribed, which in the end will be brought to a temporal close: its great and celebrated library burnt to the ground, its buildings destroyed, its surviving members scattered. In parallel with the fictional world the reader is enclosed within a textual world of his or her own, by being offered a narrative which promises closure and in a sense delivers it: a mystery to be resolved, an investigator to triumph – and even if the mystery is solved for the wrong reasons, or it turns out to be the wrong mystery, and the investigator as investigator is defeated, nothing at the most basic level is left unexplained, the story concludes, life resumes.

The investigator, William of Baskerville, pulls off a first, demonstrative and diplomatically important feat of detection, when he tracks and identifies the abbot's runaway horse Brunellus, of which he knows nothing, not even its name. The deductions that he makes from the hoofprints on the ground and other contextual hints depend on convention and cultural knowledge, not least the qualities

of equine beauty described by an *auctoritas*, Isidore of Seville, and
the name, Brunellus, by which 'the great Buridan, who is about to
become rector in Paris' always calls a horse when he wants to use
such an animal in one of his logical examples. 'This was my master's
way,' concludes the admiring Adso, Benedictine novice, secretary
to the Franciscan William, and now elderly narrator. 'He not only
knew how to read the great book of nature, but also knew the way
monks read the books of Scripture, and how they thought through
them' (*NRE*, pp. 24–5).[22] For William, follower of Roger Bacon and
friend of William of Ockham, his success in helping the cellarer to
find the horse testifies not to the vastness of his intellect but to the
poverty of his deduction: 'the ideas, which I was using earlier to
imagine a horse I had not yet seen, were pure signs as the hoofprints
in the snow were signs of the idea of "horse"; and signs and the
signs of signs are used only when we are lacking things' (*NRE*,
p. 28). In a more recent book, *Kant e l'ornitorinco*, we shall be told
that human language has few names and few definitions for an
infinity of single things, and so 'recourse to the universal is not a
power of thought but an infirmity of discourse' (*KO*, p. 13). But here
Adso will learn, and the reader with him, that signs, and signs of
signs, are all we have, or at any rate, that the pursuit of hypothetical
things that might lie 'beyond' the signs is never completed. William
is a nominalist, the medieval equivalent of a 'methodological' as
opposed to an 'ontological' structuralist, who would be a realist in
medieval terms and is represented in the novel by William's antagonist Jorge of Burgos. From the nominalist perspective, signs 'are
understood to be historically and culturally determined, just as
their denotations are, because they are not the objective counterparts of signs but "cultural elements" which, in turn, can be differ-
entiated from other "cultural elements" only with the help of
signs'.[23] It may be that unicorns do not exist, or not in the form in
which they are depicted, but it is certain that, even if they do not
exist, the 'trace' of them does point to something. 'The print does
not always have the same shape as the body that impressed it, and
it doesn't always derive from the pressure of a body,' William
explains in Socratic dialogue with the young Adso. 'At times it
reproduces the impression a body has left in our mind: it is the print
of an idea. The idea is a sign of things, and the image is sign of the
idea, sign of a sign. But from the image I reconstruct, if not the body,
the idea that others had of it.' True learning, however, must not be
content with ideas, but must discover things in their individual
truth. 'And so I would like to go back from this print of a print to the

individual unicorn that stands at the beginning of the chain.' That can only be done with the help of other signs, from which Adso concludes: 'Then I can always and only speak of something that speaks to me of something else, and so on. But the final something, the true one – does that never exist?' Perhaps it does, William assures him, it is the individual unicorn (*NRE*, pp. 316–17) – where 'unicorn' stands not for the impossible, but for that which is spoken of in many different ways.

William proceeds as an investigator by trying to reconstruct the sequence which gave rise to the signs whose interpretation is puzzling. He wants to get inside the mind of the murderer; in order to penetrate the labyrinthine structure of the library he needs to retrace 'the operations of the artificer' (*NRE*, p. 218). It is a procedure that will be followed at a turning-point in the narrative by the shipwrecked Roberto in *The Island of the Day Before* (p. 236) and, all too effectively, by the meta-plotters of *Foucault's Pendulum*. Happenstance and inspired guesswork play their part: the key that unlocks the secret door is provided unawares by Adso, and it is Adso's dream, itself shaped by the *Coena Cypriani*, that persuades William to follow up the one hypothesis among others that will lead to the solution of the mystery. Yet the semiotic skills which William deploys appear to lead only to impasse, for, despite his 'fanaticism', despite his 'insane passion for the truth' unrelieved by the ability to laugh (*NRE*, p. 491), the criminal Jorge proves no less adept than his tracker in reconstructing and foreseeing the mind of his adversary in an end-game of chess played with mirrors which is indebted, perhaps a homage to, the trap which Scharlach sets for the investigator Lönnrot in Borges's 'Death and the Compass'. Worse, William's reconstruction is almost his undoing: he had been foolishly convinced that the series of crimes followed a certain sequence (the seven trumpets of the Apocalypse) and, having conceived a false pattern to interpret the moves of the guilty man, finds that the guilty man has taken the initiative and pretended to follow that same pattern (*NRE*, pp. 469–70).

At this point, the reader might feel, survival and death, the punishment of the wicked and the reward of the righteous, are matters of chance: Jorge perishes with his library in the flames, the innocent, nameless, girl has been put to death, William is lost track of, perhaps to fall victim eventually to plague, Adso gets older and little wiser. We may feel ourselves obscurely implicated by the worrying contradiction between the sense that William in some ways points towards a future which is a part of what we readers have become and the fact that in the novel that future has been cut off. Only the names remain.

Yet the narrative does contain one small triumph which is replicated on a larger scale. William achieves one reconstruction which is both correct and cannot be matched by Jorge, only admired by him. He reconstructs the second book of Aristotle's *Poetics*, the hidden manuscript and murder weapon all in one, the longed-for object which you die for touching.

> 'Gradually this second book took shape in my mind as it had to be. I could tell you almost all of it, without reading the pages that were meant to poison me. Comedy is born from the komai – that is from the peasant villages – as a joyous celebration after a meal or a feast. Comedy does not tell of famous and powerful men, but ... Is that it?' 'Fairly close [*Abbastanza*. Close enough]. You reconstructed it by reading other books?' 'Many of which Venantius was working on'. (*NRE*, pp. 471–2)

Many years later, as a grown man, Adso returns to the ruins of the abbey and poking about among the rubble begins to gather fragments of parchment.

> Some fragments of parchment had faded, others permitted the glimpse of an image's shadow, or the ghost of one or more words. At times I found pages where whole sentences were legible; more often, intact bindings, protected by what had once been metal studs. . . . Ghosts of books, apparently intact on the outside but consumed within; yet sometimes a half page had been saved, an incipit was discernible, a title. (*NRE*, p. 500)

Back in his own monastery at Melk, Adso attempts to decipher these remains; he acquires other copies of the same titles, until, at the end of his 'patient reconstruction', he has before him 'a kind of lesser library, a symbol of the greater, vanished one: a library made up of fragments, quotations, unfinished sentences, amputated stumps of books' (ibid.). Unlike William confronting Jorge, however, Adso receives no confirmation of the value of his reconstruction. The more he rereads his list, the more he is convinced it is the result of chance and contains no message, but he has consulted it like an oracle in the intervening years. He has almost had the impression that what is written in the pages of the chronicle which we have just read 'is only a cento, a figured hymn, an immense acrostic that says and repeats nothing but what those fragments have suggested to me, nor do I know whether thus far I have been speaking of them or they have spoken through my mouth' (*NRE*, p. 501). Less and less can this old monk understand whether there is a 'design' which goes beyond the sequence of events and the times which connect them; whether the 'letter' which he has written contains some hidden meaning, or many, or none at all (ibid.).

Adso's patient reconstruction, full of doubt and weariness after the conflagration that has closed his youth and demolished the world whose certainties, William had already shown him, were less adamantine than his insecure disciple might have hoped, is the darkened mirror image of William's. The reconstruction of the second book of the *Poetics*, though forged in a moment of extreme danger, perhaps precisely for that reason, because so much is at stake, is brimful with confidence, William's confidence in his own skill as an interpreter and the confidence that he is right, that it really is the mission of those who love mankind 'to make people laugh at the truth, *to make truth laugh*' (*NR*, p. 491). But Adso's own forlorn endeavour is itself, however implausibly, endorsed. Naturally, a manuscript – in his preface the author/editor/transcriber/ translator makes the greatest possible play of the tenuousness of the threads which tie his text to Adso's manuscript (if it ever existed) and the confusion of his motives for reproducing it: an Italian translation, drafted, it seems, in a single night, of an obscure, neo-Gothic French version (Vallet), lost or purloined, of a seventeenth-century Latin edition (Mabillon), untraceable, of a work written in Latin by a German monk towards the end of the fourteenth century, also untraceable, the only independent evidence of whose existence is provided by extracts quoted from an unidentified work by Athanasius Kircher in the Castilian translation of a work originally written in Georgian on the use of mirrors in the game of chess. All of which means nothing at all except that it is possible to construct a text, containing the stories of both William and Adso, and much else besides, out of nothing at all, except, perhaps, out of other books, which disappear or dissolve. The elaborate construction of the novel's fictionality, at its beginning and its end, is an emphatic statement, despite Adso, of the power of narrative to mean something; in short, however flimsy its support, the flimsiest possible, it is not a *flatus vocis*. And in this sense, from the point of view of (model) author and (model) reader, one might consider *The Name of the Rose* to be a book not without hope.

The narrative structure of Eco's second novel, *Foucault's Pendulum*, is more straightforward and less obviously self-reflexive than that of the first. A first-person narrative told in the twilight between a series of adventures recounted in retrospect and the present which will bring those events to their climax, it recalls the familiar scenario of classic *film noir*, the murderer or the witness, but in this case the self-selecting victim (a model reader?) reviewing the events prior to the *dénouement*. The ugly scenes which ensue when the power to create texts out of other texts runs wild and the boundaries between text and extra-text are blurred beyond the point of recognition are delegated to the story as told, not seriously addressed in the telling of it (the structure could have remained much the same if instead of spending their time constructing a fantastic Plan which would bring all the Diabolicals out of the woodwork and apparently turn fiction into reality, the three principals had decided to play at blackmailing world leaders with a suitable quantity of nuclear waste or nerve gas that had fallen into their hands). The novel incorporates egregious representations of the paranoid state which has been extensively thematized by writers such as Pynchon and DeLillo,[24] and which is discussed in more detail in chapter 7. In his excellent study of Eco's novel, Brian McHale, building on Fredric Jameson, highlights the obsession with conspiracy scenarios favoured by this literature and the interest in mechanical writing, that is, writing procedures over which the author has surrendered at least partial control (despite the active presence of the computer Abulafia, however, this aspect is marginal to *Foucault's Pendulum*). In this second novel, the 'good' reconstruction of William (and even of Jorge) has become pure fabrication (the fear of which had been perhaps the secret spring of Adso's anxiety). 'The idea', explains Casaubon, the first-person narrator, 'is not to discover the Templars' secret, but to construct it' (*FP*, p. 383). In keeping with his view that modernism tends to be marked by epistemological concerns, postmodernism by ontological ones, McHale notes of this remark that what is in view is no longer 'an epistemological quest, but an enterprise unconstrained by criteria of truth and evidence. . . . [Unlike in *The Name of the Rose*] here the epistemological quest is aborted very early in favor of a project which is from the outset explicitly ontological: an experiment in self-conscious world-making.'[25] The enterprise ends in grim defeat for its begetters; in the present of the narration, at the close of the book, Casaubon awaits *his* end, all his guilt, foolishness, and pride already exposed, there remaining nothing to be said. What we might call the neutrality of the structure of *Foucault's Pendulum* might have been difficult for Eco to avoid, but by putting all the weight on the story as told, the novel runs the risk of moralism, particularly in the figure of Lia to whom is entrusted the task of producing non-paranoid, sensible and earth(l)y, readings.[26] *Foucault's Pendulum* might present a terrifying world, or possible

world, but its mode of presentation is oddly comfortable.[27] This
is very far from being the case in Eco's third novel, published in
1994.

The Island of the Day Before, like *The Name of the Rose*, uses the
device of the found manuscript and, again like its predecessor,
suspends the reader's disbelief on the thinnest of threads:

> Nor could I elude the childish curiosity of the reader, who would want to
> know if Roberto really wrote the pages on which I have dwelt far too
> long. In all honesty, I would have to reply that it is not impossible that
> someone else wrote them, someone who wanted only to pretend to tell
> the truth. And thus I would lose all the effect of the novel: where, yes, you
> pretend to tell true things, but you must not admit seriously that you are
> pretending. (*IDB*, pp. 512–13)

Thus the anonymous narrator in the last pages of the novel, showing that he is experiencing as much difficulty in ending his narrative
as he had had in beginning it. But let us proceed with order.

The setting of the novel is one of extraordinary calm. In July or
August of 1643 the hero, Roberto de la Grive, having lost his ship,
finds himself washed up on another, deserted one, berthed about a
mile from the shore of what he takes to be an island, faced across the
huge bay by another, vaster, stretch of land. The rest is sea, sky. The
stillness is to become the determining condition of Roberto's existence. There is no boat, he cannot swim, the days and nights succeed
each other (in reverse order, for the castaway is photophobic),
Roberto is a prisoner on his life-saving ship. The calm is deceptive.
Roberto gradually discovers that there is someone else on board
'his' ship. The other is finally tracked down and identified, a
German Jesuit who like Roberto had been on a mission to reach the
Solomon Islands and with them the supposed location of the anti-
podean meridian, both of these unfortunates working on behalf of
foreign governments to crack the secret of measuring longitude.
Together they discuss theology, astronomy, cosmology and how to
escape from the *Daphne* to the shores of the Island, where Father
Caspar has left his instruments and a longboat. Caspar dies in a vain
attempt to reach land; in due course Roberto too will let himself be
carried by the current.

The state of becalmment, imposed, lost, reinstalled, is the precise
opposite, the mirror image, as it were, of the storm and strife that
rage in Roberto's head. Roberto, we are quickly given to understand, is a child of his time: thus, fascinated by stories of twins and
doubles, so fascinated that he takes to inventing one of his own

involving an imaginary evil half-brother, Ferrante; learning early the place of equivocation and reversal in the world, of dissimulation, artifice and beautiful conceit in speech; his eyes opened to the 'alien architectures' of which the world consists, the world as labyrinth, but also as theatre; introduced to dazzling concepts like those of an infinite number of possible worlds, or parallel worlds existing in the same, or different, times. From his early masters he has learnt that with language, provided that language is witty (*arguta*), not ingenuous (*aperta*), most things can be achieved, but his sceptical narrator will point out time and again how Roberto seems more carried away by his words than carrying them. But sometimes he finds what seem to be the right ones, as when he beguiles the salon of Arthénice with his elegant theory on the Powder of Sympathy and the Sympathy of Love, until this story falls into the lap of Mazarin. The times are vertiginous, and the young man setting out in society has to learn quickly the difficult art of maintaining his balance, even for a moment. Little wonder that his inner life reads like that of a seventeenth-century postmodernist, one who learns to see the universal world

> as a fragile tissue of enigmas, beyond which there was no longer an Author . . . If there [at the siege of Casale] Roberto had sensed a world now without any center, made up only of perimeters, here [on board the *Daphne*] he felt himself truly in the most extreme and most lost of peripheries; because, if there was a center, it lay before him, and he was its immobile satellite. (*IDB*, p. 146)

All this derives from the words Roberto writes during his enforced exile on the *Daphne*. The writing takes the form of letters to the Lady, Lilia, the castaway's beloved, of poems, of records of conversations with Caspar (or perhaps notes for conversations that have not yet taken place), and finally of a fine Romance. The narrator reports these words, comments on them, speculates about them, gives us the flavour of them, but very seldom reproduces them directly. The relationship that is established between the narrator and Roberto as the reported author of his tale is the most interesting feature of the novel. At one level the author plays on the gap between the narrator's knowledge and Roberto's: relying on weathered documents written in the exaggerated style of the time, the narrator does not know how much Roberto knows, doubts whether it matters (for example, whether he and Caspar are marooned at the antipodes of the zero line measured through the Isla de Hierro or the zero line measured through Greenwich), worries about reassuring or apologizing to the contemporary reader of the novel, contradicts Roberto. At another level, and intriguingly, he enacts the mystery of the date line, on one side of which it is theoretically today and on the other, theoretically, the day before.

The first half of the novel (the first nineteen chapters) serves to set the scene, furnish the world around which the *Zeitgeist* will manoeuvre, and tell Roberto's life from childhood through Casale, the salons of Paris and his perilous sea-voyage in the enforced service of Mazarin to the moment of his arrival on the *Daphne* with which the novel begins. All this is done in a prolonged retrospective which is intercut with scenes from the narrated present which edges Roberto's story on the shipwreck forward, until the point in chapter 20 when, so to speak, his past finally catches up with his present. For a few chapters, the space of Roberto's conversations with Caspar, the novel lives in a continuous present, that is to say, the narration recounts events as they unwind on board the *Daphne*, but it is all the time under strain because Roberto's thoughts and desires are always tensed outwards and away, towards the possibilities created by the thought that he might be looking at the day before, by the emblem of the Christ-like Orange Dove which Caspar tells him of, by the disorienting blankness of the surface of the ocean under which his mentor has finally disappeared. At this point, in chapter 27, Roberto conceives his plan to write a Novel in which Lilia, through amazing adventures and reversals, will arrive at the Island of the Day Before, and he will join her there; inevitably, however, that bliss will be threatened from the outset by the serpent Ferrante. It is the point at which, if we can put it this way, Roberto begins to meet himself coming back. Now the narrative follows this lead, despite the objections of the narrator ('the Art of the Romance, though warning us that it is providing fictions, opens a door into the Palace of Absurdity, and when we have lightly stepped inside, slams it shut behind us,' he proclaims in the sententious style of the century: *IDB*, p. 369). Once again, the narrative splits in two, one half continuing to follow Roberto's progress on his ship, the other documenting Ferrante's rape of Lilia. As it nears its end, Roberto enters his own fiction (chapter 39), leaving the narrator to wonder how on earth to end this narrative he has been left with.

The narrative time-structure of *The Island of the Day Before*, as the title might lead us to expect, is both more sophisticated and more disturbing than the simple *film noir* arrangement of *Foucault's Pendulum*, while the relation between the frame and the boxes within it in the most recent novel is antithetical to that same relation in *The*

Name of the Rose. In Eco's first novel, the texts that are lost are in one form or another restored; however different they may be from their irrecoverable and unknowable original, they do in some fashion continue and re-present it, whether it be the second book of Aristotle's *Poetics* or Adso's lost manuscript. In *The Island of the Day Before*, the impossibility of concluding, the tension between the narrator and the narrative he is reporting, the sense of a narrative world spinning out of control, the air of barely manageable delirium engendered by the main character, are all symptomatic of a greater malaise. This is a novel which appears to plunge into an intertextual vortex (as with *The Name of the Rose*, this is a book ostentatiously made of other books, but here the reading is feverish), the novel as genre breaks down before our eyes into its subgenres and progenitors, the Romance, the epistolary novel, cloak-and-dagger à la Dumas, as the protagonist crosses over into his own invention the fiction appears to devour its own tail, and, whatever Roberto's fate between his rotting shipwreck and the island, on this side or that side of the line, the narrative itself is dragged down, is engulfed. Adso found a few charred fragments and reconstructed his own poor copy of a library from them which is the novel that we read. The narrator of *The Island of the Day Before* may be presumed to have come by Roberto's papers somehow (he is vague on the matter), but so indistinct has become the line between fiction and reality in Roberto's mind, and so helpless is his narrator to distinguish any 'truth', that we cannot be sure that we are not swept up in that delirium too.[28] From what position, for Eco, can any future narrative be ventured?

7

Secrets, Paranoia and Critical Reading

During the 1980s Eco conducted a vigorous campaign against what in the Tanner Lectures delivered in Cambridge in 1990 he called 'the syndrome of the secret'. From one perspective, Eco saw this syndrome as affecting whole swathes of social life, activity and belief. From another, his concerns were more specific: he regarded the credit given to hidden meanings, which endlessly resist interpretation, as a failure on the part of philosophy, and particularly on the part of literary philosophy, or theory. Connected therefore with the battle against the syndrome of the secret is the assertion of the 'limits of interpretation', a principle embodied in the titles of the important collection of essays published in both Italian and English (with some variation in content), also in 1990: *I limiti dell'interpretazione* and *The Limits of Interpretation*. This strong notion of the limit will continue into Eco's non-literary writings of the later 1990s.

With *Foucault's Pendulum*, Eco devoted an entire novel to exploring the patterns and ramifications of the syndrome of the secret in its wider social and cultural sense. As a cultural critic and commentator, whose opinions on current affairs were, and are, well known to readers from his regular column for the weekly magazine *L'Espresso*, Eco the novelist has also been read as commenting on the contemporary scene, at least in his first two novels. *The Name of the Rose* was taken to allude to the contest between rebellion and power in the 1960s through its evocation of heresy, ecclesiastical authority and the emergence of new secular forces in the 1320s. *Foucault's Pendulum* seemed more explicit, not least because it is set in the present or near-present, stretching from the late 1960s to the summer of 1984. The novel concerns a trio of intellectuals who are seduced by the sheer far-fetchedness of a plan for world domination supposedly hatched by the medieval Knights Templar and pursued by the initiated through the centuries. The three sorcerer's apprentices begin to elaborate their own version of The Plan until, too late, they discover that they are fatally entangled in the entirely fictitious web which they themselves have spun. Readers had no difficulty in recognizing here the plotting and paranoia of the 1970s, a decade which for many Italians was stretched out between the threat and reality of political violence and a pervasive, not to say invasive, suspicion of conspiracy at all levels of public life: the so-called 'strategy of tension', the alleged complicity of the secret services in terrorist outrages, the ideological miscegenation of the neo-fascist right and the armed left, and the labyrinthine ramifications of the P2 Masonic lodge at the highest levels of the State. People were living the 'syndrome of the secret' every time they opened their newspapers or switched on their television.

For Eco, however, the wide-eyed belief in secrets, which he associates with a disposition to excessive wonder, goes beyond the 1970s' obsession with political conspiracy, an obsession that was by no means confined to Italy. At one level he reads it as a generalized state of mind, a resurgence of irrationalism, a 'return to the Middle Ages'. Quoting Chesterton, he tells assembled publishers at the 1986 Frankfurt Book Fair that '[w]hen men stop believing in God, it isn't that they then believe in nothing: they believe in everything' – this dictum will recur towards the end of *Foucault's Pendulum*.[1] At another, where secrecy is inextricably entangled with interpretation, he sees it reflected in contemporary literary theory, with damaging effects. Eco's disrobing of the 'Followers of the Veil', the practitioners of a hermetic literary criticism, is systematic and impassioned at the same time. This chapter, however, will raise a question about a kind of hermeticism that persists in Eco's own practice, and is implicit in his theory of interpretation.

We can begin from the 1990 lectures mentioned above, and subsequently published by Cambridge University Press in 1992 as *Interpretation and Overinterpretation*.[2] Eco dwells at some length, and very informatively, on the origins of Hermetic thought in the second century AD, its revitalization in Renaissance Neo-Platonism and Christian Cabbalism in the sixteenth century, its complex (and not entirely antagonistic) relation with the birth of modern science, its persistence in the thought of today. Hermeticism, according to

Eco, rests on the rejection of the principle of non-contradiction, the principle that something cannot both be and not be at the same time: Hermes, the presiding deity of Hermetic thought, is volatile and ambiguous, and symbolizes continuous metamorphosis, which is why he is the patron of artists, merchants, thieves and travellers – and interpreters. Rejecting non-contradiction, Hermeticism, conversely, embraces ideas of universal sympathy (the connection between all things) and similarity: ideas, incidentally, which play a significant role in *The Island of the Day Before*, published in Italy in 1994. Universal sympathy emanates from an unknowable One which, however, is the very seat of the principle of contradiction, or metamorphosis. 'As a consequence' (and here I shall quote Eco at some length):

> interpretation is indefinite. The attempt to look for a final, unattainable meaning leads to the acceptance of a never-ending drift or slide of meaning. A plant is not defined on the basis of its morphological or functional *characteristics*, but on the basis of its *resemblance*, albeit only partial, to another element in the cosmos. If it is vaguely *like* part of the human body, then it has meaning because it *refers* to the body. But that body has meaning because it refers to a star [and the latter to a musical scale, and this to a hierarchy of angels, and so on *ad infinitum*]. Every object, be it earthly or heavenly, hides a secret. Every time a secret has been discovered, it will refer to another secret in a progressive movement toward a final secret. [But] there can be no final secret. The ultimate secret of Hermetic initiation is that everything is secret. Hence the Hermetic secret must be an empty one, because anyone who pretends to reveal any sort of secret is not himself initiated and has stopped at a superficial level of the knowledge of cosmic mystery. (*IO*, p. 32; emphases and bracketed words mine)

Eco believes that this kind of hermetic thought is not confined to obscure second-century sects, or to the obsessionals who throng the pages of *Foucault's Pendulum*, or to the fantasy worlds inhabited by Breakfast TV's resident astrologers. He thinks it permeates contemporary thought, specifically literary criticism and theory in many of its post-structuralist guises, and in particular deconstruction, in which, according to Eco, the text is a sort of wonderful playground, where the interpreter can discover infinite connections and 'the glory of the reader is to discover that texts can say everything, except what their author intended them to mean; as soon as a pretended meaning is allegedly discovered, we are sure that it is not the real one' (*IO*, p. 39).

The notion of semiotic drift is one that Eco contests on numerous occasions, and we have already considered one of these, in *The Role of the Reader*, where Eco reflects on the Peircean idea of 'habit' (cf. chapter 5). On the basis of this idea, Eco challenges Derrida's reading of Peirce in the second chapter of *On Grammatology*, intended, according to Eco, 'to legitimize his [Derrida's] attempt to outline a semiosis of infinite play, of difference [*sic*], of the infinite whirl of interpretation' (*LIE*, p. 34; the essay is entitled 'Unlimited Semiosis and Drift'). Eco severs the apparent link between the Peircean notion of unlimited semiosis and the hermeneutic drift proposed by Derrida and other deconstructionists. From Peirce's point of view, Eco argues, every semiosic act is determined by a Dynamic Object, which, in Peirce's words, 'is the Reality which by some means contrives to determine the sign to its Representamen' (*Collected Papers*, 4.536), in other words, '[w]e produce representamens because we are compelled by something external to the circle of semiosis' (*LIE*, p. 38). Thus, when we speak of a complex representamen like a text, we can say that it 'can be interpreted independently of the intention of its utterer, but we cannot deny that any text is uttered by somebody according to his/her actual intention, and this intention was motivated by a Dynamic Object (or was itself the Dynamic Object)' (*LIE*, pp. 38–9). If it is the case that every sign appears to permit a multiplicity of possible textual developments, as soon as it is located within a text, the encyclopedic wealth of its virtual senses is limited by the universe of discourse in which it is inserted. When signs are organized in a text, relationships are established between them which limit their possible expansion; they are in effect subject to laws established by communicative habits which are shared by a given community of interpreters.[3] As Eco puts it in his reply to Rorty in *Interpretation and Overinterpretation*, Peirce 'tried to establish a minimal paradigm of acceptability of an interpretation on the grounds of the consensus of a community', an idea that he thinks is not so far from Gadamer's idea of an 'interpretative community' (*IO*, p. 144). Far from considering every interpretation as misinterpretation, Eco argues repeatedly that, even if it is impossible to say which is the best interpretation of a text, it is possible, on the basis of the rules or habits on which communication within a community is founded, to decide which interpretations are unacceptable. Against the notion of hermetic drift Eco raises the standard of 'the limits of interpretation'.[4]

There is a danger in Eco's argument here of setting up a straw opposition between interpretative restraint presided over by the linguistic community's neighbourhood watch and the kind of anarchic drift attributed to deconstruction – belatedly, according to Mieke Bal, who cites Derrida himself as having already endorsed Eco's plea for a distinction between indeterminacy and (Peircean) infinite regression.[5] There is a danger too, in the good fight against what Eco clearly sees as an attitude of obscurantist mysticism towards the text, of suppressing any sense of mystery about narrative at all. Yet there is a case for arguing, a case which in other contexts Eco will acknowledge, that secrecy, mystery, is the essential ingredient of all narrative: that we read stories, or listen to them, because we want to know what happens next and how it all turns out. Of course, that bald statement must be qualified. Mystery is not the *only* reason we read narrative, it is simply the essential one. Texts continually frustrate the reader's desire to know, but the effect of anticlimax or non-closure cannot be achieved without a corresponding expectation that in some way the mystery *will* be resolved. The term 'mystery' is used here in a way similar to that in which Matei Calinescu, following Barthes, has deployed the term 'enigma', to designate techniques of 'enigmatization' of narrative information and plot construction, 'the manipulation of narrative data to create suspense'.[6] Calinescu makes an operative distinction between enigma and secrets, the latter being elements of content, items that are deliberately hidden by the author of a text (secret signs directed to the faithful reader, secret signs directed to a group of initiates or those ripe for initiation, personal authorial secrets), but allows the distinction to blur in his summary of what is involved in 'a first involved reading of a work of fiction', to which the generic category of secrecy is relevant in two ways:

> First, the text may conceal and disclose information at strategic junctures to create interest in the resolution of a *linear enigma* (the ending is always perceived as important: it is the final disclosure of information, the final word). Second, secrecy is also relevant insofar as the text makes the reader a participant in a situation of imaginary gossip, in which he or she becomes privy to the characters' 'secrets'.[7]

In both of these respects, the necessity of concealment and withholding in narrative, the prolongation of incompletion, are evident conditions of interpretation itself.

The reader, we are told, cannot make a text say anything that she or he wants it to say. *The Name of the Rose* contains abundant information on medieval herbalism as well as much useful advice on how to poison people, but it cannot be read as a treatise on botany, pharmacology or toxicology. More pertinently perhaps, it would be a mistake to read *Foucault's Pendulum* as a set of instructions for the initiated (but if you are not initiated yourself, how do you know?) alluding to the next steps to be taken in the Templar plan for control of the world, when the text is buzzing with signals to the effect that this is a fiction.

But the posing of limits (to interpretation) immediately raises the question of authority. Who, or what, will establish, and then police, the boundaries? What the question means in practice is: who, or what, decides what constitutes a 'good' reading, a good interpretation, as opposed to a bad one? We approach all texts, and perhaps especially narrative texts, in a spirit of inquiry and conjecture, anticipating what is to come on the basis of what has come before, reassessing what we have already read in the light of new information, wondering what is going on when something unexpected occurs, a new character (even more an unexplained one, like Joyce's man in the macintosh) or an allusion whose reference is not obvious (but might be explained later). Eco has described the text as a 'lazy machine' (see above, p. 121) that makes its readers work, and what fuels the reader, and hence the lazy machine, is curiosity, hypothesis, suspicion.

Of course there is good suspicion and bad suspicion. To take an example from a non-fictional source: it was mentioned above that the notion of universal sympathy which Eco attributes to Hermeticism in 1990 plays a significant role in his third novel, *The Island of the Day Before*, which appeared in 1994. Not long after the lecture on Hermeticism appeared in print (1992), Eco wrote the following sentence: '[The story time of] Jules Verne's *Around the World in Eighty Days*, from the time of departure to the time of arrival, lasts eighty days – at least for the members of the Reform Club, waiting in London (for Phileas Fogg, who is travelling eastward, it lasts eighty-one)' (*SWFW*, p. 54). Having read *The Island of the Day Before*, which, as we have seen, is vitally concerned with time-zones and particularly with the slippage of one day on the 180th meridian, now the International Date Line, and furthermore, has characters rather more sinister than the members of the Reform Club anxiously waiting in London for signals from the other side of the world, one might note the connection between universal sympathy, Jules Verne and the new novel and think that, obviously, the themes of the novel were in the author's mind even while he was writing his lectures; and one might even go so far as to wonder, in the reference to Phileas Fogg, whether the preoccupations of the novel had not in some way affected the choice of this particular example or even the phrasing of the sentence. What one cannot do is to assume that by mentioning universal sympathy in 1992 and Phileas Fogg's journey around the world in eighty-*one* days in 1993, Professor Eco is signalling to his global public the themes of his next novel, published in 1994. In that case, what is a good suspicion, or, as Eco might put it, the most 'economical' hypothesis, tips into bad suspicion, amounting quite possibly to the obsessive conviction that *by* mentioning things in 1990 or 1992 or 1993, Eco is sending coded messages to the elect among his readers about what he is going to do in 1994. Nevertheless, the boundary between allowable suspicion and paranoid obsession is not always easy to establish, and the question of who or what authorizes one reading rather than another remains open.

Wherever the authority comes from, Eco reckons, it is not from the author, not the flesh-and-blood author whom he calls the empirical author. The following passage appeared on the dust cover of the first Italian edition of *The Name of the Rose* in 1980. It is presumably written by Eco himself and he elaborated on it subsequently in various places, including the *Reflections on 'The Name of the Rose'*. This is in effect Eco's blurb to his own novel:

> Difficult to define (Gothic novel, medieval chronicle, detective story, ideological narrative *à clé*, allegory), this novel . . . may perhaps be read in three ways. The first category of readers will be taken by the plot and the *coups de scène*, and will accept even the long bookish discussions and the philosophical dialogues, because it will sense that the signs, the traces and the revelatory symptoms are nesting precisely in those inattentive pages. The second category will be impassioned by the debate of ideas, and will attempt to establish connections (which the author refuses to authorize) with the present. The third will realize that this text is a textile of other texts, a 'whodunnit' of quotations, a book built of books. In any case, the author refuses to reveal to any category of readers what the book means. If he had wanted to advance a thesis, he would have written an essay (like so many others that he has written). If he has written a novel, it is because he has discovered, upon reaching maturity, that those things which we cannot theorize about, we must narrate.[8]

We shall return in a moment to the point about theorization and narration, but let us concentrate first on what is implicit rather than spelt out in this statement which Stephens rightly characterizes as a '*défi aux lecteurs*'. Eco is careful to treat his three categories of reader with apparent equity. But it is only apparent. Category 1 is 'taken by' the plot and the exciting bits, the *coups de scène*; the 'impassioned' category 2 is still passive, even though it displays more

intellectual energy, and anyway is 'attempt[ing] to establish connections'; category 3, finally, 'realizes' that there is more to this than
meets the eye: this is a book made of other books, which is what
Adso will learn (quite quickly) about the books in the abbey,
and about the monks' lives too, that they are made up of what they
have read and seen. This incipient hierarchization of the readership
underlines the obvious point that the limitation of interpretation is
not only a logical condition of semiosis in general but that this
condition has a social dimension as well; the social conditions under
which readings are authorized or variously erased, however, are
not so readily seen.

In 1993 Eco was invited to deliver the Charles Eliot Norton
Lectures at Harvard, a series which was then published in 1994
as *Six Walks in the Fictional Woods*. Thirteen years on from *The
Name of the Rose* the notion of a hierarchy of readers has become
more explicit, and as it becomes more explicit, so it becomes
more questionable. Every narrative text is now addressed to model
readers at two levels. The model reader of the first level wants
to know, 'quite rightly' Eco says, how the story ends. The
model reader of the second level is more self-conscious and self-
questioning, wondering what sort of reader that story would like
him or her to become and wanting to discover how the model
author goes about serving as a guide for the reader. 'In order to
know how a story ends, it is usually enough to read it once. In
contrast, to identify the model author the text has to be read
many times, and certain stories endlessly' (*SWFW*, p. 27). This is
the *Finnegans Wake* requirement, frequently cited by Eco, of 'an
ideal reader affected by an ideal insomnia', the demand made by
Joyce of his reader 'that he should devote his whole life to reading
my work'.[9]

There is little to quarrel with here. But then Eco gives an example
which it may be thought unclinches his argument rather than the
opposite. He takes Agatha Christie's *The Murder of Roger Ackroyd*.
'Everyone knows the story,' he states, which is just as well because
he is about to reveal the ending. A narrator, speaking in the first
person, tells how Hercule Poirot gradually comes to discover the
culprit, except that at the end we learn from Poirot that the culprit
is the narrator, who cannot deny his guilt. But while he is waiting to
be arrested and is about to commit suicide, the narrator turns directly to his readers and invites them to read the book again from
the beginning because, he states, if they had been perceptive, they
would have realized that he had never lied.

Eco takes this as a blueprint for second-level reading. In other words, the real reader will translate the narrator's instructions to the model reader and set off on a rereading to see for herself or himself how the author worked her enigma. But it is at least arguable that this translation from the model reader to the empirical reader is superfluous. It is enough for the real reader to be aware of the model that is being proposed without having to reproduce it. Indeed, one might go further and, appealing to empirical (and impassioned) experience, suggest that the last thing the actual reader wants to do at the moment of revelation is reread the novel; certainly he or she re-views it, a very rapid process of assimilation takes place and the new information is absorbed, with the help of the rereading carried out in the text by the narrator himself; and as the narrator-murderer does *his* rereading of his own text, the empirical reader becomes more and more aware of the culprit's narcissism, which proves to be another element in the climax/anticlimax of this great book. The conclusion is that in order to achieve a reading of *Ackroyd* that goes well beyond the simple question 'whodunnit?' one does not have to posit a second level of reading; in fact, the hypothetical second level adds nothing to the first level *except* that it enables readers to detach themselves from the position of reader and from that of the narrator, and establish themselves instead in the position of author. Indeed, it may be argued that what Eco is inviting the reader to do is to play at being author, taking up the position of model author in the text, with the actual author ultimately remaining in control or, even, absent, paring his fingernails.

If there is any truth in these observations, they give rise to several reflections which have to do with secrets in general, with hierarchies of readers and reading, and with the particular kind of reader and the particular kind of text which Eco appears to have in mind. The first is simply that any description of interpretation which draws on the idea of grades or levels of access, which involves metaphors of gateways, doors, an outside and an inside, partakes in some measure of the 'syndrome of the secret'. It was an earlier Norton lecturer, Frank Kermode, who had based his series entitled *The Genesis of Secrecy* (published in 1979) on these words in Mark's Gospel, themselves open to dispute and reinterpretation:

> To you has been given the secret of the kingdom of God, but for those outside everything is in parables [but the Hebrew which is translated with the Greek *parabolē* may also connote 'riddles']; so that they may

indeed see but not perceive, and may indeed hear but not understand; lest they should turn again, and be forgiven. (4: 11–12)

The rhythm if not the precise terms of the Evangelist's text is echoed in Eco's presentation of his first novel. See but not perceive; hear but not understand; be taken by but not realize; want to know how it ends but not wonder what sort of reader the story would like me to become: the repeated pattern of initiation and exclusion is what strikes the reader of Eco's words.

But why? It is a matter of common sense that some readers are 'better' than others, and likewise some readings, better informed, more insightful, richer and more rewarding. Eco, however, tends, at least for the sake of theoretical argument, to establish a binary division between two levels or kinds of reading, and this dualism merits further consideration. He describes it in various ways during the 1980s. For example, in a paper on the consumption of literature first delivered in 1983, he tells us that every work has in mind at least two different kinds of reader: 'The first is the predestined victim of the strategies of utterance which the work puts in place, the second is the critical reader who takes pleasure in the way in which he has been made into the predestined victim' (*SS*, p. 106).[10] The same idea appears in the essay on 'Interpreting Serials' in *The Limits of Interpretation*, but in softer focus:

> Once again we must remember that every text presupposes and con-
> structs always a double Model Reader – a naive and a 'smart' one, a
> semantic reader and a semiotic or critical reader. The former uses the
> work as semantic machinery and is the victim of the strategies of the
> author who will lead him little by little along a series of previsions and
> expectations. The latter evaluates the work as an aesthetic product and
> enjoys the strategies implemented in order to produce a Model Reader of
> the first level. (*LIE*, p. 92)

What is meant by 'semantic' and 'semiotic' in this context is explained in '*Intentio Lectoris*: The State of the Art'.

> Semantic interpretation is the result of the process by which an
> addressee, facing a Linear Text Manifestation, fills it up with a given
> meaning . . . [T]his type of interpretation . . . is a natural semiosic pheno-
> menon. Critical interpretation is, on the contrary, a metalinguistic activ-
> ity – a semiotic approach – which aims at describing and explaining for
> which formal reasons a given text produces a given response (and in this
> sense it can also assume the form of an aesthetic analysis). (*LIE*, p. 54)

With these two different 'levels of reading' which correspond to two different 'kinds of reader', reading (or interpretation) is either the co-operative work required of the reader in order to make the textual machine work, or it is a higher-level activity bringing other codes to bear on the text, for example reading *Il nome della rosa* as an anti-detective novel rather than as a straightforward mystery story. Readers are either 'naïve' (they co-operate in the way that the author, or text, wants them to without thinking twice about it, and so they simply enable the text to do its job) or they are 'critical', which means they not only perform as naïve readers, but are aware of the games which the author/text is playing and appreciate the work at that level too.

Three objections might be levelled against this characterization of reading and readers. Firstly, despite the pre-eminence given to the reader in the theory, the reader remains essentially passive: if and when her or his critical faculties come into play, their role is to recognize and to admire the skill of the author. The Eco of *Lector in fabula*, where these propositions first take shape, is about to become an author of fiction himself, but the foregrounding of the role of the author, against all reasonable expectation, is not due to narcissism on his part: it is inherent to the theory, which sees the work of reading and interpretation as a kind of pact between author and reader, more precisely model author and model reader, mediated by the (actual) text, a 'co-operation' precisely. Anything else that impinges on the reading of a text is not 'interpretation' but 'use'.

This leads into the second objection. Eco foresees only one position of the (model) reader vis-à-vis the (model) author: that of enjoyment of the skill deployed (or, presumably, frustration at its absence). He thereby excludes most of the responses which actual readers, including critical ones, commonly refer to when describing their enjoyment, but also their critical understanding, of a fiction: its capacity to 'enlarge' or to 'enrich' the reader's experience, for example, or the fact that empirical readers, far from being lost in admiration of the writer's skill, are more likely to enact it in more sophisticated ways, for example, by re-imagining a scene or character or by, in a sense, pretending to be the author. Except for the latter, which might in certain respects come within Eco's profile of the author–reader relation, all the rest is likely to be ascribed to 'use' (psychological, emotional, conceptual or ideological). Pragmatists like Richard Rorty prefer not to make the distinction between using and interpreting texts on the grounds that 'all anybody ever does with something is use it' (Rorty in *IO*, p. 93). Rorty's resistance to interpretation puts one in mind of an earlier American contribution to this debate, Susan Sontag's famous essay of 1964 'Against

Interpretation', even though she is arguing from a quite different position. According to Rorty, 'the notion that there is something a given text is *really* about . . . is as bad as the Aristotelian idea that there is something which a substance really, intrinsically, *is*' (*IO*, p. 102), while Sontag believes interpretation is what blocks our access to the sensuous, formal, qualities of the work, and as far as she is concerned Aristotle is a pragmatist, for whom art serves a useful medicinal function. We should not worry about the levels of meaning in *Last Year at Marienbad*, she says, 'what matters . . . is the pure, untranslatable, sensuous immediacy of some of its images'.[11] The pleasure of the immediate, unenlightened by an understanding of its modus operandi, is for Eco a form of use, something that he spells out in reply to Rorty in *Interpretation and Overinterpretation* when talking about one of his favourite texts, Nerval's *Sylvie*, about which he had first written in 1961 and which was to form a centre-piece of his Harvard lectures: 'I was not satisfied by the pleasure I experienced as an enthralled reader,' he writes; 'I also wanted to experience the pleasure of understanding how the text was creating the fog effect I was enjoying' (*IO*, p. 147).[12] Untranslatable immediacy is something which Eco profoundly distrusts. But with the rejection of 'immediacy' goes the rejection of much else besides, and behind it, one suspects, lies the one blind spot of Eco's cultural baggage, Romanticism. What the theory cannot allow is any central role to the Romantic and late-Romantic notions of 'feeling', 'intuition', the imagination, or the unconscious. They exist of course, but outside the circle of (model) author–text–(model) reader, in the shadow-lands of empirical use.

Finally, one might object to the implication that Eco's reader appears to be either 'naïve' or 'critical', or first one and then the other, while most readers are probably both in some degree at any one time, and that is, not only 'naïve' as well as 'critical', but also 'critical' as well as 'naïve'. One way in which this might happen is suggested by Calinescu when he observes that 'reading and reread-ing often go together'. Calinescu's 'rereading' is akin to Eco's 'criti-cal reading', but he notes that

> under certain circumstances the first reading of a work can in fact be a *double* reading; that is to say, it can adopt, alongside the prospective logic of reading, a retrospective logic of rereading. Such a double reading consists, naturally, of the sequential temporal movement of the reader's mind (attention, memory, hypothetical anticipation, curiosity, involve-ment) along the horizontal or syntagmatic axis of the work; but it also consists of the reader's attempt to 'construct' . . . the text under perusal,

or to perceive it as a 'construction' with certain clearly distinguishable structural properties.[13]

Here 'construction' refers not to the (re)construction of the world of the fiction (cf. chapter 6), but insight into the means whereby the text works its effects. Such switching between the two planes probably occurs more commonly than Calinescu suggests, but it may be that Eco tends to prefer the binary division between 'naïve' and 'critical' because the kind of text that he has in mind, or more precisely the approach to texts which is implicit in his writing, is effectively didactic: a text will reveal itself to those who have eyes to see and ears to hear, and those eyes and ears require training. 'Didactic' does not mean here the drumming home of a moral or political message, nor does it imply a particularly professorial approach to story-telling, nor does it solely express that sense which the reader of Eco *on* fiction sometimes has, that the theory of reading is strongly marked by the experience of reading in class, with a group of students. What it does suggest is that the text will yield more the more the reader brings to it of his or her own knowledge and experience, and knowledge and experience are variable things, affected by time, circumstance and native wit. On one of the rare occasions on which Eco is drawn to muse on a possible social function of fiction, he speaks of it, perhaps not surprisingly, as a kind of learning: 'Fiction has the same function that games have. In playing, children learn to live, because they simulate situations in which they may find themselves as adults. And it is through fiction that we adults train our ability to structure our past and present experience' (*SWFW*, p. 131). But learning, by definition, does not come all at once: it implies at least the crossing of a threshold, the line which for Eco separates the critical from the naïve.

The insistence on this threshold may betray a mild hermetic temptation on Eco's own part; at any rate, there is a case for arguing, as suggested above in the instance of *The Murder of Richard Ackroyd*, that the first level of reading is richer, fuller and more extensive than Eco allows for, and for defending that first level in its fullness. Eco clearly wants to get us off the first level as quickly as possible, and it is possible that, whatever other merits it might have, this is an enlightening way to approach Eco's own novels. What cannot be theorized must be narrated, we remember, but the narration itself may perhaps be theorized. In order to explore the possibilities, and problems, of reading Eco with Eco, and at the same time to point to a second hermetic temptation, we might take a passage from *The Island of the Day Before*. By this stage of the novel, the hero, Roberto de la Grive, shipwrecked on the 180th meridian in the year 1643, is dying, hallucinating, shaping the events of his life into that novel of his own in which his evil other half, his fictitious half-brother Ferrante, will meet his just deserts in hell. Here is Ferrante arriving, in chapter 38, pp. 488–90:

> Where the plain began to rise, Ferrante could make out a little band of men, and he moved towards them.
>
> Men – or, in any case, human beings – they seemed from the distance, but as Ferrante reached them, he saw that if they had once been human, now they had become, or were on the way to becoming, exhibits for an anatomy theater. . . .
>
> An anatomist-God had, in a different way, touched these inhabitants of the island, whom Ferrante was now seeing closer and closer.
>
> The first was a body without skin, the ropes of muscle taut, the arms in a gesture of abandonment, the suffering face turned heavenwards, all skull and cheekbones. The hands of the second had flayed skin hanging from its fingertips, barely attached, like a glove, and the skin of the legs was rolled up to the knee like a supple boot.
>
> On the next, first the skin, then the muscles had been so splayed that the whole body, especially the face, seemed an open book. As if to show skin, flesh, and bones at the same time, thrice human and thrice mortal. It seemed an insect, of which those tatters would have been the wings if there had been on that island a wind to stir them. But these wings did not move by any impulse of the air, stagnant in that twilight; they barely shifted at the movements of the body, akimbo.
>
> Nearby, a skeleton was leaning on a spade, perhaps to dig its grave, its eyesockets peering at the sky, a grimace on the crooked arc of the teeth, the left hand held out as if to beg for compassion and a hearing. Another skeleton, bent forward, proferred the curved back of its spine, walking in jerks, bony hands over a lowered face. . . .
>
> The last of them, excoriated like a Saint Bartholomew, held up in his right hand his still-bleeding skin limp as an unused cape. It was possible yet to recognize a face there, with the holes of the eyes and nostrils and the cavern of the mouth, which seemed the ultimate melting of a wax mask, dripping, exposed to sudden heat.
>
> And that man (or rather, the toothless and deformed mouth of his skin) spoke to Ferrante.
>
> 'Ill-come,' he said to him, 'to the Land of the Dead, which we call Insula Vesalia. Soon you too will follow our fate.'

Now, faced with this passage, one might suppose that an Echian first-level reader should sit back and enjoy, as it were, the juicy bits, the *coups de scène*. In fact, it is difficult to do that, because of the way that Roberto is foregrounded as the author of this fantasy, so acting as intermediary between the reader and the scene described. So let us assume that we jump immediately to the second level, or third category, armed in the knowledge that Umberto Eco's books are 'book[s] built of books', and other cultural artefacts. 'Hell' in the Italian context of the narration suggests the *Divine Comedy*, even if precise, line-for-line references do not come immediately to the reader's mind. What matters at this stage is a general effect. That opening sentence seems vaguely to recall the shores of Mount Purgatory, and the *Inferno* surely has its share of gutted, flayed and variously mutilated sinners. Visual images come to mind: the description of the St Bartholomew lookalike towards the end seems to have something of Michelangelo's empty skin in the Sistine Chapel; and the anatomy theatre: are we looking at the wonderfully preserved seventeenth-century theatre at Bologna, or at a painting of the Anatomy Lesson, or both? This is an elementary use of the encyclopedia, that store of cultural knowledge to which we refer all the time to make sense of the world, and of texts. But as with all encyclopedias, it helps if you have something to look up. Proper names are amongst the most obvious keywords, so it is tempting to think that we might find something if we look into the name of this hell, 'Insula Vesalia'.

Anatomists and bibliophiles amongst Eco's readers will have made the connection straight away. The allusion is to the seven books of Andreas Vesalius on the structure of the human body, *De humani corporis fabrica libri septem*, published in Basle in 1543, a pioneering anatomical treatise illustrated with numerous plates allegedly from the studio of Titian. Each one of the grotesques in the passage above, and those in the paragraphs omitted, is a transcription of one of these plates: a transcription in the sense of being a verbal rendering of the image that is there represented visually (with purely anatomical, not moral, intent).[14] I hope that at this point it might be legitimate to draw on my own experience of deciphering this passage in order to arrive at the more general conclusions which follow. Five brief observations:

1   The fact that I as an individual reader made a connection between Eco's Vesalia and the sixteenth-century anatomist Vesalius came about by pure chance, because the name Vesalius, if I had ever seen it, had meant nothing to me until I happened to come across it shortly after reading Eco's novel.
2   By good fortune I had an excellent library to hand, which possessed a copy of the 1543 edition of Vesalius, so I could

go and verify my hypothesis of a connection between the two.

3   When I saw that the hypothesis was correct, and I could read off Eco's text against Vesalius's plates, I felt considerable, if not inordinate, satisfaction.

4   Did the sight of Vesalius's plates add anything to the reading of Eco's text? It did: it not only multiplied the impact of the images, but it seemed to authenticate Roberto's imagination by locating it historically; it seemed, so to speak, to fill out the picture created by the 'linear text manifestation'.

5   In which case, I had to ask myself, what about the boundless tracts of Eco's text for which I had not serendipitously found a source or reference? The initiate's brief glory is spent; he is once more outside the gate, a mere first-level reader.

We appear to be coming to a point in our argument where we are saying that Eco's model reader must have access to an encyclopedia as large as Eco's own (but the copy will always fall short of the original), or at any rate to a commentary which will fill out the whole text in the way one reader's adventure with Vesalius filled out one page. If the suggestion is that novels like Eco's must follow the path trodden by secular bibles like the *Divine Comedy* or Manzoni's classic novel *The Betrothed* (1827), inflicted on generations of Italian schoolchildren, in which a small pocket of text is embedded in a sprawling undergrowth of close-printed comment, the prospect does not appeal. But it is worth lingering a moment. The relation between text and commentary is a complex one, and incidentally illustrates well the paradox of the distinction between open and closed works. The text – let us say Dante's poem or Eco's novel – is that which seems open, capable of multiple, perhaps infinite interpretations. The function of the commentary is to de-limit, mark off, say what is relevant and what is not. But a commentary can take on a life of its own; anyone who has read into the commentaries on Dante's *Divine Comedy* will know that they are a mine of more or less useless information which are difficult to resist mining. In fact, it was by reconstructing the esoteric readings of Dante practised by Gabriele Rossetti and others in the first half of the nineteenth century that Eco produced his most convincing and intriguing example of blatant overinterpretation.[15] But if the reader follows the commentary's leads beyond a certain point she or he must realize that one is leaving the text and entering other territory. The text, however, will always pull the reader back to itself; the commentary can, potentially, go anywhere, the text no. In this sense one might agree with Eco about the limits of interpretation, and paradoxically the commentary can help, because by setting the text in the context of the information that can be generated from and around it, it highlights the relative permanence, autonomy and continuity of the text. If semiotic drift occurs, it is in the commentary, not in the text, taking now as 'commentary' all that has been and might be said about a text.

8

Kant, the Platypus and the Horizon

With this last chapter, we return to the more purely 'semiotic' Eco of *La struttura assente*, *A Theory of Semiotics* and *Semiotics and the Philosophy of Language*, as seen through his most recent theoretical work, *Kant e l'ornitorinco*, published in Italy in 1997. The purpose of this brief analysis is to give some idea of what the book is about, to locate it in relation to Eco's previous work, and to point out what appear to be important developments in it.

Kant and the Platypus (to give it a provisional English title) is in part a revisiting and a revision of *A Theory of Semiotics*; in particular, it addresses head-on some of the doubts about the earlier work which have been discussed here in chapter 5. This is an aspect which Eco himself has stressed both in the Introduction to his book and in interviews with the press. History seems to repeat itself here: as *A Theory of Semiotics* had grown out of a 'failed' attempt to translate *La struttura assente*, so *Kant* is the product of a 'failure' to rewrite *Theory*, or the objective impossibility of doing so.

Eco presents the stance of the new book as a change of focus or perspective, which he explains in Peircean terms. In the first of the two major sections of *A Theory of Semiotics*, the part concerned with a theory of codes, he had started from this problem: if there is a Dynamical Object, we know it only through an Immediate Object.[1] With our manipulating of signs we refer to the Dynamical Object as the *terminus ad quem* of semiosis. In the other major section, on sign production, he had assumed, even if it had not been spelt out, that if we speak, or emit signs of any sort, it is because there is something (or Something) which impels us to speak,[2] whence the question addressed in this book of the Dynamical Object as *terminus a quo*. From this point of view, if he were systematically to rewrite the *Theory*, he would put the section on sign production first; instead, the reminder of the 'something' that is there before we produce signs serves also to put into perspective the work which followed *A Theory of Semiotics*. In fact, Eco tells us, his having put the Dynamical Object as *terminus ad quem* determined his later focus on semiosis as a sequence of interpretants, the latter being understood as a collective, public, observable product, which are deposited in the course of cultural processes, even if one does not presume a mind which receives, uses and develops them. This in turn gave rise to his writing on the problem of meaning, the text and intertextuality, narrativity, interpretation and its limits (cf. *KO*, p. xi). But *tout se tient*, as he indicated in an interview with Domenico Pacitti, echoing a sentiment already expressed in his Introduction: 'while it is true that a text is open to infinity in respect of possible interpretations, it is also true that certain things simply cannot be said. *Kant and the Platypus* is the transposition of this problem from texts to reality'.[3]

Kant and the Platypus is a recognition and exploration of the material bases of signification,[4] and at the same time a return to the theme of limits which allows the philosopher no repose. It is informed by huge reading in the areas of the cognitive sciences and the philosophy of perception and, once again, defines itself as a work-in-progress, not without self-doubt: its constituent essays are written 'under the banner of indecision and numerous perplexities' (*KO*, p. x). The themes and problems of perception had never of course been far from Eco's mind even at the time of *A Theory of Semiotics*, but the emphasis was a 'culturalist' one, the focus being on how meaning is codified, agreed and transmitted within a community. Now Eco is prepared to journey below that 'lower threshold' of semiotics which had been so much questioned by some early readers of the *Theory*. He adopts, for example, a much more nuanced position on the question of iconism (*KO*, chapter 6). While not reneging his culturalist past, he is prepared to put it into historical perspective, and to explore the area which joins rather than separates the natural object in itself and its cultural representation. The outline which you draw on a sheet of paper to produce the figure of a horse, for example – and which is precisely the feature which the natural horse does not have – is no longer seen from that point of view which stresses the conventionality of the representation, but in relation to our perception of the natural horse, the way in which the drawn outline reproduces a visual stimulus in nature.

Eco is in effect conceding that it does reproduce some conditions of the perception of the object, which had previously been denied on the grounds that any such conditions had already been selected on the basis of given recognition codes.[5] Another important issue 'left over' from *A Theory of Semiotics* concerns the subject, and here too Eco confesses to a certain embarrassment while rehearsing and in a sense confirming the historical reasons for the particular emphases of his earlier work. In an important note he restates that in the *Theory*, and in the phase which the semiotic discussion had reached at that point,

> it seemed important to underline the social and cultural nature of sign systems. The effort to find a definition of content in terms of interpretants, all of them publically exhibited by the 'public' repertoire of the encyclopedia, aimed to rescue the problem of meaning from the shoals of mentalism, or at least of a recourse to the subject which at the time was identified (dangerously, in my view) with the unconscious.

The problem which was put to one side at that time was deciding whether the inferential labour required to understand something was to be studied by the psychology of perception and cognition as something that was preliminary but not central to semiotics, or whether intelligence and signification were not a single process and a single subject of inquiry as required by the phenomenological tradition by which Eco was influenced (in *Opera aperta*, as has been indicated in chapter 1 of this book). By considering the Dynamical Object as a *terminus a quo*, as what is before semiosis and as the starting point for forming perceptual judgements, it becomes possible to move the problem of perceptual semiosis to the forefront of inquiry (*KO*, pp. 395–6).

The heart of this collection of essays is concerned with perception and cognition, the schemata of Kant (hence one half of the title) and what happens when, confronted by an unknown object (like the duck-billed platypus which racked the brains of the zoologists at the end of the eighteenth century, whence the other half of the title), before the chain of interpretants is formed, a process of interpretation of the world begins which takes on an 'auroral' air, a process of trial and error which is already semiosis in action, throwing preestablished cultural systems into question (*KO*, p. xi). It is also a rereading of, and through, Peirce. Chapter 2 having introduced both Kant and the platypus (and Peirce's reading of Kant), chapter 3 elaborates a theory of 'Cognitive Types' (here horses return, this time the horses of the conquistadores seen for the very first time by the Aztecs): the Cognitive Type, like Kant's schema, is not just a kind of multimedia image, but a rule or procedure for constructing the image of the horse; it is that which permits recognition of other examples of the same type, even though they may differ in important details from the first examples ever seen (*KO*, p. 110). Alongside the 'private' dimension of the Cognitive Type (private in the sense that it cannot be seen or touched, it can only be postulated on the basis of phenomena of recognition, identification and successful reference), there is the 'public' dimension of what Eco calls the 'Nuclear Content', which is the sum of the interpretants and represents the way in which we try to determine inter-subjectively the elements which make up a Cognitive Type (*KO*, p. 116).

Chapter 4 brings the platypus back on the scene, and has it, or rather its taxonomists, veering 'between dictionary and encyclopedia' as it tells the story of the attempts, which continued surprisingly late into the nineteenth century, to classify the new creature in view of the many 'contradictory' features observed about it which cut across existing zoological categories. The story, certainly, is one of a negotiation, and one thing we learn from it is that in the process of categorizing we are looking out for new properties (in the form of an 'untidy encyclopedia', as Eco puts it) and that the discovery of properties makes us look again at the categories that we started off with, but that at the same time our hypotheses on what categories to adopt at any one moment have an impact on what observations can be made and what statements about them are valid: in this particular case, 'those who think the platypus is a mammal do not look for eggs or refuse to recognize them as such when they appear, while those who think of the platypus as an oviparian try to ignore its breasts and its milk' (*KO*, p. 215). This is the dialectic of cognition and knowledge, but, as Eco points out, the negotiation is based on something: all those who disagreed so vehemently over whether the platypus was or was not a mammal did agree that it seemed to be like a beaver or a duck or a mole, not a cat, an elephant or an ostrich. The story of the platypus also tells us something else: that the structuralist perspective of Hjemslev (which shows us that our semantic and conceptual competence are categorial in nature, being based on a segmentation of the continuum which enables us to perceive the form of the content in terms of opposition and difference) and the cognitive-interpretative perspective of Peirce (which dissolves rigid structural organizations into the network of encyclopedic properties strung out along the potentially infinite line of unlimited semiosis), though they might seem incompatible, and though their coexistence cheek-by-jowl in *A Theory of Semiotics* might, so Eco fears, appear to be a case of syncretism, are in fact equally necessary. Neither approach on its own does justice to our way of knowing and expressing what we know, for 'in the process of knowledge the structural moment and the interpretative moment alternate with and complete each other at every step' (*KO*, p. 219). Pursuing these themes of negotiation, dialectic, alternation, which in fact recur in different guises throughout the various essays which make up this book, chapter 5 is devoted to outlining a cognitive semantics

> based on a *contractual* notion both of our cognitive schemata and of meaning and reference. . . . By doing this, I am trying to temper an eminently 'cultural' view of semiosic processes with the fact that, however great the weight of our cultural systems might be, there is something in the continuum of experience which sets limits to our interpretations.

On the basis of this tempering he would wish to propose an approach that he calls 'contractual realism' (*KO*, p. xii).

These central chapters, including the sixth on iconism, place themselves in the thick of a debate about meaning and perception to which Eco's earlier writings, drafted at a different stage in the evolution of semiotics, had already made a formidable contribution. In the density of their argument, and the thoroughness and precision with which they engage the work of many other thinkers, they resist easy or rapid summary. Rather, they expect that continuing dialogue with specialists of different disciplines, and with non-specialists to whom questions of meaning and cognition, perception and communication matter, which has been a hallmark of Eco's semiotic, and, more broadly, philosophical work. But there is one point in this book at which Eco seems to stand back from the detail of the scientific argument and to speak to an even wider audience, and this is in the opening essay entitled simply 'On Being'. His theme, once again, is the limit.

A Dynamical Object (seen as a *terminus a quo*) impels us to produce a representamen, something makes us speak: 'We produce signs because there is something which needs to be said' (*KO*, p. 5). There is a pre- or protosemiotic phenomenon which Eco calls 'primary indicality or attentionality'. Perhaps we might say 'attentiveness': Peirce wrote about 'attention', the ability to direct the mind towards an object, to pay attention to one element and ignore another. Eco here is talking about our paying attention to something in the mass of sensations by which we are bombarded and *only then* deciding to speak about it. There is a pre-semiotic drawing or catching of attention. It is not our attention which defines the something, it is the something which awakens our attention; we call this something Being (*KO*, p. 6).

Why is there something rather than nothing, being rather than non-being? Because there is: *Perché sì*.[6] The first thing that our intellect conceives is that there is something; all the rest comes after. Being is icastic, 'evidenza' (*KO*, p. 10); the question of the existence of God is subsequent to this 'evidence' of being. Being is before we speak of it. But we can only transform it from 'irrepressible evidence' into a question, seeking an answer, by speaking of it; ecstasy gives way to philosophy. Aristotle said that being is spoken of in many different ways (in chapter 5 of this book we have seen how Eco made strategic use of this dictum when writing of the sign): 'At the moment that it appears before us, being arouses interpretation; at the moment that we can speak of it it has already been interpreted. There is nothing to be done' (*KO*, p. 12).

Not only is being perceived as an effect of language, but language cannot define it. Eco explores this aporia in Aristotle, in Heidegger, in poetic discourse, and finally in Nietzsche, Vattimo, deconstruction and weak thought. If being can be spoken of in many ways, are all perspectives equally valid? Does anything go? Given that everything is already interpretation, are there limits to the interpretation, not only of texts, but also of reality? Does being have a 'hard core', not in the sense of an irreducible centre which you might reach at the end having nibbled away the rest, but in that of something that resists?

The 'resistance' of being is the strong concluding idea of this essay. Being sets limits to the discourse through which we establish ourselves in its horizon: this is not a negation of hermeneutic activity, but its condition. Following Heidegger, the question of being is posed only to him who is thrown into Being-Here. In our *Dasein* we have the fundamental experience of a limit, that of death, which language can speak in advance, can foretell, in only one way, and which then fades into silence. 'Since we speak of being knowing that there is at least one limit, we can only continue asking to see if, by chance, there are others as well' (*KO*, p. 37). If we do find such limits in the natural world, as we do,[7] it is not just that our language is too poor to do justice to the whole expanse of being, but that there is a 'resistance' there which induces us to invent general terms. Eco imagines these 'lines of resistance' as being like the grain of wood or marble, which invites us to cut in a certain way and resists us if we try not to: 'To say that there are lines of resistance only means that, even if being appears to be an effect of language, it is not so in the sense of language freely constructing it' (*KO*, p. 40). Finally, Eco seeks to put these limits in a positive light: if we are conscious of the limits of being, it is because we aspire to absolute freedom – and again there is a reference to Pareyson's late work, in a comment which, however, ends on a darker note:

> The problem is that it is not the case that if God did not exist then everything would be possible. Even before God, being comes towards us saying certain 'Noes', which is none other than the affirmation that there are certain things that we as human beings cannot say. We experience as Resistance this deep and hidden caution which exposes our every inquiry after truth and our every claim to freedom to continual risk, including the risk of evil. (*KO*, p. 391)

There is one metaphor in this essay, familiar from the philosophical literature on the topic, but which by dint of repetition, and of the careful composition of the piece, seems to acquire a particular resonance. It is that of the horizon. Being is conceived as the horizon in which our thought naturally moves, but the experience of being is implicit in the first cry of the new-born child as if to acknowledge the something which presents itself to it as a horizon; it is that to which we reach out (*protendersi*). Eco writes of the horizon of being and of the beings (*enti*) which we name, of that which imposes itself on our vision (*evidenza*), of the horizon which is the limit of 'being-for-death', of one that is ambiguous, of the infinite horizon of what is, has been and will be. The limit, the something, the horizon – the meanings often overlap, but of the three the most suggestive is the last.

If we now look back some twenty-five years, to when Eco was writing *A Theory of Semiotics*, we may surmise that the sea held few attractions for its author, who declares:

> I would put the matter this way: the object of semiotics may somewhat resemble (i) either the surface of the sea, where, independently of the continuous movement of water molecules and the interplay of submarine streams, there is a sort of average resulting form which is called the Sea, (ii) or a carefully ordered landscape, where human intervention continuously changes the form of settlements, dwellings, plantations, canals and so on. (*TSE*, p. 29)

The alternative puts the reader in mind of Walter Benjamin's famous distinction between the story-teller as resident tiller of the soil, who knows the local tales, and the story-teller as trading sea-man, who has brought his tales back from afar.[8] There is no am-biguity about where Eco stands in 1975: 'If one accepts the second hypothesis,' he continues, 'which constitutes the epistemological assumption underlying this book, one must also accept another condition of the semiotic approach which will not be like exploring the sea, where a ship's wake disappears as soon as it has passed, but more like exploring a forest where cart-trails or footprints modify the explored landscape' (ibid.). Since then Eco has always been a cultivator of the landscape and an explorer of woods; here too, in *Kant e l'ornitorinco*, fresh from his 'six walks in the fictional woods', the author presents himself as a gardener tidying the beds joined by beaten paths (not trying to design Versailles again), even though he might suspect that 'all around there still stretches a Romantic park in the English style' (*KO*, p. xii).

Nevertheless, that landlubber has in the meantime also written a novel about the sea, where the true limit is not the land lying just a mile away above the surface, or the coral reef just below it, but, in a temporal sense, the invisible line which divides one day from another and, spatially, the sea itself, where no direction is discern-ible (of Father Caspar there is no sign, whether of his point of arrival relative to his point of departure, or of his position in the depths relative to any point on the surface); a shapeless, trackless, sea which yet cannot be disjoined from its horizon. 'Now, antipodal spectator of the infinite expanse of an ocean, he saw a boundless horizon rise. And above his head he observed constellations never seen before' (*IDB*, pp. 510–11). This new-found horizon is quite different from the familiar, contained one of Roberto's childhood home, modelled in his eyes on the dome of the family chapel. Here the sky is vertiginous, like the cupola of a church he had once seen in Rome, where '[w]herever you stood under that cupola, when you looked up, you felt always at the edge' (*IDB*, p. 512). Eco, in his farewell to the Harvard audience at the end of *Six Walks in the Fictional Woods*, describes yet another extraordinary sky, one that had been designed specially for him: the reconstruction in the plan-etarium at La Coruña of the night-sky, in accelerated time, as it had appeared over Alessandria on the night of his birth. 'You will for-give me,' he enjoins his audience, 'if during those fifteen minutes I had the impression that I was the only man, since the dawn of time, who had ever had the privilege of being reunited with his own beginning' (*SWFW*, p. 140). His most recent writings enrich our vision of Umberto Eco. As always, he is the extraordinarily gifted, yet skilled and patient tiller of the soil, a master designer of rich and complex landscapes. But now there is also something in him of the voyager, inviting us to rediscover other dimensions in these tableaux of sea and night sky, and that ever-present horizon by which we are contained, to which we reach out.

Notes

Chapter 1 Form, Interpretation and the Open Work

1 B. Croce, *Breviario di estetica*, p. 15.
2 *KO*: For the abbreviations used to refer to Eco's works, see section A of the Select Bibliography. Eco's article, 'Croce, l'intuizione e il guazzabuglio', was first published in *La Rivista dei libri* in October 1991. There is a temptation to see Eco as a latter-day, Northern, version of Croce: see, for example, F. Cordelli, 'Per una umbertoecologia'. Such comparisons are superficially attractive; they boil down, however, to little more than saying that both thinkers have been enormously influential, while ignoring the great differences in the content of that influence and in the means by which it has been transmitted.
3 Eco 1957a, review of R. Wellek and A. Warren, *Teoria della letteratura*, p. 134.
4 L. Pareyson, *Estetica*, p. 7.
5 Ibid., p. 9.
6 See, for example, D. Robey, 'Introduction', pp. xxiff.
7 G. Bedani notes that the characteristic feature of what Croce called his 'crushing victory' over positivism 'was that in refusing to grant his opponents the status of interlocutors it closed discussion and left the shattered remains to be reassembled by later generations': 'Art, Poetry and Science', p. 110.
8 Notably Eco 1954, review of Bayer's *Essais sur la méthode en esthétique*, Eco 1957b, review of his *Traité d'esthétique*, and the review-essay 'L'estetica di Bayer: la cosa e il linguaggio' (1960), the last of these then in *DA*, pp. 79–101.
9 The formula will return in a new guise, to designate the novel as 'a machine for generating interpretations', in *PNR*, p. 7/*RNR*, p. 2.
10 'Poetic' in Eco's understanding of the term, and as is common in Italian aesthetics and criticism, is not the purely objective study of the linguistic structures of a literary work, intrinsically considered, as it was for the Russian Formalists, the Prague structuralists and their latter-day descendants (cf. Introduction to second edition, *OA*, pp. 17–18). It always carries a

charge of 'intentionality'. Where that intentionality is located is an issue to which Eco will return in the 1980s, but here it can for convenience be regarded as belonging primarily to the author.

11 The 'core' essays in *Opera aperta*, with their dates of original publication, usually under different titles, are: 'La poetica dell'opera aperta' (1959; in *OW* as 'The Poetics of the Open Work', and previously in *RR* with the same title); 'Analisi del linguaggio poetico' (1961; in *OW* as 'Analysis of Poetic Language'); 'Apertura, informazione, comunicazione' (1960; in *OW* as 'Openness, Information, Communication'); 'L'opera aperta nelle arti visive' (1961; in *OW* as 'The Open Work in the Visual Arts'); 'Il caso e l'intreccio. L'esperienza televisiva e l'estetica' (1956; in *OW* as 'Chance and Plot: Television and Aesthetics'); 'Lo Zen e l'occidente' (1959; not translated). The essay 'Del modo di formare come impegno sulla realtà' (1962; in *OW* as 'Form as Social Commitment') was added to the second edition; 'Generazione di messaggi estetici in una lingua edenica', first published in Italian in *FC* in 1971, is added as an appendix to the third edition; it is translated in *RR* as 'On the Possibility of Generating Aesthetic Messages in an Edenic Language'. Eco's introductions to the three successive editions of *Opera aperta* have not been translated into English, to the best of my knowledge.

12 The memorable title, Eco tells us, was a *trouvaille* of his publisher, Valentino Bompiani; his own more ponderous 'Forma e indeterminazione nelle poetiche contemporanee' ('Form and Indeterminacy in Contemporary Poetics') was relegated to a sub-title (*OA*, p. vi).

13 *OA*, p. v; D. Osmond-Smith, *Berio*, pp. 61–2.

14 Only four issues of *Incontri musicali* were published, 'all of them historic', as Eco says. But its distribution left something to be desired, if credit is to be given to a note in *Il verri* 3, 6 (Dec. 1959), in which the composer Luigi Pestalozza gave vent to his irritation at the 'clandestinity' of the review, 'its scrupulous efforts to ensure that its appearance goes unnoticed' (p. 96).

15 '...the very fact of our uncertainty is itself a positive feature: it invites us to consider *why* the contemporary artist feels the need to work in this kind of direction, to try to work out what historical evolution of aesthetic sensibility led up to it and which factors in modern culture reinforced it' (*OA*, p. 35/ *OW*, p. 4).

16 The term 'definiteness' (*definitezza*) is used in an earlier version of the arguments later elaborated in 'La poetica dell'opera aperta', originally given as a conference paper in 1958 and subsequently republished with the title 'Il problema dell'opera aperta' in *DA*, pp. 163–70.

17 Eco 1992a, 'Foreword', p. ix.

18 See the brief reception history in the Introduction to the 1976 edition: *OA*, pp. ix–xxii.

19 On the parallels between Joyce's and his own 'apostasy', see *OA*, p. xiii. The medieval aspects of Joyce are emphasized in the subtitles of both the Italian and the English editions and in the short chapter, 'The Medieval Model', added to the English translation of the essay, where, in his 'Author's Note', Eco speaks of Joyce's importance to him as 'the node where the Middle Ages and the avant-garde meet' (*AC*, p. vii). But already in his 1954 graduation thesis, published two years later, Eco, somewhat Stephen-like, had

introduced Joyce as an oblique authority on Aquinas's aesthetics, especially on the notion of *claritas* (*PETA*, p. 152 n. 57/*ATA*, p. 253 n. 130).

20 While the earlier and later phases of this history are described more or less explicitly in *The Name of the Rose* and *The Island of the Day Before*, the contemporary setting of *Foucault's Pendulum* may disguise the fact that one of its most significant aspects is the revival of hermetic beliefs and practices which had their heyday, but were by no means exhausted, in the Renaissance. The parallels between *Foucault's Pendulum* and *Finnegans Wake*, or rather Eco's account of the latter, as indeed between *The Name of the Rose* and his analysis of *Ulysses*, are suggestive: for *FP* and the *Wake* see L. P. Zamora, 'The Swing of the "Pendulum": Eco's Novels', pp. 330–1, as well as Eco himself in T. Stauder, 'Un colloquio con Umberto Eco', p. 6.

21 The passage is summarized and toned down in *AC*, p. 77. This is even more the case with the passage from p. 162 quoted below, which is barely summarized in *AC*, p. 84.

22 Tr. Charles Singleton, Princeton University Press, 1975.

23 Subsequently in E. Garroni, *La crisi semantica delle arti*, ch. 3.

24 In F. Pansa and A. Vinci, *Effetto Eco*, p. 71.

25 Cf. T. De Lauretis, *Umberto Eco*, pp. 17–18.

26 Ibid., p. 17.

27 D. Robey, 'Introduction', p. viii, draws attention to its anticipation of the concern of literary theory from the mid-1960s on with 'the element of multiplicity, plurality or polysemy in art, and the emphasis on the role of the reader, on literary interpretation and response as an interactive process between reader and text'.

28 P. Bondanella, *Umberto Eco and the Open Text*, p. 23.

Chapter 2   A Critical View of Culture: Mass Communications, Politics and the Avant-garde

1 The same point was made by Alfredo Giuliani in his Introduction to *I novissimi*, the anthology of Neo-avant-garde poetry published the previous year: 'What poetry does is precisely its "content"... its way of doing coincides almost entirely with its meaning' (p. 17).

2 Founded by Elio Vittorini and Italo Calvino in 1959, its tenth and last issue, published in 1967, was dedicated to the work of Vittorini, who had died the previous year; each number contained both critical essays and substantial original works.

3 G. Scalia, 'Dalla natura all'industria', p. 100.

4 For further details, and more generally on the Neo-avant-garde, see, in English, C. Wagstaff, 'The Neo-avant-garde'. In Italian, see in particular F. Gambaro, *Invito a conoscere la neoavanguardia* and L. Vetri, *Letteratura e caos*.

5 See in particular Eco 1976a, 'Per una indagine sulla situazione culturale', 'La generazione di Nettuno' [1964], in *CC*, pp. 267–74 and Eco 1966, contributions to *Gruppo 63. Il romanzo sperimentale*.

6 Apart from Eco himself in 'La generazione di Nettuno' (see n. 5), see R. Barilli, *La neoavanguardia italiana*, p. 202.

7 Notably 'The Death of the Gruppo 63' [1971], now in *OW*, pp. 236–49 and 'Il Gruppo 63, lo sperimentalismo e l'avanguardia' [1984], in *SS*, pp. 93–104.

8 For a further development of this point, see M. Caesar, 'Umberto Eco and the Death of the Avant-Garde'.

9 Eco began contributing to one of the most important weeklies, *L'Espresso*, in 1965; he has been writing a regular column for it since 1985.

10 R. Lumley, Introduction to *AP*, p. 3.

11 It is partially translated as *Misreadings* (see Bibliography for details).

12 'Nonita' (1959: *DM*, pp. 11–16; in *M* as 'Granita', pp. 7–14); 'Esquisse d'un nouveau chat' (1961: *DM*, pp. 36–41; in *M* with the same title, pp. 47–52).

13 'My exagmination round his factification for incamination to reduplication with ridecolation of a portrait of the artist as Manzoni' (1962: *DM*, pp. 54–65; in *M* with the same title, pp. 165–80); 'Elogio di Franti' (1962: *DM*, pp. 85–96; not in *M*).

14 'Lo strip-tease e la cavallinità' (1960: *DM*, pp. 26–9; in *M* as 'The Socratic Strip', pp. 27–32); 'Fenomenologia di Mike Bongiorno' (1961: *DM*, pp. 30–5; in *M* as 'The Phenomenology of Mike Bongiorno', pp. 156–64).

15 'Frammenti' [report from the Fourth Intergalactic Conference of Archaeological Studies] (1959: *DM*, pp. 17–25; in *M* as 'Fragments', pp. 15–26); 'Industria e repressione sessuale in una società padana' [the village of Milan observed by Melanesian anthropologists of varying persuasions] (1962: *DM*, pp. 66–84; in *M* as 'Industry and Sexual Repression in a Po Valley Society', pp. 69–93); 'Dove andremo a finire?' [mass society and the culture industry seen from the point of view of an aristocrat experiencing the changes being brought about in Periclean Athens] (1963: *DM*, pp. 97–114; in *M* as 'The End Is at Hand', pp. 94–116).

16 Notably the compilation with G. B. Zorzoli, the friend who guided him through information theory, of *Storia figurata delle invenzioni*, published by Bompiani in 1961 and in English as *A Pictorial History of Inventions* by Weidenfeld and Nicolson in 1962.

17 Eco 1965a, 'The Heavy Industry of Writing', p. 844.

18 Much the same ground is covered in Eco 1979a, 'Tre donne sulle donne per le donne'.

19 'Le strutture narrative in Fleming', in O. Del Buono and U. Eco (eds), *Il caso Bond*, 1965, translated as *The Bond Affair*, 1966; in French as 'James Bond: Une combinatoire narrative', in *Communications*, 8, 1966, pp. 77–93 (issue devoted to 'L'Analyse structurale du récit'); reprinted in Italian, *inter alia*, in *SM*, pp. 145–84, and in English, 'extensively revised', in *RR*, pp. 144–72; note that Eco regards the 1966 translation of his essay as 'completely unreliable' (personal communication. August 1998).

20 Apart from *DM/M*, see *CC*, *DPI*, *SAD* and *SDM*; selections in English in *TH* and *HTWS*.

21 In 1965, Eco announced to the readers of *Marcatré*, a cultural journal of whose editorial board he was a member, that he was changing the name of his section from 'Cultura di massa' (Mass Culture) to 'Problemi di comunicazione' (Problems of Communication) because it was only by dealing consciously with questions of communication in a modern society that one could move on to the question of standard communications addressed to a supposedly standard public by industrial producers of escapist messages; and, further, that these were problems that needed to be addressed not only on the basis of analyses of texts, but also with the

help of linguistics, information theory, the sociology of culture and the study of how messages are received: Eco 1965b, 'Una mutazione genetica', p. 43.

22 Eco 1964, 'Rotocalchi di cinque secoli fa', p. 31.

23 First given as a conference paper in 1956, now as 'Il caso e l'intreccio. L'esperienza televisiva e l'estetica', in *OA*, pp. 185–209, translated as 'Chance and Plot: Television and Aesthetics', in *OW*, pp. 105–22.

24 1963, then in *AI*, pp. 317–57.

25 Paper given in New York in 1967, then in *CC*, pp. 290–8; translated as 'Towards a Semiological Guerrilla Warfare', in *TH*, pp. 135–44.

26 Eco 1973, 'Lignes d'une recherche sémiologique sur le message télévisuel', p. 540. The focus on reception led Eco to pay particular attention to the different ways in which content is segmented by and within different cultures, until now, as he says in an essay originally published in 1973, 'an area studied by cultural anthropology, [but which] is currently giving rise to a new branch of semiotics, namely the *semiotics of culture*' ('Does the Audience Have Bad Effects on Television?', *AP*, p. 96).

27 Eco 1971, 'Guida all'interpretazione del linguaggio giornalistico'.

28 Eco 1979b, 'Can Television Teach?', p. 24.

29 D. Robey, 'Umberto Eco: Theory and Practice in the Analysis of the Media', p. 174.

30 Ibid., p. 175; the descriptions of 'closed' systems and 'open' processes are based on the fifth and final section of *La struttura assente*.

31 See Eco 1963, 'The Analysis of Structure', p. 755.

32 The other leading journal, *Lingua e stile*, edited at Bologna, was, and is, more specifically linguistic.

33 C. Segre, 'Structuralism in Italy', pp. 215–19.

34 See in particular C. Segre (ed.), *Strutturalismo e critica* and C. Segre and M. Corti (eds), *I metodi attuali della critica in Italia*, which included an essay by Eco (1970) on 'La critica semiologica'. Within the specific field of structural linguistics, Segre draws particular attention to the 'originality in assimilation and admirable completeness of information' in G. Lepschy's 1966 historical synthesis of structuralism from Saussure up to the study of generative grammar and machine translation, *La linguistica strutturale*: 'Structuralism in Italy', p. 222.

35 See also Eco 1977, 'The Influence of Roman Jakobson on the Development of Semiotics', in particular p. 47 on 'the extension of the principles of Prague poetics to different forms of art, thus establishing the bases of a semiotically oriented aesthetics'.

36 It was in fact published by Einaudi in 1966, in homage to Vittorini; the Italian translation was the first book-version of the *Eléments*. For the background to this (amicable) episode, see a letter dated 30 January 1996 from Eco to Peter Bondanella in Bondanella, *Umberto Eco and the Open Text*, p. 65 and n. 40.

37 T. De Lauretis, 'Semiotica, teoria e pratica sociale', p. 65. (This essay was originally published in English as 'Semiotics, Theory and Social Practice').

38 On this point see in particular F. Marsciani, 'Modelli e modelle', pp. 144–6. Marsciani stresses the importance of Merleau-Ponty at this stage of Eco's thinking as a crossroads between phenomenology, structuralism and

hermeneutics, with his insistence that there is always and necessarily permanence and change, system and process, being and becoming. Change is the 'great theme', Marsciani insists.

39 Cf. T. De Lauretis, *Umberto Eco*, p. 31. Eco adapted his critique of Lacan in the translations of *La struttura assente*, including the French one, in the early 1970s. He explains the reasons for this and publishes the revised version, for the first time in Italian, in the Preface to the 1980 edition of *SA*, pp. v–xxv. It is an episode in Eco's relations with French (post-)structuralism which would repay detailed study.

40 T. De Lauretis, *Umberto Eco*, p. 33.

41 Two of Eco's main contributions to *Quindici*, 'Vietando s'impara' and 'Pesci rossi e tigri di carta' can now be read in *CC*, pp. 303–16 and 317–31; on the events leading to its closure, see Eco 1971, 'The Death of the Gruppo 63' (see n. 7 above).

42 T. De Lauretis, 'Semiotica, teoria e pratica sociale', p. 65.

43 L. Escudero, 'Apocalittico e integrato', pp. 343–4.

Chapter 3   Introducing the Study of Signs

1 The International Association of Semiotics adopted the term 'semiotics' at its founding meeting in Paris in January 1969 and thereafter Eco followed that usage. I shall retain the terminology employed by Eco at the time that he wrote the work in question.

2 M. Corti, in *Strumenti critici*, 4, Oct. 1967, pp. 447–50; P. P. Pasolini, 'The Code of Codes'.

3 '"Culture" in this study is taken in the sense given it by cultural anthropology: every human intervention on a natural given, modified in such a way that it can be inserted in a social relationship' (*SA*, p. 17). But the acknowledgement of the researches of zoosemiotics on animal communication suggests that the remit of semiology extends to non-human societies as well.

4 C. K. Ogden and I. A. Richards, *The Meaning of Meaning*, p. 14.

5 F. de Saussure, *Course in General Linguistics*, p. 16.

6 C. S. Peirce, *Collected Papers*, 2.228.

7 A. Martinet, *Elements of General Linguistics*, pp. 22–3.

8 L. Hjelmslev, *Essais linguistiques*, p. 104.

9 This weirdly surrealistic pun, a standard school example from before the war, means either 'Go, Vitellius, to the sound of war of the Roman god' in the former language or 'The calves of the Romans are beautiful' in the latter (cf. *TSE*, p. 140).

10 B. Croce, 'Il carattere di totalità dell'espressione artistica' [1931], in his *Breviario di estetica*, p. 126.

11 R. Jakobson, 'Linguistics and Poetics', p. 356.

12 For Morris on iconicity, see T. A. Sebeok (ed.), *Encyclopedic Dictionary of Semiotics*, vol. 1, p. 329.

13 T. De Lauretis, *Umberto Eco*, pp. 35–9.

14 C. Metz, 'Le cinéma: langue ou langage?'; P. P. Pasolini, 'La lingua scritta della realtà'.

15 Eco 1992b, 'Joyce, Semiosis and Semiotics'; a shorter version of this paper, with the same title, is in *LIE*, pp. 137–51. For a detailed discussion, see H. van der Heide, 'On the Contribution of Umberto Eco to Joyce Criticism', pp. 334–6. Eco revisits Joyce in Eco 1998, 'A Portrait of the Artist as a Bachelor'.
16 J. Culler, *The Pursuit of Signs*, pp. 199–202.
17 See a robust discussion of Eco's castigation of some lines by the Baroque poet Claudio Achillini (which had already been mocked by Manzoni) in M. Riffaterre, 'The Interpretant in Literary Semiotics', pp. 179–82.

Chapter 4   A Theory of Semiotics

1 *Le Signe*, Brussels, Labor, 1988, and Paris, Librairie Générale Française, 1992.
2 On this aspect, see G. Manetti, 'Trame, nodi, repressioni', p. 5.
3 *VS* (or, to give it its full title, *VS Versus. Quaderni di studi semiotici*) was published for the first three issues by Achille Mauri, and then passed with the Jan.–April 1973 issue to Bompiani, who still publish it; Eco remains the editor.
4 'A semiotic approach to semantics', in *VS*, 1, Sept.–Dec. 1971, pp. 21–60; 'Introduction to a semiotics of iconic sign [*sic*]', in *VS*, 2, Jan.–Apr. 1972, pp. 1–15; 'Is the present King of France a bachelor?', in *VS*, 7, Jan.–Apr. 1974, pp. 1–52.
5 F. de Saussure, *Course in General Linguistics*, p. 67.
6 L. Hjemslev, *Prolegomena to a Theory of Language*, especially pp. 65–7.
7 Eco insists elsewhere on the *mathematical* (non-Jakobsonian) sense in which Hjemslev uses the term 'function', 'as a relation which expresses a connection between variables' (*LII*, p. 128), as is already clear from the context.
8 C. Hookway, *Peirce*, p. 119.
9 C. Hubig, 'Is It Possible . . . ?', p. 71. Hookway, however, seems much more inclined to see the strength of the claims for a general cultural application of Peirce's insights nothwithstanding their 'scientific' origin: see his pp. 119–20 and, in general, the whole of his ch. 4, 'Assertion and Interpretation: The Theory of Signs'.
10 Cf. S. Mitchell, 'Semiotics, Codes and Meanings', p. 391.
11 M. R. Quillian, 'Semantic Memory', pp. 223ff.
12 T. De Lauretis, *Umberto Eco*, pp. 56–7.

Chapter 5   Semiotics Bounded and Unbound

1 The chapters of the most recent book, for example, 'relate to each other but should not be read as "chapters" of a work with ambitions to system'; they are 'essays, wandering explorations' (*KO*, pp. ix, xi).
2 'La cooperazione interpretativa nei testi narrativi'. In the same year, *The Role of the Reader: Explorations in the Semiotics of Texts* was published. About half the book draws on *LF*, but the central theoretical section of the latter is much shortened. *RR* includes, on the other hand, material from *OA*, *FC* and *SM* not previously available in English, as well as a revised translation of the Bond essay, which was no longer easy to find.

3 There are differences between the Italian and English versions of this volume, both in their contents (there are two additional chapters in the English, as well as various cuts and additions *passim*) and sometimes in their wording as well. This is usually explained by cultural context; some of these divergences will become apparent in the pages which follow.

4 *Enciclopedia*, 16 vols, Turin, Einaudi, 1977–84.

5 An English version of the title essay is included in *SPL* as 'Mirrors'; three others, 'A Portrait of the Elder as a Young Pliny', 'Abduction in Uqbar' and 'Pirandello *Ridens*' appear in *LIE*.

6 By, for example, G. Lepschy who in his 1977 review was audibly relieved that *Theory*, which overall he judged to be useful and important, in the end 'puts semiotic phenomena back where they belong, in their social context', given that semiotics is a form of social criticism and indeed of social practice (pp. 711–12): the book has little to offer the linguist.

7 Not included in *LIE*, the paper was originally published in English as 'On Semiotics and Immunology', in E. Sercarz et al. (eds), *The Semiotics of Cellular Communication in the Immune System*; on curiosity and caution, cf. the introduction to the Italian edition (*LII*, p. 12): 'resto in posizione di cauta e incuriosita attesa'.

8 S. Mitchell, 'Semiotics, Codes and Meanings', p. 393.

9 R. Scholes, review of *Theory*, 1977, p. 477.

10 M. McCanles, 'Conventions of the Natural and Naturalness of Conventions', p. 55.

11 Ibid., p. 58. It should be noted that Eco substantially revises his position on iconism (in a 'naturalistic' direction) in *KO*: see below, pp. 163–4.

12 T. De Lauretis, *Umberto Eco*, p. 65.

13 See, for a metacritical position on this issue, T. Coletti, 'Bellydancing: Gender, Silence, and the Women of *Foucault's Pendulum*', pp. 300–3.

14 T. De Lauretis, 'Semiotics and Experience', p. 167. See also her prosecution of the psychoanalytic critique in relation to Eco's first novel in her 'Gaudy Rose: Eco and Narcissism', *passim*.

15 J. Deely, 'The Doctrine of Signs: Taking Form at Last', p. 171.

16 R. Scruton, 'Possible Worlds and Premature Sciences', p. 14.

17 Eco 1984a, 'On Fish and Buttons: Semiotics and the Philosophy of Language'.

18 Deely had made a similar point in his 1976 review; in the revised version of that article (1997) he distinguishes between 'theoretical' and 'applied' semiotics: 'Looking back on *A Theory of Semiotics*', p. 89.

19 Eco 1984b, 'Proposals for a History of Semiotics', p. 75; see, most recently, Eco 1997, 'History and Historiography of Semiotics'; cf. G. Manetti, 'Trame, nodi, repressioni'.

20 U. Volli, 'Il campo e la soglia', p. 76.

21 Ibid., p. 82. On boundaries, cf. I. Znepolsky, 'L'obsession des frontières dans la sémiotique', which is largely though not exclusively devoted to Eco and touches on all the issues raised in this section.

22 Eco 1976b, 'Peirce and Contemporary Semantics'.

23 C. S. Peirce, *Collected Papers*, 8.332.

24 A detailed analysis and application of the workings of inference in relation to the canonical types of sign (index, icon, symbol) is carried out in P. A. Brandt, 'Signe et inférence'.

25 Published in English as Eco 1979c, 'Texts and Encyclopedia'.
26 Eco 1981, 'Dall'albero al labirinto', pp. 49–50.
27 T. A. Sebeok (ed.), *Encyclopedic Dictionary of Semiotics*, vol. 1, p. 203.
28 Cf. P. Violi, 'Le molte enciclopedie', pp. 99–100. Violi, like De Lauretis, draws attention to Eco's particular understanding of subjectivity, confirmed in his model of the encyclopedia, as being our cultural inscription: subjectivity is social and intersubjective. On the encyclopedia, see also G. Cosenza, 'I limiti dell'enciclopedia'.
29 S. Schillemans, 'Umberto Eco and William of Baskerville: Partners in Abduction', p. 264. This paragraph and the next are heavily indebted to Schillemans's limpid account, especially pp. 264–6. See also G. Proni, 'L'influenza di Peirce sulla teoria dell'interpretazione di Umberto Eco', *passim*.
30 Eco 1983, 'Horns, Hooves, Insteps. Some Hypotheses on Three Types of Abduction', pp. 206–7.
31 Cf. Eco 1986, 'L'invenzione si può anche inventare', pp. 241–2: human inventiveness, 'genius', 'inspiration' etc. happen here, where I have to invent a rule which will give a meaning to that result, 'where the human brain does not need to make a *combinatoire* of all possible rules, but possesses an instantaneous capacity of "pertinentization".'

Chapter 6   Theory and Fiction

1 A moment marked by the appearance in 1980 of the anthology of essays edited by Susan R. Suleiman and Inge Crosman, *The Reader in the Text: Essays on Audience and Interpretation.* Suleiman's Introduction delineates the principal lines of reader-oriented criticism and theory as they had developed in the 1960s and 1970s; the story is taken up for the fifteen years following in the editor's Introduction to Andrew Bennett, *Readers and Reading*, 1995. The appearance of Eco's book in Italy coincided with the publication of Italo Calvino's 'reader-oriented' novel *If on a Winter's Night a Traveller.*
2 As indicated above (ch. 5, n. 2) there are substantial differences between *LF* and *RR*. For the purposes of this analysis, *RR* will be taken as the principal point of reference, supplemented by *LF* where necessary.
3 As well as Iser's best-known books (*The Implied Reader*, 1974, and *The Act of Reading*, 1978), see his essay 'Interaction between Text and Reader'.
4 G. C. Colomb, 'Semiotics since Eco', Part 2, pp. 454–5.
5 W. Iser, 'Interaction between Text and Reader', p. 21.
6 M. Olsen, ' "Lecteur modèle", codes et structures', p. 84.
7 *LF*, p. 61. Eco refers his readers to R. Jakobson, 'Shifters, Verbal Categories and the Russian Verb'.
8 Invernizio, a writer for 'Turinese seamstresses', he says in *LF*, p. 57, is a particular bête noire of Eco's. She seems to function for him as a model of an author who gives her public what it, unknowingly, wants and thus, herself unwittingly, does something new in Italian writing: her naïvety is the condition of her success. Cf. Eco 1979a, 'Tre donne sulle donne per le donne', pp. 22–4.

9 See in particular J. S. Petöfi, 'A Frame for Frames' and 'Structure and Function of the Grammatical Component of the Text-Structure World-Structure Theory', both 1976.

10 Cf. M. Olsen, ' "Lecteur modèle", codes et structures', p. 90.

11 Eco refers to his treatment of the lower levels of the text in *TSI/TSE* 3.7.4., and notes that many instances of invention by *ratio difficilis* are realized at this level (ibid., 3.4.9., 3.6.7., 3.6.8.).

12 The example is taken from a short story by Alphonse Allais, 'Un drame bien parisien', which is analysed by Eco as a testing of his hypothetical model at the end of *LF/RR*.

13 *LF*, p. 83; another example, illustrated, in *SWFW*, pp. 50–1.

14 R. Ronen, *Possible Worlds in Literary Theory*, p. 8.

15 Ibid., pp. 48, 52–3.

16 Ibid., p. 61.

17 D. R. Hofstadter, *Gödel, Escher, Bach: An Eternal Golden Braid*, p. 98.

18 The terms are borrowed from L. Doležel, who comments on Eco's variations on the 'thema' of possible worlds in 'The Themata of Eco's Semiotics of Literature', pp. 117–19.

19 First published in Italian as an essay in *Alfabeta*, 49, June 1983, then as a separate booklet by Bompiani, and subsequently appended to the text of the novel; translated into English in 1984.

20 The bibliography is by now immense, in English as well as in Italian and other languages. On aspects of the fictional world, see G. Zecchini, 'Il medioevo di Eco: per una lettura de *Il nome della rosa'*; T. Coletti, *Naming the Rose*; D. Kurzon, 'Nomen Rosae: Latin and the Ambience of the Period in Eco's Novel'; L. P. Zamora, 'Apocalyptic Visions and Visionaries in *The Name of the Rose'*; C. Della Coletta, 'Transhistorical Narratives: The Apocalypse and the Carnival in Umberto Eco'. On semiotics applied and narrated, see W. E. Stephens, 'Ec[h]o in Fabula'; W. Hüllen, 'Semiotics Narrated: Umberto Eco's *The Name of the Rose'*. On the reader's learning process, see R. Capozzi, 'Intertextuality and Semiosis: Eco's *éducation sémiotique'* and (in Italian) his earlier 'Scriptor et "Lector in fabula" ne *Il nome della rosa* di Umberto Eco'; B. McHale, 'The (Post)modernism of *The Name of the Rose'*. On the related theme of the detective, see S. Tani, *The Doomed Detective*; J. Cannon, 'Semiotics and Conjecture in *Il nome della rosa'*; D. Richter, 'The Mirrored World: Form and Ideology in *The Name of the Rose'*. On Eco's much-studied relation with Borges, see especially D. Parker 'The Literature of Appropriation: Eco's Use of Borges in *Il nome della rosa'*. There are some refreshing signs of reading against the grain of the constructed reader, for example E. Neppi, 'Love and Difference in *The Name of the Rose'*.

21 *Foucault's Pendulum* and *The Island of the Day Before*.

22 The episode is modelled on the episode of Zadig and the queen's small spaniel bitch described by Voltaire in *Zadig* (1747), which in turn is discussed by Eco 1983 in 'Horns, Hooves, Insteps. Some Hypotheses on Three Types of Abduction', pp. 207–15.

23 W. Hüllen, 'Semiotics Narrated', p. 47. For the distinction between 'methodological' and 'ontological' structuralism see *La struttura assente*, Section D, discussed above in ch. 2.

24 The relation between Eco's fiction and that of his American contemporaries remains to be explored in depth; at the simplest level it would be intriguing

to know how far Eco's growing familiarity with the United States in the 1970s led him towards a certain kind of novel-writing. The traffic is not of course all one way: 'Aristotle on Comedy, always wanted to read thah', – ,' says Mason to Dixon in Thomas Pynchon's 'post-paranoid' novel *Mason & Dixon*, p. 559 – a discreet homage? On post-paranoia, see M. Wood's review of D. DeLillo's *Underworld* ('Post-Paranoid').

25 B. McHale, 'Ways of World-Making: On *Foucault's Pendulum*', p. 173.

26 Cf. T. Coletti, 'Bellydancing: Gender, Silence and the Women of *Foucault's Pendulum*', p. 310: despite the author's endorsement of her as representing 'a logic of the body, a logic of nature' (Eco's words in T. Stauder, 'Un colloquio con Umberto Eco', p. 5), 'Lia's critique of the metaphysical pretensions of the symbolic systems and hierarchical binaries of hermeticism nevertheless preserves the gender coding of the very hierarchical oppositions she seeks to undo, as does her ambiguous fate in the novel.' For a more sympathetic view of the novel, and of Lia's position in it, see L. Hutcheon, 'Irony-clad Foucault'.

27 For the extra-textual reach of 'the syndrome of the secret', however, with which this is the most closely associated of the three novels, see ch. 7.

28 R. Cotroneo, in a brilliant essay on the three novels, rightly observes that Roberto is the great 'loser' of Eco's fiction: 'Not only does logic give him no assistance, but literature does not allow him to get beyond the fixed point in which he is suspended either. He cannot reach the island either by logic and artifice or by imagination and story-telling' (*La diffidenza come sistema*, p. 51).

Chapter 7   Secrets, Paranoia and Critical Reading

1 JoAnn Cannon, 'The Imaginary Universe of Umberto Eco: A Reading of *Foucault's Pendulum*', p. 900. This essay also discusses the social and political background to the novel.

2 With an Introduction by the editor, Stefan Collini, and contributions by Richard Rorty, Jonathan Culler and Christine Brooke-Rose.

3 Cf. G. B. Tomassini, 'Continuità e mutamento nella teoria dell'interpretazione di Eco', p. 241.

4 Eco had already engaged with Derrida in Section D of *La struttura assente* (cf. ch. 2, above), and his manner is always attentive. Disagreeing here with Searle's view that Derrida has a distressing penchant for saying things that are obviously false, Eco suggests that on the contrary, 'Derrida has a fascinating penchant for saying things that are nonobviously true, or true in a nonobvious way' – even though, in order to stress these things, he also 'disregards very obvious truths that nobody can pass over in silence' (*LIE*, p. 36). Lubomir Doležel, reviewing *The Limits of Interpretation* in 1993, doubts whether Eco's respectful account of Derrida actually captures 'the subversive theory and practice of deconstruction'; it is rather, he suggests, 'a summary of postulates and assumptions which have been reached in contemporary semiotics irrespective of, and outside of, deconstruction' (p. 589).

5 M. Bal, 'The Predicament of Semiotics', p. 549; her reference is to J. Derrida, *Limited Inc.*, 1988.

6 M. Calinescu, *Rereading*, p. 240.
7 Ibid., p. 256.
8 *Il nome della rosa*, dust cover; translated by Walter E. Stephens in his 'Ec[h]o in Fabula', p. 51.
9 As reported in M. Eastman, *The Literary Mind*, p. 100.
10 Commenting on the idea in *Lector in fabula* of the narrative text as an 'open machine' soliciting the co-operation of the reader, Raul Mordenti remarks that 'the image of an intelligent, open, machine which, however, is not working at the moment suggests, not by chance, that of the *trap*; the text, like a trap, does not simply *wait for* the intervention of the reader, but *foresees* it (in the strong sense of this word)' ('Adso da Melk, chi era costui?', pp. 38–9). The related images of 'trap' and 'victim', applied to text and reader respectively, are already present in Eco's analysis of Alphonse Allais's 'Un drame bien parisien', in *LF*, pp. 196 and 215 and *RR*, p. 206 (second reference not translated); cf. the reader as 'prey' in *RNR*, p. 53, quoted above, p. 135.
11 S. Sontag, *Against Interpretation*, p. 19.
12 See Eco 1961, 'Il tempo di "Sylvie"'.
13 M. Calinescu, *Rereading*, pp. 18–19.
14 The extracts correspond to the following plates in Vesalius: Liber II, pp. 170, 181, 187; Liber I, pp. 163, 165; I have not been able to locate the 'St Bartholomew'.
15 See M. P. Pozzato (ed.), *L'idea deforme*, the outcome of a seminar directed by Eco who provides an introduction to the volume; the argument is summarized in English in the second chapter of *Interpretation and Overinterpretation*.

Chapter 8   Kant, the Platypus and the Horizon

1 Eco assumes that his readers will be familiar with these Peircean terms. In T. A. Sebeok (ed.), *Encyclopedic Dictionary of Semiotics*, the Dynamical Object is explained as the 'object proper' while the Immediate Object is defined, concisely, as follows: 'the logically prior understanding – the sign S2 – of what the object of S1 is by means of which both S1 and S1's interpretant refer to the same object' (vol. 2, p. 680).
2 Eco uses the verb *spingere*, whose meanings include 'to push', 'to impel', 'to drive', even 'to prod'; whatever the degree of energy involved, there is the connotation of motivation, even obligation: something makes us speak.
3 D. Pacitti, 'Parables and the Pursuit of Everyday Meaning', p. 18.
4 The phrase is borrowed from G. Prodi, *Le basi materiali della significazione*; cf. *KO*, p. 88.
5 *KO*, pp. 305–9; the drawing of the horse was first discussed in *SA*, pp. 113–14. See also D. Marconi, 'Il nome della bestia', p. 6.
6 This is Eco's blunt formulation of the proposition put rather more formally by his teacher Pareyson towards the end of his life: 'It cannot be said of reality as pure reality either that it is because it could be or that it is because it could not not be, but only that it is because it is. It is wholly gratuitous and unfounded, entirely attached to freedom, which is not a foundation but an abyss, or a foundation which always denies itself as a foundation': L. Pareyson, *Filosofia della libertà*, p. 12 (cited by Eco: *KO*, p. 389).

7 With different intent, and in a different context, Eco has also written of basing a secular ethics on certain 'natural' conditions of our existence, all of which refer back in the end to the position of our bodies in space: 'Quando entra in scena l'altro', in *CSM*, pp. 83–4, 88.
8 W. Benjamin, 'The Storyteller', pp. 84–5.

Select Bibliography

The Bibliography is divided as follows:

A: Works by Eco published in volume form and cited in the text by the *initial letters* derived from their title;
B: Short works by Eco (essays, reviews, etc.) not collected in works cited in A, and cited in the text by *date and title*;
C: Secondary works relating to Eco, cited in the text by *author and title*.

None of these lists has any pretension to completeness; mostly only those works from which extracts are cited in the text are included. A full Eco bibliography comprising primary and secondary works would require several dozen pages.

A Works by Eco published in volume form

AC   *The Aesthetics of Chaosmos: The Middle Ages of James Joyce* [tr. of *PJ*], tr. Ellen Esrock, Tulsa, University of Tulsa, 1982.
AI   *Apocalittici e integrati. Comunicazioni di massa e teorie della cultura di massa*, Milan, Bompiani, 1988; first edn 1964; second edn with new pref. 1974; third edn with new pref. 1977; Eng. tr.: see *AP*.
AP   *Apocalypse Postponed* [partial tr. of *AI*], ed. Robert Lumley, tr. Jenny Condie, Liz Heron, Robert Lumley, Geoffrey Nowell-Smith and William Weaver, Bloomington, Indiana University Press and London, British Film Institute, 1994.
ATA   *The Aesthetics of Thomas Aquinas* [tr. of *PETA*], tr. Hugh Bredin, Cambridge, Mass., Harvard University Press, 1988 and London, Hutchinson, 1989.
CC   *Il costume di casa. Evidenze e misteri dell'ideologia italiana*, Milan, Bompiani, 1973.
CSM   *Cinque scritti morali*, Milan, Bompiani, 1997.

DA   *La definizione dell'arte*, Milan, Mursia, 1985; first edn 1968.
DM   *Diario minimo*, Milan, Mondadori, 1988; first edn 1963; second rev. edn 1975; Eng. tr.: see *M*.
DPI   *Dalla periferia dell'impero*, Milan, Bompiani, 1977.
FC   *Le forme del contenuto*, Milan, Bompiani, 1971.
FP   *Foucault's Pendulum* [tr. of *PF*], tr. William Weaver, London, Secker & Warburg, 1990; first edn 1989.
HTWS *How to Travel with a Salmon and Other Essays* [partial tr. of *SDM*], tr. William Weaver, London, Secker & Warburg, 1994.
IDB   *The Island of the Day Before* [tr. of *IGP*], tr. William Weaver, Orlando, Fla., Harcourt Brace & Co. and London, Secker & Warburg, 1995.
IGP   *L'isola del giorno prima*, Milan, Bompiani, 1994; Eng. tr.: see *IDB*.
IO   *Interpretation and Overinterpretation*, with Richard Rorty, Jonathan Culler and Christine Brooke-Rose, ed. Stefan Collini, Cambridge, Cambridge University Press, 1992.
KO   *Kant e l'ornitorinco*, Milan, Bompiani, 1997.
LF   *Lector in fabula. La cooperazione interpretativa nei testi narrativi*, Milan, Bompiani, 1979; partial Eng. tr.: see *RR*.
LIE   *The Limits of Interpretation* [partial tr. of *LII*], Bloomington, Indiana University Press, 1990.
LII   *I limiti dell'interpretazione*, Milan, Bompiani, 1990.
M   *Misreadings* [tr. of 1975 edn of *DM*], tr. William Weaver, London, Cape, 1993.
NRE   *The Name of the Rose* [tr. of *NRI*], tr. William Weaver, London, Secker & Warburg, 1992; first edn New York, Harcourt Brace Jovanovich, 1983.
NRI   *Il nome della rosa*, Milan, Bompiani, 1984; first edn 1980; Eng. tr.: see *NRE*.
OA   *Opera aperta. Forma e indeterminazione nelle poetiche contemporanee*. Milan, Bompiani, 1976 (third edn); first edn 1962; second edn 1967; French tr. *L'oeuvre ouverte*, Paris, Seuil, 1965; Eng. tr.: see *OW*.
OW   *The Open Work* [partial tr. of *OA*], tr. Anna Cancogni, Cambridge, Mass., Harvard University Press and London, Hutchinson Radius, 1989.
PETA *Il problema estetico in Tommaso d'Aquino*, Milan, Bompiani, 1970 (second rev. edn); first edn, as *Il problema estetico in San Tommaso*, Turin, Edizioni di 'Filosofia', 1956; Eng. tr. [of 1970]: see *ATA*.
PF   *Il pendolo di Foucault*, Milan, Bompiani, 1988; Eng. tr.: see *FP*.
PJ   *Le poetiche di Joyce. Dalla 'Summa' al 'Finnegans Wake'*, Milan, Bompiani, 1982; first edn in *OA*, 1962, then separately 1966; Eng. tr.: see *AC*.
PNR   *Postille a 'Il nome della rosa'*, Milan, Bompiani, 1983; Eng. tr.: see *RNR*.
RLP   *La ricerca della lingua perfetta*, Bari, Laterza, 1993; Eng. tr.: see *SP*.
RNR   *Reflections on 'The Name of the Rose'* [tr. of *PNR*], tr. William Weaver, London, Secker & Warburg, 1985; first edn New York, Harcourt Brace Jovanovich, 1984.
RR   *The Role of the Reader: Explorations in the Semiotics of Texts* [partial tr. of *LF*], London, Hutchinson, 1981; first edn Bloomington, Indiana University Press, 1979.
S   *Il segno*, Milan, Istituto Editoriale Internazionale (Isedi), 1973.
SA   *La struttura assente. Introduzione alla ricerca semiologica*, Milan, Bompiani, 1989. First edn 1968; reissued, with new introduction, 1980.

186 *Select Bibliography*

SAD *Sette anni di desiderio*, Milan, Bompiani, 1986; first publ. 1983.

SDM *Il secondo diario minimo*, Milan, Bompiani, 1992; Eng. tr.: see *HTWS*.

SFL *Semiotica e filosofia del linguaggio*, Turin, Einaudi, 1984; Eng. tr.: see *SPL*.

SM *Il superuomo di massa. Retorica e ideologia nel romanzo popolare*, Milan, Bompiani, 1988; first edn Milan, Cooperativa scrittori, 1976; second, enlarged, edn Milan, Bompiani, 1978.

SP *The Search for the Perfect Language* [tr. of *RLP*], tr. James Fentress, Oxford, Blackwell Publishers, 1995.

SPL *Semiotics and the Philosophy of Language* [tr., with additions, of *SFL*], Bloomington, Indiana University Press and London, Macmillan, 1984.

SS *Sugli specchi e altri saggi. Il segno, la rappresentazione, l'illusione, l'immagine*, Milan, Bompiani, 1988; first publ. 1985.

SWFW *Six Walks in the Fictional Woods*, Cambridge, Mass., and London, Harvard University Press, 1994 [in Italian as *Sei passeggiate nei boschi narrativi*, Milan, Bompiani, 1994].

TH *Travels in Hyperreality*, tr. William Weaver, New York, Harcourt Brace Jovanovich, 1986 and London, Pan Books in association with Secker & Warburg, 1987; also publ. under the title *Faith in Fakes*, London, Secker & Warburg, 1986.

TSE *A Theory of Semiotics*, Bloomington, Indiana University Press, 1979; first edn 1976.

TSI *Trattato di semiotica generale*, Milan, Bompiani, 1978; first edn 1975; English version: see *TSE*.

B Short works by Eco

1954. Review of R. Bayer, *Essais sur la méthode en esthétique*, *Filosofia*, 5, 4, Oct. 1954, pp. 680–5.

1957a. Review of R. Wellek and A. Warren, *Teoria della letteratura*, *Rivista di estetica* 2, 1, 1957, pp. 130–5.

1957b. Review of R. Bayer, *Traité d'esthétique*, *Rivista di estetica*, 2, 2, 1957, pp. 267–72.

1961. 'Il tempo di "Sylvie"', *Poesia e critica* 1, 2, 1961, pp. 51–65.

1963. 'The Analysis of Structure', *Times Literary Supplement*, 27 Sept. 1963, pp. 755–6.

1964. 'Rotocalchi di cinque secoli fa', *Rivista Italsider* 5, 3–4, 1964, pp. 29–32.

1965a. 'The Heavy Industry of Writing', [unsigned], *Times Literary Supplement*, 30 Sept. 1965, pp. 843–4.

1965b. 'Una mutazione genetica', *Marcatré* 16–18, July–Sept. 1965, pp. 42–3.

1966. Contributions to debate in N. Balestrini (ed.), *Gruppo 63. Il romanzo sperimentale*, Milan, Feltrinelli, 1966, pp. 72–8 and 84–6.

1970. 'La critica semiologica', in C. Segre and M. Corti (eds), *I metodi attuali della critica in Italia*, Turin, ERI, 1970, pp. 371–88.

1971. 'Guida all'interpretazione del linguaggio giornalistico', appendix to V. Capecchi and M. Livolsi, *La stampa quotidiana in Italia*, Milan, Bompiani, 1971, pp. 333–77.

1972. 'Towards a Semiotic Inquiry into the Television Message' [first publ. in Italian in 1965], *Working Papers in Cultural Studies*, 3, autumn 1972, pp. 103–21.

1973. 'Lignes d'une recherche sémiologique sur le message télévisuel' [paper given in 1968], in J. Rey-Debove (ed.), *Recherches sur les systèmes signifiants*, The Hague, Mouton, 1973, pp. 535–40.

1976a. 'Per una indagine sulla situazione culturale' [fusion of two articles first publ. in 1963], in R. Barilli and A. Guglielmi (eds), *Gruppo 63. Critica e teoria*, Milan, Feltrinelli, 1976, pp. 289–311.

1976b. 'Peirce and Contemporary Semantics', *VS*, 15, 1976, pp. 49–72.

1977. 'The Influence of Roman Jakobson on the Development of Semiotics', in D. Armstrong and C. H. van Schoonefeld (eds), *Roman Jakobson: Echoes of his Scholarship*, Lisse, De Ridder, 1977, pp. 39–58.

1979a. 'Tre donne sulle donne per le donne', in U. Eco, M. Federzoni, I. Pezzini and M. P. Pozzato, *Carolina Invernizio, Matilde Serao, Liala*, Florence, La Nuova Italia, 1979, pp. 5–27.

1979b. 'Can Television Teach?', *Screen Education*, 31, summer 1979, pp. 15–24.

1979c. 'Texts and Encyclopedia', in J. S. Petöfi (ed.), *Text vs. Sentence: Basic Questions of Text Linguistics*, Hamburg, Buske, 1979, pp. 585–94.

1981. 'Dall'albero al labirinto', in A. Bonito Oliva (ed.), *Luoghi del silenzio imparziale*, Milan, Feltrinelli, 1981, pp. 39–50.

1983. 'Horns, Hooves, Insteps: Some Hypotheses on Three Types of Abduction', in U. Eco and T. A. Sebeok (eds), *The Sign of Three: Dupin, Holmes, Peirce*, Bloomington, Indiana University Press, 1983, pp. 198–220.

1984a. 'On Fish and Buttons: Semiotics and Philosophy of Language', *Semiotica*, 48, 1–2, 1984, pp. 97–117.

1984b. 'Proposals for a History of Semiotics', in T. Borbé (ed.), *Semiotics Unfolding*, Berlin/New York/Amsterdam/Mouton, 1984, vol. 1, pp. 75–89.

1985 [with Patrizia Magli]. 'Sémantique greimassienne et encyclopédie', in H. Parret and H. G. Ruprecht (eds), *Exigences et perspectives de la sémiotique. Recueil d'hommages pour A. J. Greimas*, Amsterdam, Benjamins, 1985, vol. 1, pp. 161–77; translated as 'Greimassian Semantics and the Encyclopedia', *New Literary History*, 20, 3, spring 1989, pp. 707–21.

1986. 'L'invenzione si può anche inventare', in R. Boeri et al. (eds), *La forma dell'inventiva*, Milan, Unicopli, 1986, pp. 239–42.

1989. 'Introduzione – La semiosi ermetica e il "paradigma del velame"', in M. P. Pozzato (ed.), *L'idea deforme. Interpretazioni esoteriche di Dante*, Milan, Bompiani, 1989, pp. 9–37.

1992a. Foreword to O. Calabrese, *Neo-Baroque: A Sign of the Times*, Princeton, Princeton University Press, 1992, pp. vi–x.

1992b. 'Joyce, Semiosis and Semiotics', in R. M. B. Bosinelli et al. (eds), *The Languages of Joyce: Selected Papers from the 11th International James Joyce Symposium, Venice, 12–18 June 1988*, Philadelphia, Benjamins, 1992, pp. 19–38.

1997. 'History and Historiography of Semiotics', in R. Posner, K. Robering and T. A. Sebeok (eds), *Semiotik Semiotics. Ein Handbuch zu den zeichentheoretischen Grundlagen von Natur und Kultur. A Handbook on the Sign-Theoretic Foundations of Nature and Culture*, vol. 1, Berlin/New York, Walter de Gruyter, 1997, pp. 730–46.

1998. 'A Portrait of the Artist as a Bachelor', in L. Santoro-Brienza (ed.), *Talking of Joyce*, Dublin, University College Dublin Press, 1998, pp. 7–40.

C Secondary works

Bal, Mieke, 'The Predicament of Semiotics', *Poetics Today*, 13, 3, fall 1992, pp. 543–52.

Barilli, Renato, *La neoavanguardia italiana. Dalla nascita del 'Verri' alla fine di 'Quindici'*, Bologna, Il Mulino, 1995.

Bedani, Gino, 'Art, Poetry and Science: Theory and Rhetoric in Croce's Early Anti-Positivist Epistemology', *Italian Studies*, 49, 1994, pp. 91–110.

Benjamin, Walter, 'The Storyteller: Reflections on the Works of Nikolai Leskov', in his *Illuminations*, London, Jonathan Cape, 1970, pp. 83–109.

Bennett, Andrew (ed.), *Readers and Reading*, London, Longman, 1995.

Bondanella, Peter, *Umberto Eco and the Open Text: Semiotics, Fiction, Popular Culture*, Cambridge, Cambridge University Press, 1997.

Brandt, Per Aage, 'Signe et inférence', *VS*, 54, Sept.–Dec. 1989, pp. 97–107.

Caesar, Michael, 'Umberto Eco and the Death of the Avant-Garde', in J. Petitot (ed.), *Au nom du sens. Autour d'Umberto Eco*, Paris, Grasset, 1999.

Calinescu, Matei, *Rereading*, New Haven and London, Yale University Press, 1993.

Calvino, Italo, *Se una notte d'inverno un viaggiatore*, Turin, Einaudi, 1979; *If on a Winter's Night a Traveller*, tr. William Weaver, London, Secker & Warburg, 1981.

Cannon, JoAnn, 'Semiotics and Conjecture in *Il nome della rosa*', *Italian Quarterly*, 27, 103, winter 1986, pp. 39–47.

Cannon, JoAnn, 'The Imaginary Universe of Umberto Eco: A Reading of *Foucault's Pendulum*', *Modern Fiction Studies*, 38, 4, winter 1992, pp. 895–909.

Capozzi, Rocco, 'Scriptor et 'Lector in fabula' ne *Il nome della rosa* di Umberto Eco', *Quaderni d'Italianistica*, 3, 2, autumn 1982, pp. 219–29.

Capozzi, Rocco, 'Intertextuality and Semiosis: Eco's *éducation sémiotique*', *Etudes Sémiotiques/Semiotic Inquiry*, 3, 3, 1983, pp. 284–96.

Capozzi, Rocco (ed.), *Reading Eco: An Anthology*, Bloomington and Indianapolis, Indiana University Press, 1997.

Coletti, Theresa, *Naming the Rose: Eco, Medieval Signs and Modern Theory*, Ithaca, NY, and London, Cornell University Press, 1988.

Coletti, Theresa, 'Bellydancing: Gender, Silence, and the Women of *Foucault's Pendulum*', in Capozzi (ed.) 1997, pp. 300–11.

Colomb, Gregory C., 'Semiotics since Eco: Part 1, Semiotic Texts', *PLL*, 16, 3, summer 1980, pp. 329–48; 'Part 2, Semiotic Readers', *PLL*, 16, 4, fall 1980, pp. 443–59.

Cordelli, Franco, 'Per una umbertoecologia', *Leggere*, 33, July–Aug. 1991, pp. 10–12.

Cosenza, Giovanna, 'I limiti dell'enciclopedia', in Magli et al. (eds) 1992, pp. 115–28.

Cotroneo, Roberto, *La diffidenza come sistema. Saggio sulla narrativa di Umberto Eco*, Milan, Anabasi, 1995.

Croce, Benedetto, *Breviario di estetica* [1912], Bari, Laterza, 1988.

Culler, Jonathan, *The Pursuit of Signs: Semiotics, Literature, Deconstruction*, London, Routledge & Kegan Paul, 1981.

Deely, John N., 'The Doctrine of Signs: Taking Form at Last', *Semiotica*, 18, 2, 1976, pp. 171–93.

Deely, John N., 'Looking Back on *A Theory of Semiotics*', in Capozzi (ed.) 1997, pp. 82–110.

De Lauretis, Teresa, 'Semiotica, teoria e pratica sociale. Una storia critica della semiotica italiana', *VS*, 23, May–Aug. 1979, pp. 58–79 [translation of 'Semiotics, Theory and Social Practice: A Critical History of Italian Semiotics', *Cine-Tracts*, 2, 1, 1978, pp. 1–14; references are to the Italian version].

De Lauretis, Teresa, *Umberto Eco*, Florence, La Nuova Italia, 1981.

De Lauretis, Teresa, 'Semiotics and Experience', ch. 5 of her *Alice Doesn't: Feminism, Semiotics, Cinema*, London, Macmillan, 1984, pp. 158–86.

De Lauretis, Teresa, 'Gaudy Rose: Eco and Narcissism' [1985], in her *Technologies of Gender: Essays on Theory, Film, and Fiction*, London, Macmillan, 1989, pp. 51–69.

Deleuze, Gilles and Guattari, Félix, *Rhizome: introduction*, Paris, Editions de Minuit, 1978.

Della Coletta, Cristina, 'Transhistorical Narratives: The Apocalypse and the Carnival in Umberto Eco's *The Name of the Rose*', in her *Plotting the Past: Metamorphoses of Historical Narrative in Modern Italian Fiction*, West Lafayette, Ind., Purdue University Press, 1996, pp. 153–94.

Della Volpe, Galvano, *Critica del gusto* [1960], Milan, Feltrinelli, 1966; *Critique of Taste*, tr. M. Caesar, London, Verso, 1991.

Derrida, Jacques, *Limited Inc*, Evanston, Ill., Northwestern University Press, 1988.

Doležel, Lubomir, review of *LIE*. *Journal of Pragmatics* 19, 6, 1993, pp. 585–9.

Doležel, Lubomir, 'The Themata of Eco's Semiotics of Literature', in Capozzi (ed.) 1997, pp. 111–20.

Eastman, Max, *The Literary Mind*, New York and London, Charles Scribner's Sons, 1931.

Escudero, Lucrecia, 'Apocalittico e integrato', in Magli et al. (eds) 1992, pp. 343–55.

Gambaro, Fabio, *Invito a conoscere la neoavanguardia*, Milan, Mursia, 1993.

Garroni, Emilio, *La crisi semantica delle arti*, Rome, Officina Edizioni, 1964.

Giovannoli, Renato (ed.), *Saggi su 'Il nome della rosa'*, Milan, Bompiani, 1985.

Giuliani, Alfredo (ed.), *I Novissimi* [1961], Turin, Einaudi, 1977.

Hjemslev, Louis, *Prolegomena to a Theory of Language* [1943], tr. Francis J. Whitfield, Madison, University of Wisconsin Press, second rev. edn, 1961.

Hjemslev, Louis, *Essais linguistiques*, Copenhagen, Nordisk Sprog- og Kulturforlag, 1959.

Hofstadter, Douglas R., *Gödel, Escher, Bach: An Eternal Golden Braid. A Metaphorical Fugue on Minds and Machines in the Spirit of Lewis Carroll*, Harmondsworth, Penguin Books, 1980.

Hookway, Christopher, *Peirce*, London, Routledge & Kegan Paul, 1985.

Hubig, Christoph, 'Is it Possible to Apply the Concept "Interpretant" to Diverging Fields Uniformly? Something about the Relationship between Semiotics as Philosophy of Science and Semiotics of Arts', in K. Ketner et al. (eds), *Proceedings of the C. S. Peirce Bicentennial International Congress*, Lubbock, Graduate Studies, Texas Tech University, 1981, pp. 71–4.

Hüllen, Werner, 'Semiotics Narrated', *Semiotica*, 64, 1–2, 1987, pp. 41–57.

Hutcheon, Linda, 'Irony-clad Foucault', in Capozzi (ed.) 1997, pp. 312–27.

Inge, Thomas M. (ed.), *Naming the Rose. Essays on Eco's 'The Name of the Rose'*, Jackson, University Press of Mississippi, 1988.

Iser, Wolfgang, *The Implied Reader: Patterns of Communication in Prose Fiction from Bunyan to Beckett*, Baltimore, Johns Hopkins University Press, 1974.

Iser, Wolfgang, *The Act of Reading: A Theory of Aesthetic Response*, Baltimore, Johns Hopkins University Press, 1978.

Iser, Wolfgang, 'Interaction between Text and Reader', in Bennett (ed.) 1995, pp. 20–31.

Jakobson, Roman, 'Shifters and Verbal Categories' [1957], in R. Jakobson, *On Language*, ed. L. R. Waugh and M. Monville-Burston, Cambridge, Mass., and London, Harvard University Press, 1990, pp. 386–92 [omits the sections on the verbal system in Russian].

Jakobson, Roman, 'Closing Statement: Linguistics and Poetics' [1958], in Thomas A. Sebeok (ed.), *Style in Language*, Cambridge, Technology Press of Massachusetts Institute of Technology, 1960, pp. 350–77.

Kermode, Frank, *The Genesis of Secrecy: On the Interpretation of Narrative*, Cambridge, Mass., and London, Harvard University Press, 1979.

Kurzon, Dennis, 'Nomen Rosae: Latin and the Ambience of the Period in Eco's Novel', *HSLA*, 17, 1989, pp. 36–51.

Lepschy, Giulio, *La linguistica strutturale*, Turin, Einaudi, 1966.

Lepschy, Giulio, review of *A Theory of Semiotics*, *Language*, 53, 3, Sept. 1977, pp. 711–14.

Lumley, Robert, Introduction to *AP*, pp. 1–14.

McCanles, Michael, 'Conventions of the Natural and Naturalness of Conventions', *Diacritics*, 7, 3, fall 1977, pp. 54–63.

McHale, Brian, 'The (Post)modernism of *The Name of the Rose*' and 'Ways of World-Making: On *Foucault's Pendulum*', in his *Constructing Postmodernism*, London and New York, Routledge, 1992, pp. 145–64 and 165–87.

Magli Patrizia et al. (eds), *Semiotica: storia teoria interpretazione*, Milan, Bompiani, 1992.

Manetti, Giovanni, 'Trame, nodi, repressioni. Umberto Eco e la storia della semiotica', in Magli et al. (eds) 1992, pp. 5–24.

Marconi, Diego, 'Il nome della bestia', *L'Indice dei libri del mese* 14, 10, Nov. 1997, p. 6.

Marsciani, Francesco, 'Modelli e modelle. Rileggendo la sezione D', in Magli et al. (eds) 1992, pp. 143–50.

Martinet, André, *Elements of General Linguistics* [1960], tr. E. Palmer, London, Faber & Faber, 1964.

Metz, Christian, 'Le cinéma: langue ou langage?', *Communications*, 4, 1964, pp. 52–90; in English in his *Film Language*, tr. M. Taylor, New York, Oxford University Press, 1974, pp. 31–91.

Mitchell, Sollace, 'Semiotics, Codes and Meanings. Or: Meanings Are Not Always What They Seme', *PTL*, 2, 1977, pp. 385–96.

Mordenti, Raul, 'Adso da Melk, chi era costui?', in Giovannoli (ed.) 1985, pp. 38–44.

Neppi, Enzo, 'Love and Difference in *The Name of the Rose*', *HSLA*, 17, 1989, pp. 52–81.

Ogden, C. K. and Richards, I. A., *The Meaning of Meaning*, London, Routledge & Kegan Paul, 1923.

Olsen, Michel, ' "Lecteur modèle", codes et structures', *Orbis Litterarum*, 37, 1, 1982, pp. 83–94.

Osmond-Smith, David, *Berio*, Oxford and New York, Oxford University Press, 1991.

Pacitti, Domenico, 'Parables and the Pursuit of Everyday Meaning' [based on interview with Eco], *Times Higher Education Supplement*, 23 Jan. 1998, pp. 18–19.

Pansa, Francesca and Vinci, Anna, *Effetto Eco*, Preface by Jacques Le Goff, Rome, Nuova Edizioni del Gallo, 1990.

Pareyson, Luigi, *Estetica. Teoria della formatività* [1954], with Preface by the author, Milan, Bompiani, [1988] 1991.

Pareyson, Luigi, *Filosofia della libertà*, Genoa, Il Melangolo, 1989.

Parker, Deborah, 'The Literature of Appropriation: Eco's Use of Borges in *Il nome della rosa*', *Modern Language Review*, 85, 4, Oct. 1990, pp. 842–9.

Pasolini, Pier Paolo, 'La lingua scritta della realtà' [1966]; in English as 'The Written Language of Reality' in his *Heretical Empiricism*, tr. B. Lawton and L. K. Barnett, Bloomington, Indiana University Press, 1988, pp. 197–222.

Pasolini, Pier Paolo, 'Il codice dei codici' [1967]; in English as 'The Code of Codes', in his *Heretical Empiricism* [see previous entry], pp. 276–83.

Peirce, Charles Sanders, *Collected Papers*, Cambridge, Mass., Harvard University Press, 1931–58 [reference by conventional numeration, not page number].

Petöfi, Janos S., 'A Frame for Frames', in *Proceedings of the Second Annual Meeting of the Berkeley Linguistic Society*, Berkeley, University of California, 1976.

Petöfi, Janos S., 'Structure and Function of the Grammatical Component of the Text-Structure World-Structure Theory', Workshop on the Formal Analysis of Natural Languages, Bad Homburg, 1976 [mimeograph; reference in *RR*, p. 271].

Prodi, Giorgio, *Le basi materiali della significazione*, Milan, Bompiani, 1977.

Proni, Giampaolo, 'L'influenza di Peirce sulla teoria dell'interpretazione di Umberto Eco', in Magli et al. (eds) 1992, pp. 89–98.

Pynchon, Thomas, *Mason & Dixon*, London, Cape, 1997.

Quillian, M. Ross, 'Semantic Memory', in Marvin Minsky (ed.), *Semantic Information Processing*, Cambridge, Mass., MIT Press, 1968, pp. 216–70.

Richter, David H., 'The Mirrored World: Form and Ideology in *The Name of the Rose*', in Capozzi (ed.) 1997, pp. 256–75.

Riffaterre, Michael, 'The Interpretant in Literary Semiotics', in Capozzi (ed.) 1997, pp. 173–84.

Robey, David, 'Introduction' to Eco, *OW*, pp. vii–xxxii.

Robey, David, 'Umberto Eco: Theory and Practice in the Analysis of the Media', in Z. G. Baranski and R. Lumley (eds), *Culture and Conflict in Postwar Italy. Essays on Mass and Popular Culture*, London, Macmillan, 1990, pp. 160–77.

Ronen, Ruth, *Possible Worlds in Literary Theory*, Cambridge, Cambridge University Press, 1994.

Saussure, Ferdinand de, *Course in General Linguistics*, tr. Wade Baskin, introd. Jonathan Culler, London, Fontana/Collins, 1974.

Scalia, Gianni, 'Dalla natura all'industria', *Il menabò*, 4, 1961, pp. 95–114.

Schillemans, Sandra, 'Umberto Eco and William of Baskerville: Partners in Abduction', *Semiotica*, 92, 3–4, 1992, pp. 259–85.

Scholes, Robert, review of *A Theory of Semiotics*, *Journal of Aesthetics and Art Criticism*, 35, 4, summer 1977, pp. 476–8.

Scruton, Roger, 'Possible Worlds and Premature Sciences', *London Review of Books*, 2, 2, 7 Feb. 1980, pp. 14–16.

Sebeok Thomas A. (ed.), *Encyclopedic Dictionary of Semiotics*, 3 vols, Berlin/New York/Amsterdam, Mouton de Gruyter, 1986.

Segre, Cesare (ed.), *Strutturalismo e critica*, Milan, Il Saggiatore, 1965.

Segre, Cesare, 'Structuralism in Italy', tr. John Meddemmen, *Semiotica*, 4, 3, 1971, pp. 215–39.

Sercarz, Eli et al. (eds), *The Semiotics of Cellular Communication in the Immune System*, Berlin, Springer, 1988.

Sontag, Susan, *Against Interpretation*, London, Eyre & Spottiswoode, 1967.

Stauder, Thomas, 'Un colloquio con Umberto Eco su *Il pendolo di Foucault*', *Il lettore di provincia*, 21, 75, Sept. 1989, pp. 3–11.

Stephens, Walter E., 'Ec(h)o in Fabula', *Diacritics*, 13, 2, summer 1983, pp. 51–64.

Suleiman, Susan R. and Crosman, Inge (eds), *The Reader in the Text: Essays on Audience and Interpretation*, Princeton, Princeton University Press, 1980.

Tani, Stefano, *The Doomed Detective*, Carbondale, Southern Illinois University Press, 1984 [chapter on *The Name of the Rose*, pp. 68–75].

Tommasini, Giovanni Battista, 'Continuità e mutamento nella teoria dell'interpretazione di Umberto Eco', *Quaderni d'Italianistica*, 13, 2, autumn 1992, pp. 231–44.

Van der Heide, Herman, 'On the Contribution of Umberto Eco to Joyce Criticism', *Style*, 26, 2, summer 1992, pp. 327–39.

Vetri, Lucio, *Letteratura e caos. Poetiche della 'neoavanguardia' italiana degli anni Sessanta*, Milan, Mursia, 1992.

Violi, Patrizia, 'Le molte enciclopedie', in Magli et al. (eds) 1992, pp. 99–114.

Volli, Ugo, 'Il campo e la soglia. Riflessione sulle definizioni degli oggetti della semiotica nell'opera di Umberto Eco', in Magli et al. (eds) 1992, pp. 75–88.

Wagstaff, Christopher, 'The Neo-Avant-Garde', in M. Caesar and P. Hainsworth (eds), *Writers and Society in Contemporary Italy*, Leamington Spa, Berg and New York, St Martins Press, 1984, pp. 35–61.

Wood, Michael, 'Post-Paranoid', *London Review of Books*, 20, 3, 5 Feb. 1998, pp. 3–5.

Zamora, Lois Parkinson, 'Apocalyptic Visions and Visionaries in *The Name of the Rose*', in Inge (ed.) 1988, pp. 31–47.

Zamora, Lois Parkinson, 'The Swing of the 'Pendulum': Eco's Novels', in Capozzi (ed.) 1997, pp. 328–47.

Zecchini, Giuseppe, 'Il medioevo di Eco: per una lettura de *Il nome della rosa*', in Giovannoli (ed.) 1985, pp. 322–69.

Znepolsky, Ivailo, 'L'obsession des frontières dans la sémiotique', *VS*, 67, Jan.–Apr. 1994, pp. 3–33.

Index

abduction (hypothesis), 97, 98,
    117–19, 132
addressee, 11, 12, 56, 63, 81, 120
aesthetic message, the, 64, 69–70,
    73–5, 94–8
Alembert, Jean d', 114
Alighieri, Dante see Dante
Allais, Alphonse, 134
ambiguity, 11, 24, 44–5, 63, 64, 65,
    66, 73, 96
Anceschi, Luciano, 7, 16, 40
Antonioni, Michelangelo, 30, 34
'apocalyptic' and 'integrated'
    intellectuals, 29, 38–9
Aquinas, Thomas, 1, 21, 114
Arbasino, Alberto, 32
Aristotle, 109–10, 156, 167
author, the, 123–5, 149, 151, 155
Avalle, D'Arco Silvio, 78
avant-garde, the, 1, 17, 28, 29,
    32–6, 52

Bal, Mieke, 149
Balestrini, Nanni, 16, 17, 31, 32, 52
Bally, Charles, 112
Baroque, the, 75
Barthes, Roland, 41, 48, 60, 149

Baudelaire, Charles, 48
Bayer, Raymond, 10
Beauvais, Vincent de, 114
being, 166–8
Benjamin, Walter, 168
Berberian, Cathy, 16
Berio, Luciano, 16, 25, 27, 34
Berlusconi, Silvio, 46
Bernard of Clairvaux, 43
binary method, 56–7, 61
Bohr, Niels, 20
Bologna, University of, 2, 78, 101
Bompiani (publishers), 17, 32, 48,
    78
Bompiani, Valentino, 172 n. 12
Bongiorno, Mike, 41
Bopp, Léon, 10
Borges, Jorge Luis, 137
Boulez, Pierre, 16, 27, 50
Brecht, Berthold, 18

Cage, John, 16
Calder, Alexander, 27
Calinescu, Matei, 149, 156–7
Calvino, Italo, 173 n. 2, 179 n. 1
Carmi, Eugenio, 4
Carnap, Rudolf, 120

Chesterton, G. K., 146
Chomsky, Noam, 60
Christie, Agatha, 152–3
cinema, 68
circumstance, 63
code, 57–8, 59–60, 62–3, 69–71,
    73–4, 81, 82–3, 84–5, 86–9, 91,
    99, 116–17, 122, 128, 162–3
cognition, 164–6
Colomb, Gregory C., 121
communication, 11, 12, 23, 26, 55,
    56, 60, 62, 66, 81, 82, 91, 98,
    122
community, 148, 163
connotation/denotation, 60, 63, 65
Contini, Gianfranco, 48
correlation (expression plane and
    content plane), 83–5, 95, 96
Corti, Maria, 48, 54
Cotroneo, Roberto, 181 n. 28
Croce, Benedetto, 6–7, 8, 10, 12, 31,
    47–8, 64, 66, 171 nn. 2, 7
Culler, Jonathan, 72–3
'culture industry', the, 37, 39, 40,
    41
    see also mass culture

Dante, 18, 23–4, 73, 160
De Amicis, Edmondo, 41
deconstruction, 51, 147, 149, 167
Deely, John N., 108
De Lauretis, Teresa, 27, 51, 52–3,
    67–9, 92–3, 106–7
Deleuze, Gilles and Guattari, Félix,
    115
DeLillo, Don, 140
Della Volpe, Galvano, 7, 15, 96
denotation *see* connotation/
    denotation
Derrida, Jacques, 51, 75, 148, 149,
    181 n. 4
Dewey, John, 7, 29
dictionary/encyclopedia, 113–17,
    120, 130–1, 148, 165
discourse, 69
Dorfles, Gillo, 7

double articulation, 61, 67, 68
Dumas, Alexandre, 38, 144

Eco, Umberto
    academic career, 2, 78
    biographical information, 1–2
    cultural journalism, 4, 42
    single works [*NB: titles are cited
    in the language of the edition to
    which primary reference is made; for
    further details concerning
    translations and differences between
    editions, see text and Select
    Bibliography*]:
    The Aesthetics of Chaosmos (cf. *Le
    poetiche di Joyce*), 15, 21–2;
    Apocalittici e integrati (cf.
    Apocalypse Postponed), 1, 28, 29,
    30, 31, 37–40, 42, 43, 44, 79; *Art
    and Beauty in the Middle Ages*, 4;
    Beato di Liébana, 4; *Come si scrive
    una tesi di laurea*, 4; *La definizione
    dell'arte*, 10; *Diario minimo*, 40–1;
    Le forme del contenuto, 70–5, 76;
    Foucault's Pendulum, 3, 101, 139–
    41, 143, 145–6, 150; *Interpretation
    and Overinterpretation*, 102, 124,
    146–7, 148, 155–6; *The Island of
    the Day Before*, 3, 101, 137, 141–4,
    150–1, 158–60, 169; *Kant e
    l'ornitorinco*, 3, 101, 162–9; *Lector
    in fabula* (cf. *The Role of the
    Reader*), 3, 101, 102, 108, 111–12,
    113–14, 118, 120, 121–4, 125–33,
    134, 155; *The Limits of
    Interpretation*, 3, 102, 118, 133–4,
    145, 147–8, 154; *The Name of the
    Rose*, 3, 45, 100, 101, 135–9, 140,
    143–4, 145, 149, 151–2; *Opera
    aperta* (cf. *The Open Work*), 1, 3,
    7, 9, 10, 15–27, 28, 55, 70, 75, 79,
    95; *Reflections on 'The Name of
    the Rose'*, 134–5; *The Search for
    the Perfect Language*, 101; *Il segno*,
    76–7; *Semiotics and the Philosophy
    of Language*, 3, 77, 101–2, 107,

108–10, 112–13, 115–16; *Six Walks in the Fictional Woods*, 123–4, 134, 152, 157, 169; *La struttura assente*, 9, 49–52, 54–70, 76, 80, 95, 101; *Sugli specchi*, 102; *A Theory of Semiotics*, 2, 3, 64, 75, 77, 78–99, 100, 101, 102–6, 107, 110, 113, 120, 122, 162–3, 164, 168; *Vocali*, 4
Einstein, Albert, 19
encyclopedia *see* dictionary/encyclopedia
entailment *see* implication
entropy, 57
Erlich, Victor, 48
Escher, M. C., 134
L'Espresso, 4
evaluation, 14
experimentalism, 32–3, 36, 51, 52
extension *see* intension/extension

Ferraresi, Mauro, 124
Fleming, Ian, 42, 46
form, 7–10, 17, 70
Formaggio, Dino, 7
Fortini, Franco, 32
Foucault, Michel, 51
frames, 113–14, 130–1
Freud, Sigmund, 99, 106
Futurism, 75

Gadamer, Hans-Georg, 148
Gainsborough, Thomas, 94
Galilei, Galileo, 51
Garroni, Emilio, 25
Giuliani, Alfredo, 16, 52, 173 n. 1
Gramsci, Antonio, 31, 38
Greimas, A. J., 78, 116
Gruppo 63 [Sessantatre], 26, 31, 32, 36

habit, 111–12
Hauser, Arnold, 10
Heidegger, Martin, 51, 75, 167
hermeticism, 102, 111, 144, 145, 146–7, 173 n. 20

hermetic semiosis *see* hermeticism
Hjemslev, Louis, 50, 60, 61, 75, 83–4, 87, 96,165, 177 n. 7
Hofstadter, Douglas R., 134
Hubig, Christoph, 88
hypothesis *see* abduction

icon *see* iconism
iconism, 66, 67–9, 80, 92–3, 103–4, 163–4
idiolect, 65, 66, 96, 97
impersonality, 9
implication, 113, 130
ineffability, 12, 116
inference, 91, 98, 100, 112, 131
information theory, 12, 23, 25–6, 39, 55, 57, 83
Ingarden, Roman, 121
intension/extension, 86, 88, 128–34
International Association of Semiotics, 78, 176 n. 1
interpretant, 59–60, 86, 87–8, 163
interpretation, 7–10, 64, 65, 70, 91, 100–1, 112–13, 121–3, 126, 145, 148–9, 150, 160, 163, 167
Invernizio, Carolina, 126, 179 n. 8
Iser, Wolfgang, 121–2
Italian Communist Party, 27, 49

Jakobson, Roman, 25, 26, 48, 64, 69, 75, 95, 103
Joyce, James, 1, 14, 15, 18, 20, 21–2, 23–4, 48, 70–2, 75, 126–7, 150, 152, 172–3 n. 19, 173 n. 20

Kafka, Franz, 18
Kant, Immanuel, 12, 164, 165
Kermode, Frank, 153
Kristeva, Julia, 75, 105–6, 107

Lacan, Jacques, 51, 106, 176 n. 39
langue, 60, 67
Leonetti, Francesco, 32
Lepschy, Giulio, 175 n. 34
Lévi-Strauss, Claude, 48, 50–1, 60–1, 62

lexicon, 60, 62, 63, 70
Lingua e stile, 175 n. 32
literature and industry, 30–1
Locke, John, 83
Lombardi, Germano, 32
Longinus (pseudo-), 13

McCanles, Michael, 103–4
McHale, Brian, 140
Mad, 131
Magli, Patrizia, 116
Mallarmé, Stéphane, 14, 22, 75
Manzoni, Alessandro, 40, 160
Marcatré, 48, 174–5 n. 21
Marinetti, Filippo Tommaso, 35
Mark (evangelist), 153–4
Martinet, André, 61
mass culture, 1, 28, 29, 30, 37–9, 41, 43
mass media and communications, 28, 31, 36, 37, 39, 42, 43
meaning, 58, 59, 76
Il menabò, 30
mentions, theory of, 86
Merleau-Ponty, Maurice, 19, 175–6 n. 38
message, 56, 58, 62, 63, 64, 65, 66, 121, 122
see also 'aesthetic message', the
metaphor, 70, 71–3, 85
metonymy, 71–3
Metz, Christian, 68
Middle Ages, the, 1, 4, 21–2, 43, 146, 172–3 n. 19
Milan, 1, 16, 52, 78
Mitchell, Sollace, 103
Model Reader, the see the reader
Morris, Charles, 23, 66, 68, 92
Mozart, Wolfgang Amadeus, 33, 35, 36

Neo-avant-garde, 17, 31, 32–6, 49, 52
Neo-Marxism see New Left
New Criticism, 7, 9

New Left, 49
Nietzsche, Friedrich, 38, 51, 167
noise, 56, 58, 63, 64
I Novissimi, 16

Ogden, C. K. and Richards, I. A., 23, 59, 86
openness, 11, 12, 15, 16, 17, 18–23, 47, 48, 52, 65, 70, 96, 126, 160–1
'open work', the see openness
order/disorder, 57, 64, 75
Osmond-Smith, David, 78
overinterpretation see interpretation

Pacitti, Domenico, 163
Pagliarani, Elio, 16
paranoid fiction, 140
Pareyson, Luigi, 6–10, 18, 31, 168, 182 n. 6
Pascal, Blaise, 79, 83
Pasolini, Pier Paolo, 32, 54, 68
Peirce, C. S., 3, 59–60, 66, 68, 86, 87–8, 92, 100, 111–12, 113–14, 117–19, 128, 148, 162, 164, 165
pertinent features, 58, 69, 80, 82, 93, 95, 179 n. 31
Pestalozza, Luigi, 172 n. 14
Petöfi, Janos, 117, 128
poetics, 14, 31, 171–2 n. 10
popular culture see mass culture
popular fiction, 38, 42, 46
Porta, Antonio, 16
possible worlds (in literary theory), 133–4
postmodernism, 142
post-structuralism, 116, 120, 147
Pousseur, Henri, 16
pragmatics, 80, 90, 100
Prague School, the, 96, 171 n. 10
Propp, Vladimir, 131
Putnam, Hilary, 117
Pynchon, Thomas, 140, 180–1 n. 24

Queneau, Raymond, 4
Quillian, M. Ross, 89; the Model Q,
    89, 130
Quindici, 29, 52, 176 n. 41

RAI Studio di fonologia, 16, 36
RAI-TV (Italian State Radio and
    Television), 16, 32
ratio facilis/difficilis, 92–3
reader, the, 121–3, 125, 126–8, 130–
    4, 151–5, 156–7
reading *see* the reader
reception (of messages), 39–40, 44–
    5, 66, 175 n. 26
recipient *see* addressee
redundancy, 56
reference *see* mentions
referent, 56, 58, 80, 84, 85–6
repertoire (of symbols), 56, 62
representamen, 59–60, 86, 148, 166
Riffaterre, Michael, 177 n. 17
Rimbaud, Arthur, 75
Riva, Valerio, 26
Robey, David, 46, 173 n. 27
Romanticism, 68, 75, 156
Ronen, Ruth, 133
Rorty, Richard, 148, 155–6
Rossetti, Gabriele, 160
rule-governed creativity, 70–1
Russian Formalism, 25, 48, 171 n.
    10

Sanguineti, Edoardo, 16, 17, 32
Saussure, Ferdinand de, 25, 48, 59,
    67, 83–4, 112
Scalia, Gianni, 30
Schillemans, Sandra, 118–19
Schklovsky, Viktor, 103
Scholes, Robert, 103
Scruton, Roger, 108
Sebeok, Thomas A., 116, 118
secrets *see* hermeticism
Segre, Cesare, 48
semantics, 70, 73, 80, 82, 87, 88, 90,
    91, 92

semiology *see* semiotics
'semiotic drift', 116, 147–8, 148
semiotics, 26, 29, 42, 44–5, 46–7,
    51, 52–3, 54–5, 58–9, 60, 66,
    67, 69–70, 77, 78, 79–80, 83,
    86, 87, 99, 102–4, 107–11, 176
    n. 1
'sense', 59
sign, 55, 59, 67, 68, 76–7, 80, 81, 83–
    5, 86, 87, 90, 91–4, 162–3
signal, 55–6, 82, 84, 91
signification, 80, 81, 83, 86, 87
signified *see* signifier/signified
signifier/signified, 56, 59, 61, 62,
    64, 68, 83, 84
Sontag, Susan, 155–6
Spitzer, Leo, 48
Stein, Gertrude, 96
Stephens, Walter E., 151
Stockhausen, Karlheinz, 18, 27, 47
structuralism, 25, 29, 36, 47–51, 52,
    54, 62, 77
structural linguistics, 23, 25
structure, 11–15, 39, 42, 47–51, 55,
    60–1, 62, 65–7, 69, 83, 95, 97,
    98, 106, 113–14, 122, 130,
    132
Strumenti critici, 48, 78
subject, the, 105–7, 164, 179 n. 28
Sue, Eugène, 38, 46, 126
Suger, Abbot of St Denis, 43
symbol, 58, 59, 62
Symbolism, 14, 18
the 'syndrome of the secret' *see*
    hermeticism

television, 31, 43–4, 46
Tel quel, 48
text, 91, 100, 113–14, 119, 120–34
text pragmatics, 99, 100, 101
textual co-operation, 121, 122–3,
    126, 128–34, 155
type/token, 92–4

unlimited semiosis, 60, 87, 111–12,
    148

use (vs. interpretation), 127–8, 155–6

the user [*fruitore*] of the work of art *see* addressee

Vattimo, Gianni, 167
  and Rovatti, Aldo, 116
Verne, Jules, 150
Il verri, 16, 17, 32, 40
Vesalius, Andreas, 159–60
Vittorini, Elio, 31, 173 n. 2, 175 n. 36

Volli, Ugo, 110–11
VS Versus, 78, 79, 111

Wahl, François, 48
Wellek, René and Warren, Austin, 7
Wittgenstein, Ludwig, 125
Wols, 27

Zolla, Elemire, 29
Zorzoli, G. B., 174 n. 16